SHAKESPEARE AT THE GLOBE

Shakespeare
at the Globe

⋙ 1599-1609 ⋘

BERNARD BECKERMAN

THE MACMILLAN COMPANY 1962
New York

Macmillan Paperbacks Edition 1962

The Macmillan Company, New York
Brett-Macmillan Ltd., Galt, Ontario

Printed in the United States of America

Library of Congress catalog card number: 62-7159

ACKNOWLEDGMENTS

Mʏ debts of gratitude, which this acknowledgment can hardly hope to pay, are especially due to Professors Oscar J. Campbell, S. F. Johnson, and Dr. John Cranford Adams, President of Hofstra College. To detail the extent of Professor Campbell's assistance would be futile. I merely count myself fortunate in having enjoyed his guidance and encouragement. From Professor Johnson this study received a careful and perceptive scrutiny, to the excellence of which I trust these pages testify. In supporting my work as Director of the Hofstra College Shakespeare Festival, Dr. Adams provided me with the opportunity not only to explore the authentic staging of Shakespeare's plays but also to draw upon his knowledge and advice. Although my present views of Shakespearean staging differ from his, nonetheless they owe much to the initial stimulus he gave and the rigorous scholarship he exemplified. In addition, I have benefited from the indulgence of various friends and scholars. Dr. Raymond W. Short read and criticized the original draft of the chapter on dramaturgy. Dr. James G. McManaway and Irwin Smith offered valuable suggestions for the entire manuscript, and Mr. Smith, together with Dr. Robert De Maria, Howard Siegman, and my wife, Gloria, has assisted me in the final preparation of the book.

CONTENTS

INTRODUCTION

FROM 1599 to 1608 or 1609 the Globe playhouse was the home of the Chamberlain-King's company and the only theater where it publicly presented its plays in London. The Globe was imitated by Henslowe, the theater magnate, and lauded by Dekker, the playwright. Upon its stage Shakespeare's major tragedies enjoyed their first performances. Located among the stews and marshes of the Bankside, it drew across the Thames its audience, men and women, gentlemen and journeymen, sightseeing foreigners and native playgoers.

Yet for us the playhouse signifies more than a physical structure for the presentation of plays. It has become the symbol of an entire art. Its construction initiated a glorious decade during which the company achieved a level of stability and a quality of productivity rarely matched in the history of the theater. So rich was the achievement that virtually all interest in the Elizabethan drama radiates from the work of these years.

Circumstances attendant on the building of the Globe playhouse were instrumental in developing the distinctiveness of this endeavor. The new playhouse itself was regarded as the last word in theaters. Alleyn and Henslowe modeled the Fortune upon it. Dekker, in a widely known paragraph from *The Gull's Horn-book,* praised the wonder of it. In the design of the Globe there were significant changes from former playhouses. It was a theater built by actors for actors. To subsidize it a new financial system was instituted which more fully than heretofore interrelated theater and actors.

Furthermore, young men had recently taken over the entire enterprise, playhouse and company. Until 1597 James Burbage had maintained some connection with the Lord Chamberlain's men. Builder and owner of the Theatre, lessor of Blackfriars, he had exercised a strong influence on the course the company took.

In the midst of the uncertainty marking the negotiation for a
new lease on the Theatre, James Burbage died, bequeathing to
his sons and, by association, to the actors an equivocal inherit-
ance. From his death in 1597 to the building of the Globe in
1599, the company was adrift, playing mainly at the Curtain.
How much responsibility and authority the elder Burbage had
relinquished to the young men before 1597 is virtually impossible to determine, but the records indicate that he played an
active part in the management of theatrical affairs until the end
of his life.[1] After his death the erection and success of the Globe
devolved upon young, presumably enthusiastic, but not green
men of the theater.

At this time Shakespeare, even then the leading playwright of
the Lord Chamberlain's men, was passing into a new phase of
dramatic activity. The major tragedies were soon to come from
his pen. The romantic comedies, in a style which he had developed earlier, were shortly to reach their perfection in *Twelfth
Night*. The histories were to appear no longer. None of the plays
written between 1600 and 1609 was considered a history by the
editors of the First Folio. Since *Henry V*, dated 1599, probably
appeared before the completion of the Globe, Shakespeare wrote
no history play for the Globe company. On the other hand,
Titus Andronicus and *Romeo and Juliet* are the only plays, written before the opening of the Globe, which were labeled tragedies. Such categorization is somewhat artificial, but it does ac-
centuate the fact that the settlement of the company at the
Globe was followed shortly by a shift of emphasis in Shakespeare's work.

One more significant change occurred at this time. Either a
dispute with his fellows or an irrepressible wanderlust led the
leading clown, Will Kempe, to break with the company. Apparently before the stage of the Globe was painted and the
spectators admitted, he severed his connection with the Lord
Chamberlain's men, though he had been among the original five
who had taken a moiety of the lease on the projected playhouse.
After his departure, there followed a period of great stability in
the acting company. In the entire decade there were only two re-
placements, owing to the deaths of actors, and three additions
with an expansion from nine to twelve members in 1603.

This nexus of events does not necessarily prove that there was a stylistic or artistic change in 1599. Nor does it imply that little in procedure, tradition, and equipment was carried over from the Theatre and the Curtain to the Globe. But it does indicate that circumstance and planning combined to modify the character of the enterprise, to make it not merely a continuation of the past but the start of a new theatrical endeavor. As such, the opening of the Globe serves as an excellent point of departure for a special study of the company sometimes dubbed "Shakespeare's" but in this book termed "the Globe."

In 1608–1609 the King's men, acquiring the private indoor theater of Blackfriars, brought the distinctive period to a close, for with the leasing of Blackfriars, according to Professor Gerald Bentley, came a change of outlook.[2] He emphasizes two major factors which led to this change. First, the audience at the private theater differed markedly from that at the public playhouse: the former audience was sophisticated and exclusive whereas the latter was rude and representative. The contrast has been fully elaborated by Alfred Harbage in *Shakespeare and the Rival Traditions*. Secondly, the indoor theater, relatively intimate, lit by candles, required an alteration in style of acting and provided a subtler control of mood. To substantiate the theory that the King's men faced these differences squarely, Bentley cites the employment of Jonson, skilled in writing for Blackfriars and the Children of the Queen's Revels; the appearance of a new type of play from the leading playwright, now writing with Blackfriars in mind; and the engagement of Beaumont and Fletcher, neither of whom had previously written for this company. Altogether the events grouped around the move to Blackfriars indicate that then too a new start was made, and Bentley convincingly demonstrates that within a short time Blackfriars became the leading playhouse for the King's men in point of prestige and profit.

Until now I have alluded rather generally to the building of the Globe in 1599 and to the acquisition of Blackfriars in 1608–1609. Since the assignment of several plays depends upon a more exact dating, there is a need to arrive at more precise limits.

Shortly after the 26th of February, 1599, construction of the Globe commenced under the supervision of Peter Streete, the

man with whom Philip Henslowe and Edward Alleyn contracted
a year later to erect the Fortune theater along the same lines.
From Streete's building schedule for the Fortune, we can estimate that the Globe took twenty-eight to thirty weeks to complete, and thus the earliest opening date would have been in
late August or early September, 1599.[3]

At the Blackfriars playing by the King's men began sometime
between June 24, 1608, when the company took a lease of the
premises, and the autumn of 1609, when the decline of a severe
plague permitted a resumption of playing. In January, 1609,
the players received a reward from His Majesty "for their private
practise in the time of infeccon." Testimony by Richard Burbage
and John Heminges in 1612 indicates that playing commenced
some time during the winter of 1608–1609. A temporary reduction of plague deaths in February and March, 1609, makes this
the likely period during which Shakespeare and his fellows first
played at Blackfriars and so terminated the Globe years.[4]

In the main the canon of Shakespeare's plays produced between 1599 and 1609 is set. Several plays are in dispute, but on
the whole, considering the nature of much of the evidence, the
degree of unanimity among scholars is amazing.[5]

Of about nine of the plays sufficient external evidence exists
to verify their placement between 1599 and 1608. There is general agreement that Platter is referring to Shakespeare's *Julius
Caesar* when he describes a performance on September 21, 1599.
Its absence from Meres' list places it after September 7, 1598,
and Chambers dates the play 1599–1600. *Twelfth Night*, first
mentioned in connection with a performance at the Middle
Temple, February 2, 1602, is variously dated 1599 to 1601. Suggestions of an initial performance at the Middle Temple by
Wilson and at Whitehall by Hotson do not affect the assignment of date and need not be discussed here.[6] Despite several
attempts to force back the date of the first draft of *Hamlet* to
1583, the year 1601 is still the accepted date for the play as we
know it. In an essay in 1944 Chambers confirmed his dating
which appeared in *William Shakespeare* (1930). Wilson supports
this date, and Gray and Kirschbaum have argued against the use
of Harvey's marginalia as evidence of an earlier date.[7]

Troilus and Cressida was written before February 7, 1603, when it is listed in the Stationers' Register "as yt is acted by my lo : Chamblens men." The implication is of a recent appearance, but Hotson has made an attempt to set the date back before 1598. The nub of his argument is that the enigmatic title "Love's Labour's Won," which appears under Shakespeare's name in Meres' list, really means "Love's Pains Are Gained," thus fitting the subject of *Troilus and Cressida*.[8] This line of reasoning has yet to win support.

The upper limits of *Othello, Measure for Measure*, and *King Lear* are set by their performances at Court on November 1, 1604, December 26, 1604, and December 26, 1606, respectively. The lower limits are unknown, but no responsible authority has suggested dating any of these plays before 1602.[9]

The limits for *Antony and Cleopatra* are set at the upper end by the listing in the Stationers' Register of May 20, 1608, and at the lower by Daniel's corrections to his *Cleopatra* in the new edition of *Certain Small Workes* (1607). On the same day on which the entry for *Antony and Cleopatra* was inserted, *Pericles* was registered. This play, however, had been witnessed by the Venetian ambassador sometime between January 5, 1606, and November 23, 1608.[10]

Stylistic evidence or contemporary allusion serves to date four plays in this period. *All's Well That Ends Well* is dated in 1602–1603 by Chambers, in 1602 by Kittredge and Harbage; all do so on stylistic evidence. Allusions to the doctrine of equivocation (II, iii, 9–13) place *Macbeth* in 1606, and this date is widely accepted.[11] Stylistic evidence leads most scholars to place *Timon of Athens* in 1607–1608, and this type of evidence, combined with allusions of a tenuous nature, leads them to assign *Coriolanus* to 1608.

Several plays are on the borderline at either end of the period. *As You Like It, Much Ado About Nothing*, and *Henry V* were "staid" from printing according to the Stationers' Register entry of August 4, 1600. Since none of them appears in Meres' listing in 1598, they all fall within the two-year intervening period. In dating *As You Like It* and *Much Ado About Nothing* there is very little evidence for narrowing the period. The appearance of Kemp's name in speech prefixes in *Much Ado* (IV, ii) places it before the opening of the Globe. O. J. Campbell points out that *As You Like It* must have been written after the edict against satire on July 1, 1599. These facts, together with the general consensus, lead me to include *As You Like It* in the 1599–1608 repertory and to exclude *Much Ado.* .

Henry V is more narrowly limited by the allusions to Essex's campaign in Ireland (Chorus, V, 30–34). The commencement of the campaign was on March 27, 1599, the sad conclusion on September 28, 1599. Since the Globe did not open until the end of August or early September, the weight of the evidence excludes *Henry V.* It also excludes *Cymbeline* at the end of the decade. Mentioned first by Simon Forman, who saw a performance between April 20th and 30th, 1611, the play is variously dated in 1609 or 1610. The earliest date suggested by Chambers is the spring of 1609.

One play, *The Merry Wives of Windsor,* remains in dispute. Despite the conflict with testimony from Meres, Hotson places the first performance of *Merry Wives* on April 23, 1597, when it was supposedly performed for the Knights of the Garter at Windsor. Alexander accepts this date.[12] Chambers, Kittredge, and Harbage date the play in 1600–1601, and Chambers points out the appearance of a line from *Hamlet,* "What is the reason that you use me thus?" (V, i, 312) in scene xiii of the bad quarto of *Merry Wives* (1602). On this basis and in the absence of any appropriate time when the play could have been performed before the Queen at a Garter installation, Chambers dates the play in 1600–1601. McManaway admits that many questions about the play are unanswerable at present, although he grants that there may have been revisions over a period of years beginning as early as 1597. Nevertheless, as he notes, its absence from Meres' list still remains a bar to an early dating. Consequently, we may treat it as part of the list of new plays written for the Globe playhouse.[13]

For supplementary evidence about the staging of Shakespeare's plays at the Globe, we turn to the pieces of his less gifted colleagues who supplied the Globe company with scripts. Twelve plays are extant which we know or have reason to believe were performed *only* by the Chamberlain's or King's men between 1599 and 1609. Of these, three were written by Jonson: *Every Man Out of His Humour, Sejanus,* and *Volpone.* The first was written "in the yeere 1599" according to the 1616 Folio, and the revised epilogue refers to presentation at the Globe. *Sejanus,* according to Jonson, was "acted, in the yeere 1603. By the K. Maiesties Servants." *Volpone,* again according to Jonson, was acted "in the yeere 1605. By the K. Maiesties Servants."

Barnes, Wilkins, and possibly Tourneur each contributed one play to the King's men's repertory now extant. Barnes provided *The Devil's Charter,* played before the King "by his Maiesties Servants" on February 2, 1607.[14] Wilkins supplied *Miseries of Enforced Marriage.* Q. 1607 contains the advertisement "As it is now played by his Maiesties Servants." *The Revenger's Tragedy,* uncertainly linked with Tourneur's name, appeared in quarto with the inscription: "As it hath beene sundry times Acted, by the Kings Maiesties Servants." Chambers dates the play 1606–1607.

The remaining six plays are all anonymous and all ascribe production to the Chamberlain's or King's men on the title pages of their quartos. *A Larum for London* was registered on May 27, 1600, and printed in 1602. *Thomas Lord Cromwell* was registered August 11, 1602, "as it was lately acted." [15] *Fair Maid of Bristow,* entered in the Stationers' Register February 8, 1605, is dated 1604 by Chambers. *The London Prodigal* appeared in quarto in 1605 and was probably produced in 1603–1605. *The Merry Devil of Edmonton,* although registered on October 22, 1607, is mentioned in T. M.'s *Black Book* in 1604. Chambers dates the play about 1603. Lastly, *A Yorkshire Tragedy,* entered May 2, 1608, may have been written a year or two earlier.[16]

The final additions to the 1599–1608 repertory consist of two plays which were presented by the Chamberlain-King's men as well as by another company. The first, Dekker's *Satiromastix,* presented between the production of *Poetaster* in the spring of 1601 and its entry in the Stationers' Register on November 11th of that year, contains on the Q. 1602 title page the information that it had been "presented publikely by the . . . Lord Chambelaine his Servants; and privately, by the Children of Paules."

Certainly this was unusual procedure and must be taken into consideration in applying the play to Globe stage conditions. The second, Marston's *The Malcontent*, dated 1604, was "found" and played by the King's men, presumably in retaliation for the theft of one of their plays by the Children of the Queen's Revels. The title page and induction of Q. 1604 refer to additions by Marston and Webster in order to accommodate the play to an adult company. About the status of *The First Part of Jeronimo*, the stolen play, it is difficult to be exact. Boas dates the play after 1600.[17] Since the extant Q. 1605 may reflect the copy of the Revels' production, *Jeronimo* has been cited for supplementary evidence only.

Thus, the final list of extant works first produced at the Globe playhouse between 1599 and 1609—the Globe plays—consists of fifteen Shakespearean and fourteen non-Shakespearean plays. Upon the evidence of these scripts, the bulk of this study is based.

Chapter One

THE REPERTORY

THE magnificent dramas of Shakespeare that assumed flesh and motion upon the Globe stage in its golden decade shared the boards with hack plays, near cousins to the present-day soap operas and grade-B westerns. It is easy to forget that the company which produced *Hamlet* also presented *The London Prodigal,* and that the same Burbage who shook the superflux as Lear may well have portrayed the ranting, melodramatic husband of *A Yorkshire Tragedy,* a model indeed of a figure tearing a passion to tatters. Masterpieces and minor pieces followed one another in rapid succession in the same playhouse, and the customs of their production were the result of a single repertory system.

Among the various contending works on Shakespearean stage production the one subject that is invariably neglected is this repertory system. And yet, an understanding of how a theatrical company goes about the business of presenting its plays is a necessary step in working out a theory of staging. Who sees the show and who pays the bill more often determine the possibilities of production than other high-minded considerations. To know what the Elizabethan repertory system was and how it operated requires the answers to certain basic questions: How many performances was a play likely to receive? In what sequence were these performances given? How long did a play remain in repertory? How long were the rehearsal periods for new plays? How many roles did an actor have to command at one time? Where were new plays first presented? In essence, all these questions can be contained in one all-embracing question:

How did an acting company market its wares? for let us remember that in the Elizabethan theater we find one of the earliest examples of theater as a commercial enterprise.

The pattern of performing which I call the repertory system came into being with the appearance of the first permanent playhouses. Their erection in London was a sign that the actors had discovered the means as well as the possibility of gaining the patronage of the large city populace for long periods of time. No longer did the players have to be nomads. No longer was it necessary for a handful of sharers with their apprentices and hired men to trudge from village to village in order to find paying audiences. After 1570 the nomadic troupes that played London for short engagements matured into resident companies that toured occasionally. Though even the most illustrious of the companies continued to travel in the provinces when conditions demanded, their welfare and status were tied to the fortunes of the public playhouses. Touring was an act of desperation. That way lay poverty. Well-being depended upon permanence and permanence depended upon the effective exploitation of the potential audience.

Naturally not every Londoner was a playgoer. The average play might have been witnessed by 30,000 people over a period of a year and a half. The assumption here is that the play performed to a capacity audience, each member of which saw the play once. More likely, however, not more than 15,000 to 20,000 people saw the average play. To calculate the size of the usual theater-going populace in London is difficult. One conclusion is evident, however. Given the capacity of the public playhouse, somewhat between two and three thousand persons, the companies had to change their bills frequently if they were to attract sufficient spectators. Their practices in doing so are the bases of the repertory system.

By 1599, the year in which the Globe playhouse was constructed, these practices were well established. A five-year period of growth in the theater preceded the construction of the Globe. A decade of relative stability in theatrical affairs followed. During those years it may not have appeared to the professional players that the time was settled, for a serious plague in 1603 severely curtailed playing schedules and lively competition from the children's companies drew customers to the private theaters after 1600. But a retrospective survey of the years from 1599 to 1609 makes it evident that the decade was one of peak prosperity for the public theaters.

From 1597 to 1602 the Lord Chamberlain's men and the Lord Admiral's men shared a virtual monopoly of public stage presentation. In 1597 the production of *The Isle of Dogs* by Pembroke's men had aroused the ire of the Privy Council, for what offense it is not now clear. One of the authors, Nashe, fled; Ben Jonson, either as part-author or as actor, together with two other actors, was imprisoned for some months. On July 28 all plays were prohibited. Disastrous as this event was for the Pembroke's men, it served to strengthen the Lord Admiral's and Lord Chamberlain's men, for in a minute of the Privy Council, dated February 19, 1598, they alone of the men's companies were permitted to play in London. Not until 1602 was the monopoly successfully challenged. In that year Worcester's men received permission to perform in London, and in actuality became a party to a new tripartite monopoly. Final confirmation of their privileges came in 1603–1604 when the Stuart family, drawing the theater under its patronage, dispensed royal patents to each of them.

A fourth company to receive a patent was the Children of the Queen's Revels. The patent is proof that the competition of the private theaters was a serious matter. For several years between 1600 and 1605 the boys and their literary foster fathers had achieved a fashionable popularity. But by 1606 the most successful of these troupes, the Children of the Queen's Revels, seems to have forfeited the protection of Her Majesty. Whatever may have been the reasons, the children's companies never were able to maintain the continuity of the men's companies.

From time to time throughout the decade minor adult companies drifted into London, played several performances, and departed. An Earl of Derby's company appeared at Court for three performances in 1600 and 1601, thereafter passing into the provinces whence they had come. Henslowe records two performances by Pembroke's men on October 28–30, 1600. No further word is heard of them. One performance at Court, on January 6, 1603, is noted for Hertford's men, otherwise a provincial company. But no professional group successfully challenged the supremacy of these three leading companies which, in the course of the decade, became entrenched in their grand playhouses: the Chamberlain-King's men at the Globe, the Admiral-Prince's men at the Fortune in 1600, and the Worcester-Queen's men at the Red Bull about 1605.

Concerning two of these companies, the Lord Admiral's and Worcester's, there is substantial evidence of the ways in which they functioned. The evidence appears in the diary of Philip Henslowe, wherein he noted dealings with both companies. The bulk of the records pertains to the Admiral's company, for which we have performance lists from 1592 to 1597 and debit accounts from 1597 to 1603. Records of Worcester's men appear for a shorter time in Henslowe's *Diary,* but the material, debit accounts from 1602–1603, reveals that both companies operated in essentially the same ways.

For the third of these companies, the Lord Chamberlain's men, no similar body of evidence exists. The law cases involving Heminges with Witter and Thomasina Ostler reveal the presence of a unique financial arrangement in this company, yet one which continued alongside the traditional theatrical organization. Like the other public companies, the Lord Chamberlain's men were organized into a partnership of sharers who managed and maintained the group. As sharers they purchased plays, bought costumes, hired actors, tiremen, and bookkeepers, paid licensing fees, rented a theater, shared profits and expenses, and carried on the manifold duties of a theatrical enterprise. The novelty of the arrangement was that the company rented the theater from some of its own members. Richard Burbage, William Shakespeare, Augustine Phillips, John Heminges, Thomas Pope, in varying proportions, owned profitable shares in the Globe playhouse. This overlapping of proprietary interests may tend to obscure the actual similarity of the Chamberlain's theatrical organization to that of its rivals, for though the financing of the companies differed, the system of management was the same.

Evidence pertaining to actual performances by the Lord Chamberlain's men is rare. What clues we have take the form partly of letters or notes discovered among nontheatrical documents and concerned only secondarily with the stage and partly of records of Court performances or title pages of texts that provide us with occasional information about what was appearing on the boards of the Globe. Alone, these items bear little weight. Their principal value lies in their agreement with the conditions reflected in Henslowe's *Diary*, and it is to this source that we must turn to secure a picture of how plays were produced in the Elizabethan age.[1]

The theatrical periods for which Henslowe kept records cannot be considered seasons in the modern sense. During the severe plague of 1592–1594, playing all but ceased. After the abatement of the disease and a false start at Newington Butts, the Lord Admiral's men commenced regular performances at the Rose on June 17, 1594. Playing continued without unusual interruption until the following March 14, 1595. After the Lenten season, the company recommenced playing on Easter Monday, April 21st, and played through June 26th. During the summer season the tour in the provinces was brief, for the company reopened on August 25th and again played without exceptional interruption through February 28, 1596. Performances resumed on April 12th, again after Lent, and continued through July 18, 1596. Here occurred an unusually long summer break which lasted until October 27th, during which time the company traveled in the provinces. Save for a curious suspension from November 16th through the 24th, the company played at the Rose from October 27th until February 12, 1597. A brief Lenten observance followed, and performances began again on March 3rd and continued until July 19th. The presentation of *The Isle of Dogs* halted general theatrical activity on July 20th,[2] and although the Rose opened on July 27th and 28th, the Privy Council order of the latter date suspended all playing until "Alhallontide next."

In the preceding schedule we may discern a more or less regular pattern of playing. A Lenten suspension is almost invariably observed, though the duration of the observance varies. A less regular summer break, usually from mid-July to October, intervenes, the length of time depending upon the severity of the plague. Finally, during the Christmas holidays performances are given about half the days of the month. During each December from 1594 through 1596 this interruption occurs, and is presumably the result of the company's activity at and about the Court.

The day by day program of the Lord Admiral's men follows the same sort of irregularity, as a glance at two weeks of performances will show.

Let us choose a time from an ordinary, uneventful season. On Monday afternoon of November 10, 1595,[3] if we had crossed the Thames to the Rose on the Bankside, we should have seen *Longshank,* a reasonably new play. Already it had had four performances, having opened for the first time on the previous August 28th. However, we might have discovered that this was an old play newly revived, Peele's *Edward I.* On Tuesday, the 11th, the company presented *The Disguises,* an even newer play, having opened on the previous 2nd of October. It had already been played five times and oddly enough this day's performance, the sixth, would be its last. On Wednesday and Thursday, we could have seen the first and second parts of *Tamberlaine.* Both plays had been doing brisk business, Part I from the time of its revival on August 30th, 1594, and Part II, from its revival on December 19, 1594. Typical of the Elizabethan theater would be the performance of Part II of a play the day after Part I. We should have been particularly fortunate in seeing the *Tamberlaines,* for these performances were to be the last in this revival. On Friday, November 14th, we could have attended the premiere of *A Toy to Please Chaste Ladies,* which proved to be a moderately successful piece. *The Seven Days of the Week,* a very successful play, which had opened the previous June, would receive its fourteenth performance on Saturday, and was to continue to hold the stage until the following December 31st, totaling twenty-two performances in all. There was to be no playing on Sunday, which was usual, nor on Monday, which was unusual.

From Tuesday through Thursday, November 18th–20th, we

should have seen *Crack Me This Nutte, Barnardo and Fiametta,* and *Wonder of a Woman,* all recent plays. The first had opened as a new play the previous September 5th and enjoyed some success. In 1601 it would be revived. The second play had had its premiere several weeks earlier, on October 30th, and was not as successful as the first. The third piece also had opened recently, on October 16th, and it too had excited only a moderate response. On Friday, a week after its premiere, we would have had the chance to hear *A Toy to Please Chaste Ladies* once again. It was to continue in the repertory for another year, with a total of nine performances, making it an average success. Finally, on Saturday, November 22nd, at the end of our two-week visit, *Seleo and Olempo* was on the bill, a play which had opened initially the 5th of the previous March. This performance, its eighth, would bring it near the end of its run of ten performances. On February 19, 1596, a little less than a year after its opening, the play would leave the boards, its prompt-book lost in the dust of the Rose playhouse.

Thus, in two weeks we could have seen eleven performances of ten different plays at *one* playhouse. On no day would we have found the theater repeating the play of the day before. Among the plays the majority, six of the ten, would have been new works, produced since the return of the company from its summer tour. Two others were carry-overs from the previous spring and two were older plays which had been revived. Nor would these plays have appeared regularly in the succeeding weeks. If we had remained in London for two additional weeks, we should have found some repetition of the plays we had already seen as well as some plays that would be new to us.

Again there would be eleven performances in two weeks.[4] Five performances would repeat works of the previous fortnight's bill. The remaining six performances would have been divided among five plays: a new play for two performances; another play which had opened that autumn; two parts of a play from the previous spring, whose performances, like those of *Tamberlaine,* would have been arranged on successive days; and a play which would appear once and disappear. Altogether, in four weeks we should have been able to see fifteen different plays, only five of which would be repeated, and one of which would attain three performances. Most of the plays would be less than one season old, a few, holdovers from the previous season, and only two or possibly three could be considered "old" plays. Of the fifteen, two would have been completely new plays, and, in fact, the only play to have had three performances in four weeks would have been a recent addition to the repertoire, *A Toy to Please Chaste Ladies.*

The alternation of the plays was irregular. The choice of play from day to day must have followed the exigencies of the moment. Over an extended period, on the other hand, a broad pattern may be observed. A new play or revival usually opened to a good house despite the doubling of admission prices. Several days or a week later a second performance would be given, and then, depending on the enthusiasm of the audience response, the play would be repeated several times a month at first, then less frequently, the intervals between performances becoming longer and longer until the play would be presented once a month. Within a year or a year and a half, it would fade from the theater. Such was the usual course. Naturally, a popular work would continue longer and be revived more often, whereas a "flop" would leave the boards almost immediately.

In the total winter season from August 25, 1595, through February 28, 1596, of which we have considered four weeks, the company gave one hundred and fifty performances of thirty different plays. Eighty-seven performances, or 58 per cent of the total, were of the fourteen new plays produced that season. Five performances, 3.3 per cent, were of one play, *The Jew of Malta,* revived that season. Forty-six performances, or 30.7 per cent, were given by the eight plays from the previous season which were less than a year old, counting from December 1, 1594. Only twelve performances, 8 per cent, were of the seven plays which were more than a year old. This distribution, which is similar for all the seasons covered by Henslowe's records, emphasizes how dependent the company was on the continuous addition of new plays to its stock in order to maintain itself in London.

The sheer volume of production is staggering. How strenuous the demands must have been upon the actors! Although we are familiar with the extensive repertory which an opera singer must command, at least it is a repertory which in large measure has assumed classical limitations. The Elizabethan actor, on the contrary, had to remember the old and learn the new at the same time. He had to retain the lines of the older plays, for not only might he wait weeks and months between performances of a particular play, but occasionally he might be asked to give a single performance of a long neglected play.[5] He also had to commit to memory an amazing number of new plays each season. In the three-year period from June 5, 1594, to July 28, 1597, a leading actor of the Lord Admiral's company, such as Edward Alleyn or Thomas Downton, had to secure and retain command of about seventy-one different roles, of which number fifty-two or fifty-three were newly learned.

The manner in which the acting companies secured new plays has been fully discussed by Greg and Chambers[6] so that a brief summary will suffice. Sometimes the actors would buy a finished book, as evidenced by the purchase of *Strange News Out of Poland* for £6 on May 17, 1600. However, the more usual way of dealing with the impecunious poets who supplied them with scripts was for the Admiral's men to approve a plot outline of a play, upon which approval they would pay the playwright or playwrights an advance. As portions of the book were received, further advances were given until the entire work was submitted and full payment, usually £6 in this period, was made. Although the names of a large number of playwrights appear in Henslowe's records, most of the new plays performed by the Admiral's men came from the pens of less than a dozen men.[7]

Three different types of relationships seem to have existed between actors and the playwrights. In one type Shakespeare and Heywood, actors of their companies, presumably wrote for their own fellows exclusively. In another Ben Jonson went free-wheeling in his passage from one company to another and back again. Between these extremes was a man like Dekker who

generally confined his writing to the Admiral's men, at least
at this time, although he did write occasionally for other companies.

Upon receipt of the play from the author, the actors put it
into production without much delay. Of the eighty-eight new
plays presented during this period by the Admiral's men, Henslowe records data on the purchase of both the book and properties for twenty-eight of them.[8] Only one, *Polyphemus*, shows
a substantial lapse between the final payment for the script on
February 27, 1599, and the purchase of "divers thinges" for
production on October 5, 1599. Since the purchase of these
"divers thinges" only totaled 8s., the play may very well have
been produced earlier, the later entry relating to properties or
costumes which were added to the production. Of the twenty-
seven other plays, the time between final purchase of the manuscript and the first indication of production extends from three
to fifty-one days, the average duration being a little over twenty
days. That many of the payments were for costumes which had
to be tailored indicates that the time lapse was even less than
the records show. For example, the longest delay, fifty-one days,
came between the purchase of *Brute* on October 22nd and the
payment for "cottes of gyantes" for the same play on December
12, 1598. Probably the order for the coats had been placed considerably earlier.

Three special cases, those of *Two Angry Women of Abington*,
Part II, and *Thome Strowd*, Part II, of the Admiral's men, and
A Woman Killed with Kindness of Worcester's men, demonstrate that in some instances production was begun before the
writing was completed. The book of *Two Angry Women* was
paid for in full on February 12, 1599, although gowns had been
paid for on January 31st and "divers thinges" on February 12th.
Payment in full is recorded for *Thome Strowd* on May 5, 1601,
although suits had been bought on April 27th. Lastly, Heywood
received £3 as final payment on *A Woman Killed with Kindness*
on March 6, 1603, although costumes had been paid for on
February 5th and March 7th.

The entire conception of play producing reflected here is one
of continuous presentation. As soon as a poet turned over his

play to the actors, they would introduce it into the repertory
with very little delay. There is no indication that special occasions provided the moment for unveiling a new play or that
long-range planning for a season was part of the Elizabethan or
Jacobean scheme. Immediate concerns, the nature of which we
know too little, probably dictated the day-to-day program of the
theatrical fraternity. Responsive to the vicissitudes of political,
hygienic, and economic conditions, the players within their
strictly traditional guild organization maintained an empirical,
nontheoretical, professional attitude.

Let us turn back to the winter season of 1595–1596 to trace
the introduction of new plays into the repertory. Four days after
the opening of the season, on August 29th, *Longshank* was
presented. Six days later, on September 5th, it was followed by
Crack Me This Nutte, another play followed on September 17th
(The New World's Tragedy), and still another on October 2nd
(The Disguises). For the rest of this season there were premieres
on October 16th *(Wonder of a Woman),* October 30th *(Barnardo and Fiametta),* November 14th *(A Toy to Please Chaste
Ladies),* November 28th *(Henry V),* and in 1596 on January
3rd *(Chinon of England),* January 16th *(Pythagoras),* January
23rd *(Seven Days of the Week,* Part II), and February 12th
(Blind Beggar of Alexandria). The longest interval between
the production of new plays was thirty-five days, November 28th
to January 3rd, though the intervening performances numbered
only twenty. The shortest interval, of six days, occurred twice,
at the beginning and near the end of the season. Obviously the
lack of regularity, apparent in other aspects of production, also
existed in the frequency with which new plays were presented.

Nor does the study of the year-to-year pattern reflect any
greater regularity. For example, in December, 1594, three new
plays were presented, in December, 1595, none, in December,
1596, four. The presentation of so many new plays in the latter
year was owing without doubt to the absence of any new plays
in November, 1596. Consequently, though we cannot determine
a fixed number, we can calculate the average number of new
plays introduced into the repertory in one year.

Over the three-year period 1594–1597 the actors of the Admiral's company had an average interval of 14.7 days or roughly two weeks between the opening of new plays. While the interval ranged from two days to fifty-seven, the mean interval was 13 days. Thus it would be accurate enough to say that the company produced a new play every two weeks during the playing season. For the years 1597–1603 we have evidence of the number of new plays produced each year but not of the number of performances given. Consequently, to correlate all the evidence it is necessary to calculate not only the average intervals between premieres of new plays but also the average number of plays produced from 1594 to 1597. The *Diary* reports the lists of performances continuously from June 5, 1594, to July 28, 1597, a total of three years and fifty-three days. Since 1596 was a leap year, the entire period consisted of 1,149 days during which fifty-four new plays were produced, averaging one play for every 21.3 days. Thus, about seventeen new plays were presented each year by the Lord Admiral's men.

Chambers, describing the repertory of the Admiral's men from 1597 to 1603, estimates that they added seventeen new plays in 1597–1598, twenty-one in 1598–1599, twenty in 1599–1600, seven in 1600–1601, fourteen in 1601–1602, and nine in 1602–1603. If we exclude the figures for 1602–1603, a season shortened by the death of Elizabeth, an average for the five years comes to 15.8 new plays each year. The unusually meager count of seven plays for 1600–1601 may reflect, as Chambers suggests, a reliance on the older repertory after Edward Alleyn's return to the company. Or it might indicate that the company toured extensively that year.

Until now we have considered only one company. Fortunately Henslowe served as banker for Lord Worcester's men from August 17, 1602, to March 16, 1603, a period of 212 days. During that time they commissioned twelve new plays. A simple equation based on the ratio of 12 plays to 212 days as x plays are to 365 days yields us twenty plays as the total this company would have reached if they had continued to produce new works at the same rate for the rest of the year. However, since the period covered by the accounts was the most active part of the theatrical year, it is likely that the total would have been nearer to seventeen. Furthermore, the average interval between the openings of new plays by the Worcester's men comes to .16.6 days. Allowing for the uncertainty of the length of this particular season, calculated as it is on expense payments, not actual performances, this average is in line with the earlier figure of 14.7 days between openings. Thus two of the three important public playhouses in London each presented about seventeen new plays a year, grouping them in two seasons so that a new play was presented every fourteen or fifteen days.

The evidence for the third of these companies, the Lord Chamberlain's men, is scanty; to determine whether or not it followed the system of the other two companies is hazardous at best. As Greg aptly noted more than half a century ago, "We know practically nothing of the internal workings of the Lord Chamberlain's company." [9] Yet, here and there, links between this company and the others suggest that in general all of them followed the same repertory practices.

Between June 5th and 15th, 1594, the Lord Admiral's and Lord Chamberlain's men played together at Newington Butts. Henslowe's performance list does not clarify whether they functioned as one company or two. In fact, only the excellent deduction of Greg, who followed Fleay in this, made it clear that the combination ceased after that date, for the list of subsequent performances proceeds without a break. Of the ten performances, five were of plays now generally ascribed to the Chamberlain's men.

Fleay, extolling the virtues of the Chamberlain's men at the expense of the Admiral's, asserts that he has been unable to trace at any time "more than four new plays produced by [the former company] in any one year." [10] This conclusion might stem from a recollection of a note by Malone: "It appears from Sir Henry Herbert's office-book that the King's company between the years 1622 and 1641 produced either at Blackfriars or the Globe at least four new plays every year." He goes on: ". . . the King's company usually brought out two or three new plays at the Globe every summer." [11] Both statements indicate that no less than four plays were produced annually. A study of Herbert's list of licenses supports them. From July,

1623, to July, 1624, licenses for thirty-five plays are recorded. Four may be discarded for our present purposes.[12] Of the remaining thirty-one, eleven were licensed for the Palsgrave's company, seven (six new and one old) for the Prince's men, eight (six new and two old) for the King's men, four (three new and one old) for the Lady Elizabeth's servants, and one for the Queen of Bohemia's company. G. E. Bentley very persuasively accounts for the greater number of plays licensed for the Palsgrave's men by pointing out that the fire at their playhouse, the Fortune, on December 9, 1621, deprived them of their prompt-books and that in 1623–1624 they were striving to repair the damage to their repertory.

The discrepancy between the six new plays of 1623–1624 and the estimated seventeen of 1594–1603 is not a mark of conflict in the evidence. Times had changed. The King's men needed only a third of the new plays that they had produced in earlier years. The use of a private theater largely accounts for this change, for the seats of Blackfriars could be filled four or five times over by the audience from a single performance at the Globe. What is really significant is that the King's men presented the same number of new plays as the Prince's men, and that the practices of Shakespeare's fellows were in harmony with those of other companies.

Only an idolatrous love of Shakespeare can lead us to conclude that from 1599 to 1609 the Lord Chamberlain's men produced appreciably fewer plays than the other companies did. All were in lively competition, in which, as Platter noted, "those which play best obtain most spectators." To maintain that the Globe company produced only four or five new plays a year, we must prove that Shakespeare's plays were of such popularity that they could be repeated again and again while other companies had to change their bills daily. However, we have no evidence to show that this was the case. Certainly, Falstaff was a perennial favorite, but so was Barabas the Jew. A play such as *Richard II* was old by 1601. *Twelfth Night,* or *Malvolio,* held the stage, it seems, but so did *The Spanish Tragedy,* or *Jeronimo.* Yet Henslowe's schedule reveals that the old war horses such as *Jeronimo, The Jew of Malta, Faustus,* and *Tamberlaine,*

altogether, provided no more than 11 per cent of the performances of the Lord Admiral's company throughout the entire
recorded period and no more than 6 per cent in any one year
(see Appendix A, chart ii). We should like to think that Shakespeare's work had more commercial appeal than Marlowe's or
Kyd's. But can we suppose that it had a popularity, let us say,
five or six times greater? A sobering thought on the enigma
of popularity must strike us when we realize that *Pericles* was,
if its succession of quartos offers any evidence, more popular
than *Antony and Cleopatra*, and that *The Winter's Tale*, if
Court performances are any measure, appealed to royalty more
than *King Lear*. Furthermore, once we eliminate the plays
which in all likelihood were given few performances, such as
Troilus and Cressida, *All's Well* and *Measure for Measure*, we
are left with too few Shakespearean plays to sustain a theatrical
company in the London of 1600. A reference to the list of Court
performances between 1603 and 1642 verifies the pattern reflected in Henslowe's records. Aside from their first appearances
before James, when they presented many old stand-bys, the
King's men usually offered the latest plays to Their Majesties,
and when Shakespeare died, the works of other writers rapidly
superseded his at Court.[13] Like the commonalty, royalty expected to see the current "hit."

The plays we now regard as great literary works were struck
off in the harassing atmosphere of a commercial enterprise. Most
of the plays were failures or temporary successes. Most of those
produced by the Admiral's men played their few, in many cases
very few, performances and passed away without any further
trace but the notation by a shrewd businessman. Of the one
hundred and thirteen plays listed by Henslowe between 1592
and 1597, sixty-seven would certainly be unknown without the
Diary and another twelve would probably be unknown (see
Appendix A, chart i). However, among the thirty-four plays that
would be otherwise known, only twenty-seven are extant, or
about 24 per cent of the plays listed by Henslowe. By assuming
that the twenty-nine extant Globe texts represent a similar percentage of the Globe repertory, we arrive at a conclusion that
116 plays were actually produced by the company between 1599

and 1609. But during these years the theater suffered closings of extraordinary duration because of the plague.[14] In addition, the Globe period is calculated from September, 1599, to March, 1609. Actual playing time, therefore, amounted to about seven and a half years. This estimate divided into the 116 new plays gives us a result of 15.6 plays as the average number of new works offered by the Globe company each year. Actually, in estimating these figures, some allowance must be made for Shakespeare's superiority. How much, however, is virtually impossible to say. Nor is an actual figure necessary as long as we realize that the repertory systems of all three companies were fundamentally the same. In effect, the figures that we have for the Lord Admiral's and Worcester's men are a far safer guide to actual Globe practice than any other evidence.

As lovers of literature, we need be grieved little by the disappearance of 75 per cent of the plays, at least judging from contemporary response. Generally the plays that have come down to us were the more popular pieces. Either they were printed, or discussed, or alluded to. At the same time they were played more frequently. The seventy-nine plays which we know only through Henslowe provided 496 performances in five years. The other thirty-four played 403 performances in the same period. On an average we find the plays otherwise known to us played nearly twice as many performances as those mentioned by Henslowe.

Those pieces that attained popularity and whose stage life extended over a period of years run like strong threads through the repertory of an Elizabethan company. But between the strands there was much filler, plays which spoke their brief piece upon the platform and departed within a few months. Seven to eight performances were the average number for a play. Many did not attain even this many representations. Three out of every ten plays had no more than one or two performances. Less than one out of ten went beyond twenty performances. An extensive and actually wonderful process of winnowing out the chaff was at work. This process was the repertory system. As a result of it, the plays that could bring back an audience year after year survived to speak for the age (see Appendix A, chart ii).

The process of winnowing out the ineffectual pieces was supplemented by the custom of revivals. Periodically, plays of the recent past would be brought back to the stage for another run. Usually the pattern of performances for a revival would follow that of a new play: close-packed performances at first and a tapering off until representation ceased. *The Spanish Tragedy,* or as Henslowe entitles it, *Jeronimo,* offers a clear example of the process at work. In March, 1592, it was presented for three performances, in April, again for three performances, in May it reached its peak with five performances, and in June played twice. The hiatus in the summer and fall of 1592 interrupted the normal cycle. On resumption of playing in December, *Jeronimo* appeared again, was repeated twice in January for the last times. These performances were by Strange's men. Four years later, on January 7, 1597, the Lord Admiral's men revived it as a "new" play, indicating that it had been substantially revised. Subsequent performances followed with diminishing frequency with intervals of 4, 6, 5, 9, 10, 28,[15] 14, 21, 26, 29 days. The play was further revived in September or October of 1601, this time with additions by Jonson.

Twenty plays in Henslowe's list show definite evidence of revival, either during the 1593–1597 period or the 1599–1601 period. Only *Doctor Faustus* shows continual performance from 1594 to 1597. Originally revived on October 2, 1594, it was performed from time to time by the Lord Admiral's company which did not allow more than four months to elapse between performances. There was a later revival toward the end of 1602.

Among the nineteen remaining plays the manner of revival varied somewhat. Nine of them seem to have been altered or enlarged considerably for the revival. Usually these plays had been off the stage for several years. *Fortunatus* was reworked by Dekker in November, 1599, after it had lain idle for three and a half years. *Jeronimo,* as we saw already, had not been offered for four years when it was revived as "new" in January,

1597. *Tambercame,* Part II, was three and a half years old when presented as "new" on June 11, 1596. Two of the plays, *Friar Bacon and Friar Bungay* and *Phaethon,* show evidence of alteration as do the rest, but specifically for Court performances. Though there is no certainty that revivals in the public playhouse occurred at the same time, it is not unlikely, as we shall discover.

One advantage of the Elizabethan method of revivals—abetted by the absence of copyright laws—was that it enabled a writer to rework his own or someone else's work. Through how many versions, for example, did the narrative of *Hamlet* pass to reach its final stage? We know of three at least: the one played by the "Lord Admeralle men & Lorde Chamberlen" at Newington Butts on June 11, 1594; the one contained in the 1603 Quarto; the one announced as "newly imprinted and enlarged to almost as much againe as it was, according to the true and perfect Coppie." The constant sifting of the repertory not only screened out hack pieces, it also provided time for the refinement of masterworks.

In instances where no proof of literary revision exists, there is evidence sometimes of theatrical revision. Four plays from four to six and a half years old were revived after 1597. The purchase of properties for them indicates that they received new productions. Of the last six of the twenty plays revived, only the cessation of playing and, after an extended lapse of time, the resumption of performances tell us that they were revived.

Revived plays, for all practical purposes, were treated as new. Instead of maintaining a play in continuous repertory over an extended period of time during which performances of the work would be given at regular intervals, the players permitted a work to fade out of the repertory for a time, to be restored later with or without changes for another cycle of performances. That this was also the method of the Lord Chamberlain's men is attested to in a letter written by Sir Walter Cope to Sir Robert Cecil in 1604. Upon inquiring for a new play for the Queen, Sir Walter was informed by Richard Burbage that Her Majesty had seen their new plays, "but they have Revyved an olde one Cawled *Loved Labore lost.*" [16] Whether or not this "olde play" had been presented since its performance at Court in 1597–1598, we do not know. But its description as an old play suggests that it had lain dormant for some time before its revival in 1604.

In the same letter Sir Walter complains of difficulty in finding "players Juglers & Such kinde of Creatures" to perform for the Queen. Yet, according to the formula which appears in the Privy Council minute of February 19, 1598, the Lord Chamberlain's men were permitted to stage plays so that "they might be the better enhabled and prepared to shew such plaies before her Majestie as they shalbe required at tymes meete and accustomed, to which ende they have bin cheefelie licensed." Why were they not ready then? Just what was the relationship between the public players and the Court? To what extent did the players prepare their plays specifically for the nobility? More than one scholar has been tempted to demonstrate that particular plays were prepared for the Court or courtly occasions. Usually the demonstration has had to rely on allusions in a script, for external evidence indicates that such a practice was extremely rare.

For example, we can trace the career of *Fortunatus* with minuteness. Its first performance is recorded in Henslowe's *Diary* on February 3, 1596; thereafter it runs through a normal cycle of six performances until May 26th. Between November 9th and November 30th, 1599, Dekker received £6 for rewriting the play. We may presume that it underwent a complete revision since £6 is the usual payment for a new work. On December 1st, he received an additional £1 for altering the work, and on December 12th £2 for "the eande of fortewnatus for the corte." In addition, sometime between December 6th and 12th £10 were laid out "ffor to by thinges for ffortunatus." The entries indicate clearly that a revival for the public playhouse had been planned, for which Dekker was commissioned to rewrite the play. The performance at Court could not have been the initial reason for the revival; otherwise the book would not have needed a new ending so soon. After the revision was completed, perhaps even before the Court performance had been spoken for, the play was publicly produced. Yet, when the company was called upon by the Queen in holiday season, it hurriedly had Dekker furbish up a graceful and complimentary conclusion for performance before the Queen on December 27, 1599.

While it is true that the plays chosen for Court performance had been proven *in* public, it is equally true that the plays were geared *to* the public. Usually with slight alteration, though occasionally with much, the essentially public play was readied for Queen Elizabeth, and later for King James and his family. The Admiral's men paid Middleton 5s. for a prologue and epilogue for *Friar Bacon* "for the corte" on December 14, 1602, surely a small sum to invest in pleasing a sovereign. Of course, for the holidays of 1599–1600, the company had paid Dekker fully £2 for alterations to *Phaethon* for the Court. An additional pound was laid out for "divers thinges" for the Court. Yet when the play was brought out two years earlier £5 had been spent on its furnishings for public presentation.[17]

Few plays produced by the professional players received their first performances at the Court. Reference to the summary of court performances (Appendix A, chart iii) will show that, of 144 plays presented at Court between 1590 and 1642, only eight seem to have been intended especially and initially for the Court. Two were presented in 1620, five after 1629. Only one comes from the first decade of the seventeenth century.[18]

During the holiday season of 1602–1603 the Lord Admiral's men gave three plays at Court. Presumably one of these was *As Merry As May Be,* for on November 9, 1602, John Day was given 40s. "in earneste of a Boocke called mery as may be for the corte" and on November 17th, Day, Smith, and Hathway were paid £6 more. What the occasion was for this extraordinary procedure we cannot now discover. The Admiral's men were at Court on December 27, 1602, March 6, 1603, and possibly March 8th. On which of these nights *As Merry As May Be* was played, we do not know. Considering the practice of the Admiral's men, it is not impossible that, despite the entry by Henslowe, the first performance of *As Merry As May Be* was at the Fortune.

All other plays, in one way or another, show the marks of public performance. In many instances insufficient evidence prevents us from concluding with any certainty whether or not a Court performance was initially envisioned; so many plays exist only as titles in the warrants. But where evidence appears, it supports the contention that public performance preceded Court performance. In eight cases we have the date of the licensing of a play by Sir Henry Herbert as well as the date of its first Court performance. Naturally, in each case the licensing came first. Herbert's records give substantial support for the assumption that the plays were acted the day they were licensed.[19] For example, Malone notes against the license for July 29, 1629: *"The Northern Lass,* which was acted by the King's Company on the 29th of July, 1629." Moreover, for *The Witts* by Davenant we have confirmation of public performance before Court performance. Licensed on January 19, 1634, the King having rejected some of the severities of Herbert's censoring on the 9th, Mildmay saw it acted at Blackfriars only three days later, on January 22nd. On the 28th it was given at Court.[20]

The type of theatrical presentation especially conceived and executed for a courtly audience was different in tone and character from that of the popular plays. Masques and entertainments, in their symbolic spectacles, learned allusions, and elaborate compliments delighted royalty through novelty and flattery. Interspersed with debate, music, and dance, these forms bore but a cousinly relationship to the drama. Professional writers such as Jonson, who wrote masques, had to alter their methods, for works commissioned for royal pleasure demanded that the poet practice his art with a difference. Sixty years later we find the same dichotomy occurring in the work of Molière.

Being commercial enterprises, the public theaters must have directed their energies to satisfying the customer who paid best. Some simple calculations will demonstrate that the players were dependent far more upon their public than their Court receipts. The involved estimates in determining the basis for the income of the various companies have been undertaken elsewhere and need not be repeated here. Briefly, we can adopt the results of various scholars.[21] From 1594 through 1596 the average number of playing days per year, according to Henslowe's

Diary, was 195⅔ (1594, 206; 1595, 211; 1596, 170). Consequently, about two hundred playing days a year in London
may be regarded as average. Baldwin concluded that the return to the actors for a 300-performance year was £1260. On
this basis the income for the minimum of 200 playing days a
year would come to £840. Harbage concludes that the average
daily attendance at the Rose was 1,250 persons. Since he divides
the total capacity of 2,494 into 870 persons in the yard at one
penny, 1,408 persons in the penny-gallery, and 216 in the two-
penny gallery (at two- and three-penny admissions respectively),
the average daily attendance in each section yields 436, 705, and
108 persons each by a simple proportionate equation. The average daily income would then be £9.0s.10d., the actors' share being £7.2s.5d. Consequently, by multiplying this figure by 200
we have the average yearly income for the actors of £1,424.3s.4d.
A final estimate, employing Harbage's attendance figures of
1250 and John Cranford Adams' arrangement of the Globe
playhouse, yields an income to the actors of £8.12s.5d. daily,
exclusive of the Lords' rooms, or £1724.3s.4d. for 200 days.
The Lords' rooms brought them 37s.6d. additional each day,
or £375 a year. In estimating income for the Globe company,
we must remember that at least five of the sharers of the
Chamberlain-King's men were also housekeepers and derived
income from the playhouse directly.

From Elizabeth, and later from James, the Chamberlain-
King's men received £873 between 1599 and 1609, of which
amount £70 was for relief of the company during plague time,
and £30 for reimbursement for expenses incurred during unusually lengthy travel to and from the Court. Thus the annual
average for playing was £77.6s., with the court payments in the
later years substantially greater than in the early ones. Grants
from Elizabeth never totaled more than 5 per cent of the income
the company earned at the Globe.[22] Under James the percentage
rose to a high of about fifteen by 1609. The increase in Court
support, evident in these figures, ultimately led the Globe
company to appeal increasingly to an aristocratic audience. But
throughout the decade we are considering, the actors depended

on the pence of a large, heterogeneous public more than upon
the bounty of their prince.

The players certainly tendered courtesy and respect to the
Court, which after all was their main defense against puritanical
suppression. No doubt, at the behest of the sovereign, each
company eagerly fulfilled the service required of it. The players'
well-being in and about London as well as their prestige depended to a significant extent on their relationship with the
prince. Yet the historical, literary, and economic evidence does
not support the attempts to demonstrate that such plays as
Macbeth, *The Merry Wives of Windsor*, or *Twelfth Night* were
first presented at Court. For example, Leslie Hotson's thesis that
Twelfth Night was a tribute to the ambassador, Virginio Orsino, Duke of Bracciano, has been challenged by Frances Keen
who has reexamined the documents.[23] Except for *Troilus and
Cressida*, it is not likely that any Shakespearean play of the
Globe decade was given its premiere anywhere else than at the
Globe.

I have dealt with the repertory system at length because
insufficient attention has been paid to it. In reconstructing the
staging of any company, the character of this system cannot be
ignored. For the Globe company as well as for the other companies, the staging of plays was conditioned by the irregular
alternation of plays, the large number of plays that had to be
ready for performance at one time, the rapidity with which
new ones were added to the repertory, the probability of revivals, and the reliance upon the public playhouse for theatrical well-being. Allowance for these conditions must be made
in any discussion of the play, the stage, and the actor.

Chapter Two

THE DRAMATURGY

S HAKESPEARE's plays of the Globe years are the highest forms of drama to result from a century of evolution. The long-fought battle between popular and private taste was to go on, finally to the defeat of popular taste in the rise of the private theaters. But in the ten years of the Globe, before the King's men saw their theatrical future in appealing to a Blackfriars trade, the artistic possibilities of the popular narrative drama were abundantly realized.

As the poet created the play, the actors rehearsed it—or very shortly thereafter. At the Globe playhouse the intimacy between Shakespeare and his colleagues gave unparalleled opportunity for artistic collaboration. Through changes in status and physical surroundings, they maintained warm personal and professional relations. From a common creative act arose the plays that Shakespeare penned and the productions that his friends presented. The record of this partnership is contained in the extant scripts, not merely in stage directions or in dialogue, but in the very substance of the dramatist's craft, the structure of the incidents.

To know this structure of incidents is no simple matter. Little contemporary Elizabethan theory of the dramatist's craft exists.[1] Of the few contemporary essays on poesy which treat the drama, Sidney's *The Defence of Poesie* (c. 1583), is not only the best known but also the most thorough. In measuring pre-Shakespearean drama by neoclassic standards, Sidney concludes that the early plays lack order. Yet the characteristic that Sidney so roundly condemned is the very one which, as we shall see, was so skillfully mastered by the turn of the century: the narration of an extended history covering much time and many places. By then classicism was no longer a fixed standard. This is nowhere more evident than in the words of Ben Jonson. The most classical of all the Elizabethan playwrights, with the possible exception of Chapman, Jonson contains in his remarks on the drama contradictory tendencies not fully reconciled in theory.

The chorus to *Every Man Out of His Humour*, a Globe play, provides the clearest expression of his views on the drama. Citing the precedent of the Greek poets, Jonson asserts, through the choral figure of Cordatus, that he does not see why the English poets should not enjoy "the same licence, or free power, to illustrate and heighten our invention as [the Greeks] did; and not bee tyed to those strict and regular formes, which the nicenesse of a few (who are nothing but forme) would thrust upon us" (Chorus, 267–270). Earlier, obliged to explain the absence of the traditional forms of classical drama, Cordatus remarks that there is no necessity to observe them. Yet, in setting the play in England, Cordatus quibbles over the nature of unity of place. He finds it acceptable for the author to have "a whole Iland to run through" but scorns those authors who, in one play, by showing "so many seas, countries, and kingdomes, past over with such admirable dexteritie . . . out-run the apprehension of their auditorie" (Chorus, 279–286). Later in the play, despite his previous deprecation of classical authority, Jonson justifies the almost tragic scene of Sordido's attempted suicide (III, ii) by resorting to the authority of Plautus (III, viii, 88 ff.). At another point he cites Cicero's definition of comedy to demolish the citadel of romantic comedy (III, vi, 202–207). Throughout, Jonson maintains a double standard, eluding adherence to classical prescription when it suits him to do so, citing classical authority when it supports his practice, but at all times aware that mere imitation is neither possible nor desirable. For, it is significant to note, Jonson does not oppose classical form to no form at all, but "strict and regular" form to personal invention.

Dramatic theory of the Elizabethan period is particularly deceptive because the little that exists is usually classical in vocabulary and orientation. Baldwin has attempted to equate the use of classical terms with the creation of the equivalent form. He cites Jonson's use of the critical terms *epitasis* and *catastrophe* in *Every Man Out of His Humour,* together with similar evidence from *The New Inn,* as proof that "Jonson knows and observes 'the Law of Comedy' as it has been laid down by the sixteenth century commentators on Terence." The epitasis is variously defined as "the intension or exaggeration of matters" or "the most busy part of a comedy" or "the progress of the turbations . . . the knot of error." [2] However, these generalizations have little to do with the way in which a play is shaped. For that we must go back to actual models. At once we see that the terms cannot be applied to both Terence and Jonson, and yet mean the same things. The interplay between Simo and Davus in *The Woman of Andros,* as they attempt to outwit each other, produces a tightly drawn comedy of situation. The display of foolery which infuriates Macilente results in an ambling satirical comedy. Comparison discloses that not only in tone and content but also in function and effect the epitasis or the "busie part of the subject" differs in each case. Clearly, in no substantial way did the Elizabethans derive their dramatic forms from classical tradition.

In the absence of such a tradition and with the lack of a generally accepted alternative, the theory has persisted that Elizabethan drama lacks structural form. "The events . . . are produced without any art of connection or care of disposition," wrote Samuel Johnson of *Antony and Cleopatra.* Substantially the same charge has been leveled against Shakespeare's plays in particular and Elizabethan drama in general. The art of Elizabethan drama, it is said, must be sought in the characterization, in the poetic expression, in the myth-making patterns of ideas, but not in the structure of events. In a currently fashionable form, this view is stated quite straightforwardly by M. C. Bradbrook. "The essential structure of Elizabethan drama lies not in the narrative or the characters but in the words. . . . [The structure] was purely poetic." [3]

It is true that Elizabethan dramatic structure appears to be irregular in form and haphazard in progression. Conditions of presentation, described in the previous chapter, indicate that any conscious artistic purpose must have been difficult to pursue. The speed of composition, the prevalence of collaboration, and the absence of formal standards contributed to what might be called pragmatic dramatization. However, pragmatic dramatization did not necessarily prevent the appearance of distinctive dramatic forms. In fact, the winnowing process of the repertory system was evolutionary, ensuring the development of drama in response not to abstract theory but to the deeply ingrained artistic practices of the age.

I. PREMISES FOR A STUDY OF SHAKESPEAREAN DRAMATIC FORM

In her constantly stimulating book *Endeavors of Art* Madeleine Doran introduces a new and provocative approach to the examination of Elizabethan dramatic structure. Adopting the thesis of Heinrich Wölfflin, expounded in his *Principles of Art History*, Doran extends it to apply to the literary artist. Wölfflin argues that "the art of one age differs from that of another because the artists have different modes of imaginative beholding . . . [As a result], any change in representational content from one period to [another is] less important to the effect of difference than the change in style arising from difference in decorative principle" or way of beholding.[4] Thus, the intent of the art work is less evident in the subject treated than in the arrangement effected. In comparing the "modes of imaginative beholding" in Renaissance and Baroque art, Wölfflin differentiates the two styles in terms of five categories of visual opposites, one of which is diffusion of effect (multiplicity) versus concentration of effect (unity). This category is the one most relevant to a consideration of dramatic literature. By demonstrating that Renaissance art "achieves its unity by making the parts independent as free members [and by relating them through a] coordination of the accents," Wölfflin reconciles the opposites of multiplicity and unity in a concept of "multiple unity."[5]

In the Elizabethan age the recurrent and popular expression of this concept is found in the image of art as a "mirror." Hamlet's use of this image need not be quoted. Substantially it was anticipated by Jonson in *Every Man Out of His Humour:*

> ASPER. Well I will scourge those apes;
> And to these courteous eyes [of the audience] oppose
>   a mirrour,
> As large as is the stage, whereon we act:
> Where they shall see the times deformitie
> Anatomiz'd in every nerve, and sinnew,
> With constant courage, and contempt of feare.
>   [Chorus, 117–122]

Both uses of the image reveal that the reflection is to be of the times and to be directed at the spectator. That the mirror is inherent in the thinking of the Elizabethan age not only as the purpose but as the *method* of poetry is expressed even more clearly in Puttenham's *The Arte of English Poesie.* In objecting to the mingling of the qualities of lightheaded or "phantasticall" men with poets, which "the pride of many Gentlemen and others" insist on to the derision of poetry, Puttenham writes that the poet's brain "being well affected, [is] not onely nothing disorderly or confused with any monstruous imaginations or conceits, but very formall, and in his much multiformitie *uniforme,* that is well proportioned, and so passing cleare, that by [the mind], as by a glasse or mirrour, are represented unto the soule all maner of bewtifull visions." Later: "There be againe of these glasses that shew thinges exceeding faire and comely; others that shew figures monstruous & illfavored." [6] Here the poet's mind, utilizing invention and imagination, is a mirror by which the soul receives vision.

The "mirror" had two principal functions in the Elizabethan period. One was to represent experience, in short, to achieve verisimilitude. Miss Doran demonstrates that the Elizabethans did not expect particular realism but universal truths. The other was to bring together many kinds of experience. Jonson clearly means to have the mirror turn this way and that in order to reflect a multiple image of the times. Shakespeare implies that in showing "virtue her own feature, scorn her own image," the mirror held up to nature reflects the allegorical figure Virtue, at the same time as it reflects her evil sister, Scorn. The actual practices of the plays illustrate that the poets sought to project multiple aspects of a situation—Puttenham's multi-formitie—as it were by a mirror. Consequently, they tended to give equal emphasis to the various elements of the drama, that is, to produce a coordination rather than a subordination of parts. What "coordination of parts" means in dramaturgy may be seen by contrasting the relative dominance and integration of character, plot, language, and theme in classical and Renaissance drama.

In classical and modern "realistic" construction, plot, or the structure of incidents, is dominant. It is an imitation of an action to which character and language are subordinated. Although Francis Fergusson rightly points out the difficulty of defining the word "action," nevertheless, he makes it clear that Aristotle specifies that plot is the prime embodiment of the action.[7] In this Aristotle describes the actual practice of ancient Greek drama. The incidents embrace the total significance of a play, for if plot, the structure of incidents, imitates the action which is the soul of tragedy, it must also contain the meaning of that action. Through plot the meaning radiates into character and language. Such a pyramid of emphasis, in which certain dramatic elements are subordinated, ensures genuine unity of action. If Greek drama did not always realize such an ideal form, it aspired toward such a realization.

In Renaissance construction, however, with its independent parts and coordinated accents, unity of action is not really possible. The structure of incidents does not implicitly contain the total meaning of the play. Character and thought have degrees of autonomy. They are not subordinate but coordinate with the plot. Therefore, the plot is not the sole source of unity. Instead, unity must arise from the dynamic interaction of the various parts of the drama: story, character, and language. Our task is to discover how this was accomplished.

Two habits of composition characterized the Elizabethan dramatists. First, the poets turned to popular romance and history for the sources of their plots. Baldwin saw one of the major problems of the dramatists to be the shaping of narrative material to dramatic ends, and this he believes was accomplished through the Terentian five-act structure. Both Hardin Craig and Doran regard the romantic story as the formative influence in English drama.[8] Following Manly, Doran sees the miracle play as the main source of the romantic story and, as such, a principal forerunner of the Elizabethan drama. Secondly, in utilizing these materials, "English dramatists almost without exception adopted the sequential method of action, and all the weight of classic drama did not prevail to change their minds about it." [9] The importance of this factor in the molding of drama is further emphasized in Miss Doran's suggestion that the source material, or the story, "is often the chief determinant of whether or not a play is well organized." [10] A glance at the play list of the Globe's company reveals that with the possible exception of *Every Man Out of His Humour* and *A Larum for London*, story plays a decisive part in the flow of the drama. But so was story or fable the groundwork of ancient Greek drama. The differences arise from the ways in which the dramatists of each age treated their stories.

To begin with, the English dramatists retained a very large portion of a given story. They arranged but did not eliminate. In fact, they frequently supplied additional events. In *A Larum for London* we find scene after scene illustrating the awful fate that befell the people of Antwerp at the hands of the Spanish. A copious montage of horrors passes across the stage. This multiplicity of events is a prime characteristic of this drama. To the Lear story Shakespeare adds the tale of Gloucester, to that of Helena and Bertram the story of Parolles.

Having taken a bustling story as his basis, the poet had to arrange all the events in dramatic order. According to Doran he had to find "a different method from the classical in two central problems of form: how to get concentration, and how to achieve organic structure, that is, how to achieve an action causally connected from beginning to middle to end." [11] However, Bradbrook has rightly pointed out that in Elizabethan drama "consecutive or causal succession of events is not of the first importance." With this observation, she dismisses narrative as not being one of the first concerns of the dramatists.[12]

Certainly Bradbrook is right about the absence of Aristotelian causality, as the briefest review of most Elizabethan plays will show. The events leading to Cordelia's death are without cause unless we choose chance as the cause. It is by chance she is captured, it is by chance that Edmund confesses too late.

The issue, however, is joined incorrectly. Organic structure, in this type of drama, is not a product of "causally connected events." Nor can the absence of such connection minimize the dependence of Elizabethan dramaturgy upon narrative progression. To appreciate this point of view, we must comprehend the difference between how we usually expect a play to be linked causally and how the Elizabethans employed dramatic causation.

I believe that I follow most critics in deriving the concept of dramatic causation from Aristotle's admonition that "the plot . . . must imitate one action and that a whole, the structural union of the parts being such that, if any one of them is displaced or removed, the whole will be disjointed and disturbed." The Aristotelian plot is compressive and retrospective. Its method is to submit man to an intolerable pressure until there is a single bursting point that shatters life. A single act, invariably occurring before the play begins, initiates a series of events which, linked together in a probable and necessary sequence, produces the catastrophe, which once again casts back to the original source of momentum. Such linear intensification is promoted by the exertion of tremendous will on the part of the leading characters. Antigone's willful piety clashes with Creon's statism, Philoctetes' desire for revenge and Ulysses' desire for victory at Troy combine within Neoptolemus in a conflict between honor and duty. All incidents develop out of the wills of the characters. Incident counteracts incident. For example, before Oedipus can fully digest the charge of Tiresias, he accuses Creon of treachery. Creon responds to the charge, but before their conflict can be resolved, Jocasta tries to reconcile them, the very act of which brings Oedipus closer to the awesome truth. Focus is upon the drama mounting to the climax: the scenes leading to Oedipus' discovery, the struggle leading to Neoptolemus' decision, or the near disaster leading to the ultimate revelation of Ion's origin. To sum up, a play linked causally dramatizes all the crucial causes of major actions, maintaining due balance between the force of the motive and the intensity of effect, the action mounting from cause to effect to cause, so that at any point we are aware of what circumstances led to one and only one result. Suspense is a natural corollary of such organization, and concentration of effect is its aim.

It is apparent that the Elizabethan dramatists did not address themselves to the organization of that type of sequence. Very few plays of theirs can be found where closely linked causation produces the denouement. First, the causes for significant changes are frequently assumed or implied and not dramatized. Why Lear divides his kingdom, why Cleopatra flees the battle, why Angelo repents remain unrevealed. Iago promises to show Roderigo "such a necessity in his [Claudio's] death that you shall think yourself bound to put it on him" (IV, ii, 247–248), and later Roderigo, waiting to assail Claudio, affirms that Iago "hath given me satisfying reasons" (V, i, 9). Between the scenes some justification, unknown to us, was given Roderigo by Iago. The revelation of Lady Macbeth's haunting nightmares actually serves as a *peripeteia* which, Aristotle warns, must be "subject always to our rule of probability, or necessity." But this reversal is not the result of a succession of events leading to a necessary end, unless we regard it as having taken place offstage. Such an end may be probable, of course, but we are given no insight into the forces that make it probable. Nor apparently did Shakespeare feel it incumbent upon him to show these forces. That we accept the sleep-walking scene is not so much because it is either inevitable or likely, but because of all things in the realm of possibility that could have befallen the woman, her nightmares so perfectly satisfy both our sense of justice and our inclination toward pity at the same time.

Secondly, the causes for significant changes, when dramatized, are not always commensurate with the effects. To make itself felt, a dramatic cause, in the Aristotelian sense, must have sufficient weight to produce the effect it does; a great cause must not produce a puny effort, nor a puny effort a great result. Yet this lack of proportion occurs often in Shakespeare. The ease with which Iago secures Desdemona's handkerchief from Emilia, though she wonders at the purpose of his request, does not balance the awful consequences. Brutus' and Cassius' meager dispute over whether or not to allow Antony to speak at Caesar's funeral is overshadowed by the fatal results. Here, as elsewhere, the perfunctoriness of the struggle between two antagonists is out of proportion to the effect that follows. The appearance of such imbalance, however, is not the result of ineptitude, but of artistic choice. Interest was not in the conflict leading to a decision, but the effect of the decision itself. The causes of action, therefore, tended to be taken for granted or conveyed with minimum emphasis; in other words, they were not regarded as being of first importance and so did not need to be dramatized with particularity. This attitude contributed largely to the looseness with which parts of a play are joined.

Causation, of course, was not completely abandoned, but it was generalized. Largely it resided in the given circumstances of the initial action, as Lear's pride leading him to reject Cordelia or Cleopatra's womanhood causing her to flee. For, within the Elizabethan scheme of man's relation to his action, tightly linked causation was incomprehensible.

Nor was the alternative to causal succession, episodic structure, "a stringing together of events in mere temporal succession [where] each complication is solved as it arises." [13] For dramatic causation of the parts, the Elizabethan substituted a rhythmic framework for the whole. The dramatization of a complete story employing many characters meant that within the scope of the narrative lay many plausible events. This gave the poet a wide choice of incidents with which to arrange his plot, the scope of the narrative imparting a limit of its own. Concurrently, the tendency for "mirroring" nature led him to choose scenes which would contrast or echo others or which would illustrate various facets of a single experience.

In such a drama the first scenes perform a vital function. They establish the premises upon which the action will be built. Little exposition is necessary, for not much has happened before the play opens. It is curious to note that almost all the principal characters are in a state of inertia at the beginning of the action. Hamlet, sorely distressed by his mother's marriage, is not about to act. Rosalind, Cordelia, Lear, Antony, Cleopatra, Brutus, Macbeth, Timon all are uncommitted to anything but the state, happy or troubled, wherein we first see them. Usually some force, either early in the first scenes or just before them, impels the characters to act. This type of opening contributes to the impression, first, that the play is a self-contained microcosm and, second, that the first scenes are illustrations.

Antony and Cleopatra offers a model for such an opening. The comments of Demetrius and Philo provide the frame for the illustration-premise of Antony's love for Cleopatra and his rejection of Rome. Though the messenger from Rome does propel the action forward, calling Antony to Caesar, his arrival is handled in a ritualistic manner. We might consider this demonstration of the premise as analogous to the statement of a theme in music. Just as a composer announces his musical idea, the Elizabethan dramatist illustrates his dramatic idea, proceeding from it to the variations which occupy the balance of the play.[14]

Stemming from these premises are two lines of progression, one narrative, one dramatic. The first, which is essentially concerned with what *happens* to the characters, follows a line of development to the very last scene. The second, which involves what the characters *undergo*, reaches fullness somewhere near the center of the play.

The narrative line, what happens, proceeds linearly to the finale. In *Lear*, this is concerned with the story of two fathers deceived by certain of their children; through deception they give these children their trust and power; they suffer at their hands; ultimately they are vindicated by their faithful children. All the plots and intrigues are part of the narrative. Not until Edgar fells Edmund are these plots unmasked.

The dramatic line, what the characters undergo, extends to heights of passion at the center of the play and then contracts. This line in *Lear* is concerned with how a proud man endures curbs on his nature and is reduced to humility. In the first half of the play Lear, asserting his arrogance to the fullest, passes to the limits of madness. In the second, he acquiesces to suffering, one might say, becomes detached from it. Extension and contraction is the pattern, extension of the potentialities of the premises of the action, contraction of the effects after they have reached their fulfillment.

Such parallel development of a play's action produces contradictory impulses in the drama. On one hand there existed the impulse to complete the story, on the other there persisted the temptation to dilate upon the effect of the action upon the individuals. One reason why modern audiences suffer from "fourth act fatigue" in witnessing a Shakespearean play stems from the fact that their interest in the play is disproportionate. They have a greater interest in the dramatic line than in the narrative. For the Elizabethan audience the interest must have been more evenly balanced. For them the finale, the completion of the narrative line, had as much appeal as the "climax," the height of the dramatic line.

II. FORM AND FUNCTION IN THE FINALES OF THE GLOBE PLAYS

We find a surprising similarity in the finales. Almost every one of the Globe plays contains a public resolution. Seldom is the conclusion private. The final scene of *Every Man Out of His Humour* containing the last of Macilente's purgations is one of the exceptions, as are the conclusions of *A Larum for London* and in some respects of *The Devil's Charter*. In the latter play a spectacular conclusion representing the damnation of Pope Alexander is appended to a grand finale. All the other eleven non-Shakespearean plays terminate in a finale that is ceremonious and public. Of the fifteen Shakespearean plays produced between 1599 and 1609 only *Troilus and Cressida* clearly dispenses with this type of finale. Thus, of the twenty-nine plays presented by the Globe company, twenty-five have a public accounting for the preceding action.

The importance of ending a play with a public exhibition is demonstrated by the amount of contrivance effected in some plays to ensure a grand finale. In the *Fair Maid of Bristow*, King Richard suddenly grants Anabell the right to produce a champion for Vallenger. By doing so, however, he permits a last, grand discovery and sacrifice scene to be played. Other examples can be found in Shakespeare's plays. One of the objections to *Measure for Measure* has been the forced manner in which the Duke succeeds in bringing the conclusion to public trial. This may equally well be the charge against *All's Well*. Yet, whether or not it evolves logically from the preceding action, the great closing scene is a marked formal characteristic of this drama.

Several things may happen in the finale, either separately or jointly. In romance and comedy love triumphs. Any punishment that deserves to be meted out is usually tempered. Angelo "perceives he's safe" in *Measure for Measure* and Malvolio will be entreated to a peace. In tragedy justice prevails, even though the hero may die in the process. In comedy, the substance of the finale is the working out of the complications or confusions which impede love, in tragedy, the overcoming of evil forces that destroy a just order. In some instances, notably *Measure for Measure,* both love and justice triumph.

Common to all the Globe plays are:

(1) a means for bringing about justice or of winning love: the most frequent means are discovery of the identity of disguised persons, trial, execution, repentance, single combat, suicide;

(2) a judge-figure who pronounces judgment: he may either deliver the verdict and/or grant mercy or, after the action has occurred, declare the purport of the action; in finales of combat he may serve as the avenging arm of justice;

(3) a ranking figure who reasserts order: invariably the person of highest authority, in many plays he is identical with the judge-figure. It is a convention of Elizabethan drama that the last lines of a play, excluding epilogues and songs, be spoken by the ranking figure.

In the non-Shakespearean plays, discovery, trial and/or execution, and repentance appear most often. *Fair Maid of Bristow* employs both discovery and execution, *The London Prodigal,* discovery and repentance. Excluding *Every Man Out of His Humour,* all the non-Shakespearean plays have judge-figures. In the *Merry Devil* it is the father, in *Volpone* the justices, in *Fair Maid of Bristow* King Richard, in *Miseries of Enforced Marriage,* Scarborrow himself.[15]

This figure, sometimes central to the story, sometimes not, usually referees the conflict and, at the conclusion, either passes judgment or grants mercy. In two plays the formal agency for bringing judgment about is indirect. In the brilliant reversal scene in *Sejanus* judgment is exercised through the absent figure of the Emperor Tiberius. His letter read to the convocation of senators provides the means. In turn, his judgment illustrates the caprice of fortune and the descent of nemesis. The other play, *Thomas Lord Cromwell,* likewise makes use of an indirect agency as a substitute for the judge: King Henry's delayed reprieve for Cromwell.

Each of Shakespeare's plays, excluding *Troilus and Cressida,* also employs a final scene in which judgment is meted out and/or love is won. The content of the finale may be one or a combination of discovery, single combat, preparation for suicide, trial, and siege.[16] In seven of his Globe plays discovery untangles the knot of error which separated the lovers. Usually reserved for comedy, it is employed to make Othello comprehend the horror of his act. Discovery is also combined with repentance in *All's Well* and with trial in *Measure for Measure.* In *Timon* the framework of the siege contains a trial.

In his use of formal agents Shakespeare is more subtle than his fellow playwrights. Only six plays contain judge-figures central to the action: the King in *All's Well,* the "lords o' the city" in *Coriolanus,* Alcibiades in *Timon* and, in an ingenious use of this device, Hymen in *As You Like It,* and finally the Dukes in *Measure for Measure* and *Twelfth Night.* In describing Shakespeare's use of the Duke as a type figure, C. B. Watson points out that "at the end of a play the role of the Duke is threefold: he acts to resolve the conflict in the interests of justice; he grants mercy to the offenders; and finally he plays the host at the festivities which are presumably to follow on the successful resolution of the dramatic conflict."[17]

Into the other eight plays Shakespeare introduced more subtle methods of passing judgment. Two of them show a common pattern. Although a judge-figure is present, the true judgment is made by the hero. Antony is the judge-figure in *Julius Caesar,* and Octavius in *Antony and Cleopatra,* but in each case the hero by committing suicide substitutes his or her own judgment for that of other authority. Both Brutus and Cleopatra prepare for self-death elaborately. It becomes a means of warding off ignominy and gaining glory. In *Othello* suicide serves the same purpose with only this difference, that Othello's own strong sense of justice makes it unnecessary to have a judge-figure. The ranking figure, in each of these plays, is handled differently. In *Julius Caesar,* Octavius has this role, in *Othello,* Lodovico, and in *Antony and Cleopatra,* Octavius is both judge and ranking figure.

In each of three other plays, *Lear, Macbeth,* and *Hamlet,* true judgment is rendered through a fateful single combat in which one combatant represents the forces of light, the other of darkness. In *Merry Wives* we find a double judgment. Mockery is the judgment passed on Falstaff and forgiveness that awarded Fenton and Ann. Like *Othello, Pericles* lacks a judge-figure during the finale. Instead, the goddess Diana (V, i) has played that role in the act of directing Pericles to the discovery of Thaisa. Thus, in both the Shakespearean and non-Shakespearean plays the same kind of formal conclusion rounds out the story. This particular kind of conclusion reflects the moral ideals of Elizabethan society, the achievement of salvation or order or love through judgment.

Another characteristic of the concluding scene is that it is a narrative conclusion in which the initial situation is brought to a complete close rather than a thematic conclusion in which the implications of the theme are ultimately dramatized. Several elements of the narrative are introduced early in *As You Like It.* They are Oliver's alienation of Orlando's heritage, Duke Frederick's usurpation of his brother's throne, and the love of Rosalind and Orlando. The thematic elements are indirectly related to the plot. They make themselves felt obliquely. But they are not embodied in the main action of the finale, nor, being contrasting expressions of the quality of love rather than moral injunctions, can they be so embodied. In fact, the thematic elements are absent from the finale, which is concerned with the tying of many a lover's knot and the appropriate resignation of Duke Frederick. The same holds true for *Hamlet*. The true issue, Hamlet's inability to "set things right," is resolved when Hamlet comes to a tranquil peace with his soul and accepts the guidance of providence in the scene with Horatio immediately preceding the duel (V, ii). However, the story has to be completed, and ironically Hamlet achieves by chance what he could not gain by design. In only a few plays do the thematic and narrative issues merge in the final moments of the action. *Othello* of all Shakespeare's plays offers the finest example of this concurrence, and perhaps because of this fact many critics regard *Othello* as Shakespeare's finest piece of dramatic construction. Such regard, however, is founded upon Aristotelian premises. For an Elizabethan the concurrence was incidental.

Particularly vital to our understanding of the conclusion is the place that climax or catastrophe occupies in the last scenes. The finales of Shakespeare's Globe plays often fail to produce a climactic effect because the completion of the narrative does not arise from the conflicting forces of the theme or action. Instead ceremony frequently serves as a substitute for climax. By the time the last scene began, the Elizabethan audience knew how the story would end. But it satisfied the Elizabethan sense of ritual to see the pageant of the conclusion acted out. The appeal of this pageant is clearly illustrated in *Measure for Measure, Macbeth,* and *As You Like It.* In these plays the rendition of judgment through trial or combat or revelation respectively supplied the excitement that a dramatic climax would have afforded. Nor should we underestimate the interest such conclusions held for an Elizabethan audience. Knight, in pointing out that the tragedies reach a climax in Act III, suggests that the "military conflicts [at the end] were probably far more important to an Elizabethan " than to us.[18] But this statement has a wider applicability. Ceremony, such as Orsino's visit to Olivia or trial-by-combat in *Lear* or a parley in *Timon*, is often the frame for the finale. Because ceremony played so vital a role in Elizabethan life, it had an unusually strong appeal for the audience who saw it represented on the stage.

III. THE NATURE AND FORM OF THE "CLIMAX" IN THE GLOBE PLAYS

The impulse to complete the story is satisfied in the finale, as we have seen. The impulse to dilate upon the story achieves maximum expansion in the center of the play. The presence of scenes of extreme complication and intense emotion at this point in the Shakespearean plays has led to the development of the theory of a third act climax. It has been expressed in various ways by various scholars. Knight merely notes this grouping of intensifications. Lawrence, anticipating Baldwin's thesis of the five-act structure, assumes a third act climax. Baldwin would call it the imitation of the Terentian epitasis, and Moulton speaks of it as the center piece at the point of a regular arch.[19]

Certainly there is marked emotional intensification at the center of a Shakespearean play. However, if we are to call it a climax, we must redefine our term, taking care that it not be confused with the climax in classical or modern drama. There the climax is taken to be a single point of extreme intensity where the conflicting forces come to a final, irreconcilable opposition. At that point a dramatic explosion, leading to the denouement, is the direct outcome of the climactic release. Hedda Gabler has schemed to accomplish the glorious ruination of Lövborg. At the very moment when she expects to exult, she discovers that she has failed. The climax occurs when she learns that instead of controlling others, she herself is controlled. The denouement, her death, is a direct consequence. Causally-linked drama, by its very nature, drives to a "highest" point. In Greek drama it is usually a moment of recognition and/or reversal. That is why we must be cautious of speaking of a climax in Shakespearean drama.

If we endeavor to isolate such a climax in Elizabethan tragedy, we run into many difficulties. For example, is the play-within-the-play scene, the prayer scene, or the closet scene the climax of *Hamlet?* All contain some reversal; all are highly intense; we are emotionally swept along by them, caught up in the melodrama of Hamlet's device, in his mad exultation at its effect upon Claudius, in the pathos of Claudius' contrition, and in the tortured uncertainty of Gertrude. But none of these scenes alone reveals a point of climax. If there is either recognition or reversal, it arises from accumulation of effect.

A more extended example of this diffusion of climax can be found in *Lear*. Commencing with the famous "Blow, winds" speech, there are four painfully intense scenes: three of Lear on the heath, one of the blinding of Gloucester, interspersed by two brief scenes leading to that cruel act. The Lear and Gloucester scenes alternate. In some ways the emotional hysteria of Lear's

> Blow, winds, and crack your cheeks! rage! blow!
> You cataracts and hurricanoes, spout
> Till you have drench'd our steeples,
>   drown'd the cocks!
>
> [III, ii, 1-3]

is the most intense moment, and yet the dramatic intensification brought about by weaving together the trials of Lear and those of poor Tom has yet to occur. Moulton regards the meeting of those two as the climax.[20] But in which scene? The first outside the hovel, or the second in the shelter, where Lear arraigns his false daughters? Granville-Barker selects an exact moment for the climax, in the second of the storm scenes "when the proud old king kneels humbly and alone in his wretchedness to pray. This is the argument's absolute height."[21] Must, as Granville-Barker goes on to suggest, the tension relax then during the two scenes Lear plays with mad Tom? The reading of the storm scenes should make it obvious that instead of a point of intensity with subsequent slackening, we have a succession of states of intense emotional experience: Lear's self-identification with raging nature, Lear's pathetic lucidity and new-forged humility, Lear's ultimate madness during a fantastic trial. Each high point subsides before the next bursts forth, not like a solitary cannon shot but like the ebb and flow of the pounding sea. The truth seems to be that we find not a climactic point in the center of a Shakespearean play, but a climactic plateau, a "coordination of intense moments" sustained for a surprisingly extended period.

Othello alone of the tragedies does not have that complete relaxation of intensity after the central "plateau." But here it is a matter of degree, for though the wringing of Othello's heart by Iago effects the maximum reversal of attitude, Othello continues to oscillate between doubt of and belief in Desdemona's guilt. Thereafter, while intensity mounts to Desdemona's death, the tone changes. Instead of the struggle of the giant to break the bonds of his strangling jealousy, we find a painful pathos arising from the gap between Othello's misconception and Desdemona's innocence.

Those plays in which the climactic plateau is most easily perceived, in addition to *Lear* and *Hamlet*, are *Twelfth Night,* III, i–iv; *Troilus and Cressida,* IV, iv, v; V, i; [22] *Macbeth,* III, iv; IV, i; and *Antony and Cleopatra,* III, xi–xiii. Both *Julius Caesar* and *Coriolanus* have intense centers of action in the third act. In these plays, however, the crucial scenes seem to take on the nature of a climax in the Greek sense. Antony's speech and the banishment of Coriolanus are points of reversal. A closer examination, however, reveals that these peaks are blunted. Antony does not seem to wish to let the mob depart. There are several moments when he rouses them to action, only to pull them back for further inspiration. The climax of *Coriolanus* is muted even more because Coriolanus and his friends struggle with the tribunes over the same issues twice (III, i, iii). The final banishment merely brings to an end a conclusion already foregone. In each scene Coriolanus' patrician pride causes him to defy both friend and enemy. These last two plays contract the plateau only in degree, *Julius Caesar* moving furthest toward a single moment of intensity. Generally in Shakespeare we will find the centers of action dispersed rather than concentrated, sustained rather than released.

As we might expect, a change in the duration and level of the climax produces a change in its nature. Lines of action leading to crisis are foreshortened, thereby throwing fuller emphasis on the response of the character, often expressed in lyrical ecstasy.

The center of intensity in *Lear* demonstrates this qualitative change. The impellent occasion for the storm scenes occurs in Act II, scene iv. Goneril and Regan's determination to divest him of his royal position is brought home to Lear. He rushes into the raging storm after the words:

> You think I'll weep:
> No, I'll not weep.
> I have full cause of weeping, but this heart
> Shall break into a hundred thousand flaws
> Or ere I'll weep. O fool, I shall go mad!
> [II, iv, 285–289]

His heart and mind have been shaken by rejection, but this is only the prelude to madness. The succeeding scenes on the heath (III, ii, iv, vi) are a prolonged reaction to the rejection. *Lear* does not mount steadily to another stage of madness, but reveals multiple effects of this madness: rage, bewilderment, fantasy, vengefulness, helplessness. Instead of self-realization at the climax, we find passionate release. Lear exceeds the limit of emotional endurance; he can go no further in anguish. That is the reason why he disappears from the play for the succeeding six scenes (III, vii; IV, i-v).[23] During this absence Gloucester loses his sight, the disguised Edgar comes to nurse his father, Goneril and Regan separately conspire to satisfy their passions for Edmund, and the British and French armies prepare to do battle. After the climactic plateau comes story progression.

The distinctness of this central climactic grouping is less clear in the non-Shakespearean plays, but the elements are there, if only in rudimentary form. Even where the "plateau" is not sustained, the intensification of action and the change of direction in the middle of a play are present. Perhaps the clearest and most consistent evidence of this is the split structure of many plays, that is, the progression of the story in one direction, followed by a full or partial shift of direction after the first half. *A Larum for London*, a not particularly well constructed play, is composed of such interlocked halves. The first half deals with the Spanish conquest of Antwerp through the improvidence and selfishness of the city's burghers (scenes i–vii). At this climactic point the Spaniards revel in their triumph as the Duke d'Alva parcels the town among the conquering leaders. The second half concerns the hopeless, yet valiant struggle of a lame soldier to fight for the town (scenes viii–xv). This same type of division is reflected in *The London Prodigal.* Scenes i–viii relate the trick by which Flowerdale gains the hand of Luce; scenes ix–xii depict his descent into the depths of prodigality before he is finally redeemed. Here, however, the climactic scene (scene viii) involves more anticipation than response though there are three relatively equal heights of intensity: the father's rejection of the daughter who remains faithful to her husband the prodigal, the daughter's plea for her husband's freedom from arrest, and the prodigal's abuse of his wife. Among the other plays which display the split structure are *Thomas Lord Cromwell* and, in part, *The Revenger's Tragedy.*

Of all the non-Shakespearean plays, Jonson's *Sejanus* comes closest to duplicating Shakespeare's use of the climactic plateau. The rise of Sejanus is steady. He encompasses the death of Drusus, he effects the destruction of his opponents, and finally he attempts the conquest of Tiberius himself by seeking permission to marry Livia of the imperial house. Blocked in this, he urges Tiberius' departure from Rome, and in a closing soliloquy, seeing himself conqueror of those who hate him, exults:

> For when they see me arbiter of all,
> They must observe: or else, with Caesar fall.
> [III, 621–622]

Sejanus shows excessive pride in his own power, a joyous release of self-esteem. After this speech he disappears from the play until the opening of the fifth act. Meanwhile, Tiberius secretly turns to Marco as a supplementary and independent agent, thus effecting a change of direction in the play. Just when Sejanus expects to "draw all dispatches through my private hands," Tiberius crosses him. Jonson, following the classical models more closely than Shakespeare, has his greatest climax fall during the last scene. Nevertheless, clear traces of a "center of action" can be found.

The architectonic superiority of Shakespeare can be seen in the way he raises his entire center of action to a markedly intensified level. Potential climactic "plateaus" can be found in all the Globe plays cited, but some are underdeveloped and do not reach the rich florescence that makes the center of a Shakespearean play such an overwhelming dramatic experience. Perhaps the absence of superior poetic powers prevented the minor playwrights from realizing the full possibilities of this form. Nevertheless, despite the gap between the levels of their achievements, Shakespeare and his fellow playwrights of the Globe generally built their plays along the same structural lines.

IV. STRUCTURAL PATTERNS IN THE DRAMATIC NARRATIVE

The absence of linked causation naturally meant that the action was not linear. Incidents leading to the finale or to the climactic plateau did not follow one another in a succession of tightly meshed events but in a series of alternating scenes. To illustrate, between the first expression of Maria's scheme against Malvolio (II, iii) and the first working of the scheme (II, v) intervenes the lyrical scene between Viola and Orsino (II, iv). Such separation of parts of the story encouraged the independence of one scene from another, the very thing complained of by some scholars. Schücking suggests that Shakespeare shows "a tendency to episodic intensification," that is, the development of a scene at the expense of the whole.[24] F. L. Lucas expresses the same idea in his introduction to the works of Webster, asserting that the Elizabethan audiences reacted to separate scenes rather than to a whole play. The tendency to which they refer can be found in the three Falstaff-Merry Wives scenes. In the first of the scenes, Falstaff, caught in his love-game, hides in the buck basket, only to be dumped into the Thames. Here we have a complete action. Falstaff makes an advance, and he is repulsed. There is no counteraction on his part. If he were in a Roman comedy, he would have plotted how to punish his offenders or how to encompass the women again, and thus the second scene would have resulted from a counteraction on the part of Mistress Ford and Mistress Page. Instead Falstaff is persuaded to repeat the same adventure with similar results. The second scene is not more farcical or more extravagant than the first; it is merely different. In place of intensification we find fresh invention. The third scene again does not grow out of the preceding scene, but out of the husbands' decision to shame the fat man publicly. All of the Falstaff-Mistress Page-Mistress Ford scenes have a beginning, a middle, and an end. They make themselves felt at the conclusion not by intensification but by accumulation.

Though in other plays of Shakespeare the scenes may be more closely joined, yet there is always a sense of their independence from one another. As I have said, *Othello*, of all the tragedies, is probably the most closely interwoven in plot. The deception scene (III, iii) is an example of an extended scene tying together several actions. But even in this play, we find an autonomous scene, and that near the end of the play. Half mad, playing the gruesome mockery of a visitor to a brothel, Othello questions first Emilia, then Desdemona (IV, ii). Othello arrives convinced of Desdemona's guilt; he leaves with the same conviction. It is neither augmented nor dispelled. That the scene does not advance the action in no way detracts from its dramatic effectiveness, but it does reflect on the handling of the story. In the advancement of the classical drama, all scenes are integrated into a single line of action. In the progression of the Shakespearean play, scenes may be regarded as clustering about the story line. If this suggests an image of a grapevine, perhaps it is apt, for the scenes often appear to be hanging from a thread of narrative.

But a scene that may be semiautonomous insofar as the story line is involved may be central insofar as the climactic plateau is concerned. Such is the closet scene in *Hamlet*. Note how quickly Shakespeare disposes of Polonius. The murder of the old man does advance the plot, of course, for it causes Ophelia's madness and brings Laertes back from France. But the murder is a minor part of the closet scene. Of its entire 217 lines, the action involving Polonius occupies, both at the beginning and at the end, forty lines (1–33, 211–217). Another eleven lines are occupied with Hamlet's recollection that he must go to England (199–210). The remaining 166 lines are devoted to the relation of mother and son and the visitation of the ghost. Certainly the scene is dramatic, in fact, one of the most dramatic in all literature. Yet it does not carry the action on to a new stage, but allows Hamlet to express his disapproval and suspicion of his mother. In fact, the central portion of the scene leaves no trace on the plot. Though Gertrude is shaken by Hamlet's accusations against his uncle and herself, there is no indication that her attitude toward Claudius changes as a result. Nor is Hamlet purged by the meeting. Neither is the decision to send Hamlet to England brought about by it, for the King had determined to send him there immediately after the nunnery scene (III, i, 175–183). The closet scene opens with Polonius' murder and closes with a return to Hamlet's responsibility for the act. In between Hamlet relieves his soul of the stifled passion against his mother.

Certainly a drama composed of these semiautonomous scenes loses not unity necessarily, but compression. What it foregoes in that direction it makes up for in extension. Instead of the story eliminating incidents not strictly contributing to a final climax, it serves as a point of departure. When Orestes meets his mother, his behavior must follow the demands of the plot, and Aeschylus allows him only one pitiful question to Pylades: Must he kill his mother? The Elizabethan form permits the full relationship of the mother and son to be explored. Like a mirror the scene casts an additional reflection of the image that is Hamlet. For this advantage of multiplicity of implication the Elizabethan sacrificed concentration of effect. Unable to grasp this shift in emphasis, many critics have treated the lack of concentration in Shakespearean structure as evidence that the poet did not know how to construct plays. As we saw, Dr. Johnson dismissed the construction of *Antony and Cleopatra* with the comment that the events "are produced without any art of connection or care of disposition." Schücking, about a hundred and fifty years later, dismisses Shakespeare's structural

practices as primitive. The conclusion is the same though the
reasons may differ. But until we can meet Elizabethan structure
on its own terms, we really do not know what its failures were.
When we deprecate the skill of the playwrights, let us remember
that the University Wits, men trained in the Terentian, Plau-
tine, and Senecan manner, were the ones who developed the
popular Elizabethan mode. The fate that awaited them if they
did not adhere to it is keenly illustrated by Kyd's failure as a
classicist.

Within the general form of extension and contraction, extension to a climactic plateau, contraction to a ceremonious finale,
appear variant structural patterns. To reduce the total structural pattern of Elizabethan drama to a single form, or even
to two or three forms, is virtually impossible. The age was
multiple in its artistic means. Yet the inability to do this does
not mean that no structural form existed, but that many existed.
Not only was there structural variety in the works of different
men, but there were differences within the work of one man.
Nevertheless, certain dominant patterns emerge, and while the
following descriptions are not exhaustive, they include a large
proportion of the Globe plays.

Three structural patterns recur frequently in the Globe
plays: the episodic, the "river," and the "mirror" patterns. In
a crude form the episodic pattern can be found in the early
Shakespearean histories. There its basic nature can be anatom-
ized. On the thread either of a historical or of a biographical
sequence a series of events is arranged in succession. The most
marked characteristic of this form is that one event or incident
is completed before another one is begun. Among the Globe
plays of our period *Thomas Lord Cromwell* is a typical example
of this type. Cromwell passes through a series of events complete in themselves: his kindness to a distraught woman in
Antwerp, his succor of an Italian merchant, his success in freeing
the Earl of Bedford from capture, his service to Wolsey, and his
downfall at the hands of Gardiner. Although the Earl of Bedford reappears during Cromwell's conflict with Gardiner, and
remembering his rescue, endeavors to help Cromwell, the two
sections of the play are not really joined. In this play, despite

the fact that Cromwell himself provides the mechanical unity that binds the play, the dramatic unity, if there is any, is multiple. The various scenes reflect Cromwell's virtues of honesty, humanity, and loyalty, thus giving a thematic wholeness to the entire play.

Since Aristotle penned his notes called *Poetics,* the episodic play has been in disrepute. Today it is difficult to imagine that it could rise to dramatic heights. Yet if we closely examine the structure of such a play as *Macbeth,* we shall realize that it is episodic in form. Of course, there are vital alterations in that form. Primarily, there is preparation for on-coming events. Instead of one event being completed before another one is initiated, we find that brief scenes are planted earlier to make the development plausible. The potential danger of Banquo to Macbeth's ambitions is established by the witches. It is touched on before the murder of Duncan, but it is not woven into the fabric of the action at that time. At first, the overwhelming emphasis is upon the triangle of Macbeth, Lady Macbeth, and the crown. Once Duncan is disposed of, the Banquo action comes into prominence, and full attention is devoted to it. Early hints of Macduff's defection are introduced, but not until Banquo is dead does the play really concentrate on Macduff. For Macbeth's second meeting with the witches there is almost no preparation. Until the end of the banquet scene, we do not even know he is aware of their abode. Until this moment, although the play reveals an episodic structure, it is more tightly knit than most of Shakespeare's other works. After the visit of Macbeth to the witches' hovel, the episodic pattern becomes more distinct. The conception of Macbeth as a character accents the episodic quality. He struggles only to reach the immediate goal; there is no ultimate point in the universe toward which he moves. Sejanus, in comparison, reduces the episodic quality of his drama because his eyes are always upon becoming Caesar, the symbol of a god on earth. Immediate intrigues are but part of the larger aim. For this concentration Jonson lost the opportunity for those very magnificent scenes which make *Macbeth* a great play. Among other of Shakespeare's plays of this period which employ the episodic pattern are *Hamlet, Corio-*

lanus, and *Julius Caesar*. What strikes many critics as a lack of unity in *Hamlet* is its particular pattern. Once the conditions imposed on Hamlet by the Ghost are revealed, we witness the following sequence: the place of love in Hamlet's mind, the testing of Claudius at the play, the relation of mother and son. Each event is prepared for, but each in turn gains full emphasis. Nor does one event bear causative relationship to another. Though Claudius is suspicious of Hamlet at the conclusion of the nunnery scene, he indicates no unusual watchfulness over Hamlet during the play-within-the-play scene. It is as though the conflict of the previous scene has been resolved with Claudius' determination to send Hamlet to England. As a point in the story this idea is established and comes into the play when needed at the end of the closet scene. And, of course, the closet scene is not a dramatic result of the play scene. The idea that Hamlet be summoned to his mother is advanced by Polonius earlier, and whether or not Hamlet had offended the King, the meeting would have taken place. Here, then, is a skillful manipulation of the structural characteristics of the episodic pattern.

The second pattern I have named the "river" pattern. I use the term because its dramatic action resembles the flow of various tributaries into a single stream. Perhaps the best example of this type of structure can be found in *Twelfth Night*. Two streams of action are of almost equal breadth and depth; the third is merely a trickle until it joins the main flow. One main stream we may call the Orsino-Olivia-Viola action. The other is the Toby-Andrew-Malvolio action. The minor stream is the Antonio-Sebastian sequence. The principal determinant of such a structure is the length of time during which each action remains independent of the others. The first two actions remain completely independent through Acts I and II. A slight link is provided in Act III, scene i, when Malvolio courts Olivia. The full merging of the two actions takes place in Act III, scene iv. Meanwhile, the Antonio-Sebastian thread was introduced into the story in Act II, scene i, and in Act III, scene iii, and partly integrated with the main action in Act III, scene iv. In the fourth act the development of the two main threads remains suspended, Viola disappearing from the stage to enable the Sebastian element to be more fully integrated with the Olivia-Orsino-Viola triangle. Finally, in the fifth act, every element is brought together, including the Malvolio sequence, even though this necessitates the unprepared revelation that Viola's womanly garments are in the hands of a captain who "upon some action/Is now in durance, at Malvolio's suit" (V, i, 282–283).

Although this form is not as prevalent as either the episodic or the "mirror," it can be found in a number of Globe plays, for example, *The Merry Wives of Windsor, The Revenger's Tragedy,* and partly in *All's Well. Twelfth Night* remains, however, its model.

Last of the three dominant forms and the most popular one is the "mirror" pattern. Usually it consists of two stories, almost equal in emphasis. Both are introduced independently and maintain a large degree of independence throughout the play, sometimes never fully coming into plot relation with each other. Their fundamental connection derives from a similarity of theme and story development. Through sharp comparison or contrast one story casts reflections upon the other as though one were the image in the mirror and one the reality. The distinctness of each story is sometimes obscured by the fact that the same individual may appear in both stories and yet maintain independence of action in each case, at least early in the play. For example, through the first two acts Gloucester functions independently in each of the two stories in *Lear.*

Fair Maid of Bristow, among the works of the Globe repertory, is an excellent example of this pattern. In fact, here we have striking evidence of the structural care with which a minor play could be organized, despite Bradbrook's assertion that structure is possible only through "literary means." This play follows the mirror pattern almost slavishly. In the first scene Challener shows his beloved Anabell to Vallenger who falls in love with her. The two men come to blows over the girl. Challener wounds Vallenger and then flees while Vallenger is taken into Anabell's house by her father. In the second scene Harbart tries to persuade Sentloe not to remain with the courtesan,

Florence. But Sentloe, blind to her fickleness and confident of her devotion, rejects Harbart. Harbart vows to follow Sentloe in disguise. In the third scene Vallenger gains the promise of Anabell's hand. In the fourth scene Challener, learning of the impending marriage, returns to Bristow in the disguise of an Italian doctor. In the fifth scene Sentloe engages Blunt alias Harbart as a servingman, and Sentloe and Florence are invited to Anabell's wedding. At this point in the play we can identify two parallel centers of action. Each contains a "loving" couple, and a friend in disguise. In one Challener hates Vallenger and loves Anabell; in the other Harbart hates Florence and loves Sentloe.

Scene vi (nearly the middle of the play, since there are four-teen scenes in all) dramatizes the first blending of the two actions. Immediately after his marriage, Vallenger falls in love with Florence and suborns the doctor to poison Sentloe and Anabell. Later, in scene vii, Florence seduces Blunt to slay Sentloe. In each case the sworn protector is asked to commit the murder. In scene vii we have a typical "digression," a comic courting scene of two servants. The theme, however, is faithful-ness. Douse, the maid, asks whether Frog, after their marriage, "will . . . not prove unkind?" Frog, in comic doggerel, vows, among other things, that only "when Lawiers have no tongues at all" will he prove unkind. The idea contrasts with the suc-ceeding scenes in which Vallenger proves unkind to Anabell, only to have Florence subsequently prove unkind to him. The two stories are more tightly joined when Blunt contrives to have Vallenger arrested for the "death" of Sentloe. The rest of the play proceeds by contrasting action. Anabell seeks to save the life of Vallenger and Blunt seeks to have Florence held responsible for her part in Sentloe's "death." The finale is brought about when King Richard, the judge-figure, permits a champion to appear for the condemned Vallenger. The final contrast comes when Anabell assumes a disguise to free Vallen-ger, and Challener throws off his disguise for the same purpose. Only when Florence is moved to contrition by the nobility of Anabell and Challener, does Blunt unveil the still-living Sent-loe, thus assuring a happy conclusion. Throughout, one line of development balances the other, and though the symmetry is not perfect, as it is rarely perfect in any Elizabethan play, the basic situations contrast with one another. Obviously the author had taken some care in organizing the plot. The disguises are well worked out, as are the balancing and interweaving of the two stories. Further evidence of the care in plotting can be seen in the foreshadowing of King Richard's appearance in the plot when Harbart, in scene ii, urges Sentloe to abandon Florence and join Richard in the Holy Land. Richard's first words are a blessing for being permitted by God to return home. Both in the larger construction and in smaller details the anonymous poet formed his work with care. What the play lacks is not organization of the story but strength of characterization, richness of poetic texture, and fresh outlook upon the prodigal son theme.

Among Shakespeare's plays of the Globe period this pattern frequently appears. *As You Like It, Troilus and Cressida, King Lear,* and, in some respects, *Antony and Cleopatra* reveal such a form. In *As You Like It, Lear,* and *Troilus and Cressida,* it is particularly well defined. Although this type of organization is best adapted to plays with double plots, it is only a little less effective in other plots. *As You Like It,* while it possesses rudimentary double plots in the Orlando-Oliver story and the Duke Frederick-Rosalind story, relies principally upon the balance of love relationships that grow in the Forest of Arden. *Lear,* on the other hand, contains a full double plot. The parallel of the two stories with the balance of cruelty of father-to-daughter and son-to-father is too well known to need repetition here. It is sufficient to point out that in situation after situation one story highlights and reflects the other. The stories join in the storm scenes, separate, join again when blind Gloucester meets mad Lear, separate, and join again when Edgar's defeat of Edmund leads to the disclosure of the plot against Lear and Cordelia. If the form does not appear to be as mechanical as I have described it and if much of the cross-reflection is implicit in the poetry and characterization, this is attributable to Shakespeare's genius, not to the absence of structural underpinning.

V. SCENE STRUCTURE IN SHAKESPEARE

In an earlier part of this chapter I emphasized the importance of the separate scenes as distinct units. At this point I should like to draw attention to certain characteristics of the scenes. Usually a portion of one action or story is not followed by an advance or counteraction, but by a new line of development, often containing completely different characters. This we take for granted in Elizabethan drama. The absence of liaison is emphasized by the way in which scenes are arranged. Some scenes, such as the one which Hamlet brings to a close with the cry

> The play's the thing
> Wherein I'll catch the conscience of the King.
> [II, ii, 632–633]

conclude with a strong emotional lift at the same time as they thrust the interest forward. Some scenes, which I shall call "leading" scenes, produce a forceful dramatic or theatrical pointing. The brief scene in which Artimedorus prepares to give Caesar a petition warning him of the conspirators is such a scene; so is the one in which Duke Frederick thrusts Oliver out of doors until he can produce Celia. These "leading" scenes are usually brief and drive the story forward with great energy. But most scenes in Shakespeare contain an anticlimactic conclusion: they are rounded off, relaxed, brought to a subdued end. Here we must distinguish between dramatic force and story development. It is the dramatic force that is softened at the same time that the story line is brought to the fore. Upon Viola's first visit Olivia falls in love with the "youth" (I, v). She sends a ring after "him" through Malvolio, then closes the scene with four lines:

> I do I know not what, and fear to find
> Mine eye too great a flatterer for my mind.
> Fate, show thy force! Ourselves we do not owe.
> What is decreed must be—and be this so!
> [327–330]

Yet compare this with her feeling before she sends Malvolio off:

> How now?
> Even so quickly may one catch the plague?
> Methinks I feel this youth's perfections
> With an invisible and subtle stealth
> To creep in at mine eyes.
>
> [313–317]

Clearly there is a diminution of intensity toward the end. The same thing occurs in the center of the play (III, iv). Viola denies knowing Antonio, but after his arrest she realizes that he has confused her with Sebastian. The scene does not end on that uplift of discovery. Viola goes off in delight; Toby sends Andrew after to beat the page. Fabian and Toby remain for a moment:

> FABIAN. Come, let's see the event.
> TOBY.   I dare lay any money 'twill be nothing yet.
>
> [III, iv, 430–431]

The final remark is almost desultory. By gradual stages the emotional pitch of the scene is lowered. Shakespeare could easily have given Toby a final line that would have carried the play forward with more vigor. But this was not the way of Shakespeare or, for that matter, of his colleagues.

The falling off of intensity toward the end of a scene is even more marked in the tragedies. In sequence the arrangement of the subdued and pointed endings of scenes helps determine the rhythm of the play. For example, the "plateau" in *Hamlet* is unified by the way in which the endings of the play-within-the-play scene and the prayer scene point forward, not only in story but in emotional level, each one concluding with Hamlet passionately wrought. Another variation, vital to the rhythm of performance, occurs in the "climactic plateau" of *Lear*. The first storm scene (III, ii) with Lear ends subdued. It is followed by a "leading" scene of only twenty-six lines in which Edmund decides to betray his father. The next storm scene (III, iv) also ends subdued after Lear's meeting with poor Tom. Another

leading scene, again of twenty-six lines, drives forward with
Edmund's betrayal of Gloucester to Cornwall who orders him
to "seek out" his father. The last storm scene (III, vi) concludes
with Edgar's realization of the similarity of his plight to that
of Lear. Though the end is keyed low, the note struck is omi-
nous. The very next scene rises to a pitch of frenzy in the blinding of Gloucester. In the Folio it concludes abruptly with Cornwall's order to drive out Gloucester, but the Quarto has a
dialogue between two servants which, serving to round out the
action, seems more typical of Shakespeare.

Within the framework of an Elizabethan scene, perhaps the
most marked characteristic is the placement of emphasis not on
the growth of action but on the character's response to crisis.
This, as we noted before, was a distinguishing feature of the
climactic plateau. Anticipation means little to the Elizabethan
dramatist. This is no more clearly seen than in the handling of
the individual scenes. Even where suspense is inevitable, it is
muted. *The Revenger's Tragedy* contains a scene (III, v) in
which Vindice, at long last, plans to take revenge upon the lascivious old Duke who murdered his beloved. The trap is set, the
Duke is near. Vindice strains forward,

> So, so; now nine years' vengeance crowd into a minute.
>
> [III, v, 124]

The Duke dismisses his train; the trap in the guise of a "lady,"
actually a poisoned manikin, is sprung; the Duke kisses "her"
and falls. All this occupies twenty-five lines. In this it reminds
us of the closet scene. Once the Duke is poisoned, Vindice and
his brother, Hippolito, triumph over the dying man; they reveal the trap and then Vindice unmasks himself. To top these
horrors Vindice discloses to the Duke that his bastard son "rides
a-hunting in [his] brow," and moreover that the son and the
Duchess are about to hold a rendezvous at the very spot:

> [Your] eyes shall see the incest of their lips.
>
> [III, v, 192]

They arrive. The father-husband watches their love-making, hears their mockery of him, and, immediately after their departure, dies. All this takes eighty-three lines. In the structure of the scene, intensification comes from double response: the horror and pain of the Duke and the diabolical delight of the revengers as they witness his pain.

Elizabethan scenes are not unique merely because they give more time to response to a situation rather than to its development. Their uniqueness comes from the fact that the full intensity and implication of the theme is realized not in the accomplishment of the event but in the effects it produces. After Caesar is assassinated, Antony comes to terms with the conspirators. Dramatic though his meeting with them is, the most intense moments are not where Antony composes his differences with Brutus and Cassius, but where he views the body of Caesar. The most compelling section of the scene is Antony's soliloquy where he envisions the ravages of war which will plague the earth as revenge for the foul deed. A glance at the proportion of lines devoted to the various parts of the scene indicates where Shakespeare placed his emphasis. Seventy-seven lines are devoted to all the tension leading to the assassination, 220 to the reactions and realignments that are its results. Ultimately we find Shakespeare dispensing completely with showing the act of murder and concentrating wholly on the psychological and philosophical responses, as in *Macbeth*.

VI. DRAMATIC UNITY IN THE GLOBE PLAYS

The repetition of dramatic forms in the Globe plays shows that there is a structural foundation for the concept of multiple unity, that unity can be found not in compression of action but in its extension. The story line links the experiences but is not identical with them. Rather the events frequently are extensions of the implications of the story exactly as the shattering of glass may be the effect of an explosion. Consequently, as the scenes seek to reach beyond the limits of the subject, it becomes requisite that means be discovered to set limits to the extension of story and theme. The Elizabethans were well aware that the dimensions of the plays threatened to overwhelm the audience. This is the essence of serious charges by Sir Philip Sidney and Ben Jonson against the popular drama. In this they may well have been following Aristotle who introduced into his definition of tragedy the concept of "magnitude." A work of art must be able to be perceived as a totality by the audience. Here, of course, we have the true determinant of unity. Training in witnessing the extended sequences of miracle plays or in listening to Sunday sermons must have contributed to a broadness of perception. Nevertheless, a major problem of the Elizabethan playwright was to observe a proper magnitude, to keep within the bounds that his plays always threatened to break. To aid him in maintaining proper magnitude he had several means at his disposal.

One of these means is the story itself; it is always brought to a conclusion. Another means, and one I have not discussed, was the concentration on character. The fact that the story is happening to Hamlet or Vindice or Sejanus is in itself a unifying factor. But I shall discuss the relevance of character to the play in the chapter on Elizabethan acting. Three other means contributed to keeping the play within perceptible bounds.

The first of these, unity through poetic diction, has been amply treated by present-day critics. Both Stoll and G. Wilson Knight have written of Shakespeare's plays as metaphorical forms.[25] Bradbrook sees the only unity as a poetic unity. Yet verbal expression is but one element of structural multiple unity. There is a close link between the dramatic form of the climactic plateau and the poetic expression, for the second requires the first. Where the playwright fails as a poet, the climactic extensions result in rant and sentimentality. But it is this form that enables the poetry to range freely, or perhaps we may consider that the same compulsion which drove the Elizabethans to copious, lyrical expression caused them to develop this particular dramatic form.

The second means relevant to multiple unity has been the subject of this chapter, precisely the arrangement of scenes about the story line. Some of the scenes that a playwright chooses to dramatize are those primarily concerned with propelling the play, such as the play-within-the-play scene in *Hamlet*. Some scenes develop traits of a character, as in the scene of Portia's plea to Brutus for confidence. But a central, repeating element within the rhythmic pattern of extension-contraction is the arrangement of scenes or incidents in a combination of contrasting and comparable circumstances. Whether the scenes used are central or peripheral to the story, they repeatedly gain illumination through mirroring similar situations. Hamlet unable to avenge his father is contrasted with Laertes too ready to avenge his father, Hamlet mad is contrasted with Ophelia mad, Rosalind's mocking love-play is heightened by comparison with Phebe and Silvius as well as with the earthy affection of Touchstone and Audrey, while Touchstone's professional mockery of the pastoral life casts light upon Jaques' melancholy. One could go on endlessly pointing out the contrast of situation with situation. Frequently we encounter scenes whose only relationship to the story is to provide dramatic contrast. I have cited the scene in *Fair Maid of Bristow* in which the servants woo each other. The Porter's scene in *Macbeth*, about which there has been "much throwing about of brains," is an example. Another is the scene where Ventidius refuses to outshine Antony, another the lynching of Cinna the poet or the valor of Lucilius (*Julius Caesar*, V, iv). Great events produce many ripples. These ripples, which found expression in the Greek choral odes, the Elizabethans sought to dramatize.

Contrast in the Globe plays, it is essential to note, is a contrast of situations, not a contrast of characters. It is true that Hamlet is contrasted with Laertes as well as Fortinbras, but the character contrast is effected by the participation of each in distinct though related incidents. In *Fair Maid of Bristow* Challener's conflict with Vallenger is contrasted with Harbart's relationship to Sentloe. Vallenger's asking the disguised Challener to murder Sentloe and Anabell parallels Florence's attempt to seduce Blunt alias Harbart to murder Sentloe. Modern drama like classic drama, however, contrasts characters caught within a single situation. Antigone and Ismene face the same dramatic circumstance; so do Electra and Chrysothemis. Character contrast is achieved through the different ways in which each person reacts to the same crisis. Lövborg and Tesman are sharply differentiated: in their reactions to the same appointment, their manner of loving, the kinds of books they write. The same holds true for Stanley and Mitch in *A Streetcar Named Desire,* or even for Stella and Blanche. But in Shakespearean drama not only is light thrown on the comparison of situations, but at times the characters are aware of this interreflection. At the end of the last storm scene in *Lear,* Act III, scene vi, Edgar has a speech which appears only in the Quarto. After witnessing the sorrow of Lear, he soliloquizes:

> When we our betters see bearing our woes,
> We scarcely think our miseries our foes.
>
> . . . .
>
> How light and portable my pain seems now,
> When that which makes me bend makes the King bow,
> He childed as I fathered!
>
> [108–116]

Certainly the Elizabethans felt that one event mirrored another, and probably that together they mirrored the common meaning of both events. This interconnection of reflected incidents contributed metaphorically to a unified impression.

The final means of achieving unity is the most difficult to define, the method of handling theme. For that reason let us turn to a play where the theme is clearly expounded. *A Larum for London* has a simple, obvious point to make: the English people will be destroyed by external enemies (the Spanish) and internal treachery unless they become aware of their dangers, forego their desire for personal profit at the expense of the defense of the commonwealth, and rally the faithful honest citizens and soldiers to their support. The point is made through dramatizing the siege of Antwerp. The scenes that are introduced arise from the initial force that propels the story: the determination of the Spanish to take advantage of the improvidence of the citizens of Antwerp. Individual scenes, however, are not causally linked. Rather they are chosen because they reflect and illustrate the basic theme. A burgher, formerly unkind to the hero, is rescued by him. This is the only scene in which the burgher appears. The play is episodic in structure but unified in theme. But the unity is a multiple one. Instead of employing the story of one family and one incident to illustrate the ravages of war, as Gorki did in *Yegor Bulichev and Others,* this play uses a multiple reflection of its theme in a number of independent scenes, each having equal emphasis. Thus the single theme is given multiple dramatization.

The weaker plays of the Globe reveal obvious ways of treating a theme. Dramas of the prodigal son reiterate their morality *ad infinitum,* providing multiple reflections of fall and redemption. The otherwise haphazardly constructed play, *The Devil's Charter,* is bound together by the theme of Man's soul sold to the devil and the final retribution that befalls him. Jonson's predilection for purging mankind with a pill of satire imposes thematic unity on disparate incidents in *Every Man Out of His Humour.* But in his other plays as well as in the plays of Shakespeare there is a more subtle interweaving of structure and theme. At the core of each play there seems to be a point of reference of which the individual scenes are reflections. Though a play moves temporally toward a conclusion, each scene may like a glass be turned toward a central referent. G. Wilson Knight has expressed fundamentally the same idea.[26] Unfortunately, he divorces this concept from the dramatic organism, with the result that his projected productions of Shakespeare's plays seem like academic and sophomoric, if not fantastic, exercises. But Shakespeare seems to have avoided, at least in his later plays, so schematic an illustration of theme as in *Richard III.* Instead, he allows the theme to permeate the characters, situations, and poetry. He concentrates on the dramatic situations and on the characters, allowing the theme to be struck off indirectly like spark from flint. That is perhaps the reason that it is so difficult to reduce the theme of any Shakespearean play to a concise statement. *Macbeth* certainly deals with the theme of the source and effects of evil, yet no single statement of this idea is sufficient, because Shakespeare dramatizes various aspects of this subject. Since, to the Elizabethan, the world was a manifold manifestation of a God whom he was unable to compress into one idea or image, in a similar way the Shakespearean play was a manifold reflection of a theme irreducible and unseen. Yet every element in a great Shakespearean play—character, structure, speech—individually and collectively, is brought into an artistic unity through a structural and poetic expression of an unseen referent at its center.

Chapter Three

THE STAGE

Two boards and a passion! Perhaps these words sum up all that was essential to the Shakespearean theater. Heightening of passion coincided with the "climax," and as for the Elizabethan stage, it was, as G. F. Reynolds remarked, a platform "upon which the story of the play was acted." [1] And so it was, a flat expanse of boards, somewhat exposed to the weather, roughly eleven hundred square feet.

The story that was acted may be best described as romantic, not because it dealt with romance, although it often did, but because it was centrifugal in impulse, ever threatening to veer from its path. Whatever direct progression narrative possessed in the medieval drama, whether moving from Adam's sin to Christ's judgment or from Everyman's ignorance to his salvation, such progression no longer existed in the Elizabethan age. Instead, the unfolding of the drama took place in a world half of man, and therefore unpredictable, half of God, and therefore moral, and was composed half of history, half of legend; half remote fantasy, half immediate reality. Such a world was wide indeed, and the poet-playwright, its creator, was shackled by neither time nor place. What he demanded of a stage was space for the unimpeded flow of scene after scene, for the instantaneous creation of any place in this world or the next. Even when a ghost in mufti made his way out the stage door in broad daylight, the poet insisted he vanished—yes, even into thin air.

Between the poet's insistence and the stage's realization lies the entire secret of Elizabethan staging. About the stage's realization there is some evidence and little knowledge. Stage directions, a much-debated sketch of a playhouse, a tantalizing incomplete building contract, other assorted fragments, invite the scholar to tilt at theory. About the poet's insistence there can be little question. Texts of play after play document the demands that the writers made upon the "unworthy scaffold." Prudence suggests, therefore, that we proceed from play to stage, discovering first what those demands were and then, if we can, how they were satisfied. To understand what the demands were in respect to the environment of an action, it is necessary to consider the following questions: how exactly was a scene located, how consistently was the location maintained, and how relevant was the location to the dramatic impact of the scene?

I. LOCALIZATION IN SHAKESPEARE'S GLOBE PLAYS

In Shakespeare's Globe plays many scenes are given an exact setting. By exact I wish to convey the notion that the action is supposed to occur in or at a particular place, such as a room, hall, gateway, garden, bridge, and that this place remains consistent throughout the scene. For example, in the scene where Martius, yet to win his name of Coriolanus, assaults the gates of Corioles (I, iv), the location is specific, consistent, and dramatically relevant. At one point in the same play Coriolanus prepares to enter the house of his enemy, Aufidius. The scene (IV, iv) takes place before Aufidius' door. Here exactness of location intensifies dramatic suspense because, as we watch Coriolanus pass through the doorway, we know he is putting himself at the mercy of his greatest antagonist. Many examples of such types of placement come to mind: Brutus' orchard, Gertrude's closet, Timon's cave, etc. Such scenes have come to be called "localized."

Usually the opposite of the "localized" setting is the "unlocalized." In this type of setting no impression of place is projected. Location is irrelevant to the progression of the scenes. Clear-cut instances of this occur in *Macbeth*, II, iv, and III, vi. In the first of these scenes Ross and an old man comment on the unnatural state of the world, then Macduff brings them news of Duncan's burial and Macbeth's election to the throne.

In the second scene, Lennox and a gentleman comment upon the web of tyranny and the hope that lies in England with Malcolm. Aside from the section containing Macduff's news, neither of these scenes contributes to the flow of the narrative. Rather they are comments upon the action and essentially perform a choral function.

That these two types of scenes are present in Elizabethan plays has long been recognized. Some scholars, such as V. E. Albright, E. K. Chambers, and J. C. Adams, have tended to divide all scenes of a play into one or the other type, the localized, usually interior and more or less realistic, the unlocalized, exterior, neutral, and somewhat less realistic. This division, according to Albright, derives from the *sedes* and *platea* of the medieval stage.[2] What had been physically separate areas earlier became united on one stage in the Tudor period. But, the argument runs, the Elizabethan dramatists continued to juxtapose the two types of scenes, stringing them in a more or less alternating order along the thread of narrative.

To what extent can this dichotomy be supported by the evidence from the Globe? Naturally there is no sharp distinction between these two types of localization. The differentiation depends upon the sequence a scene assumes in the narrative. Consequently, there are scenes which clearly fit into one or the other category. But even if all the localized and unlocalized scenes are counted, the total amounts to only 136. Since there are 345 scenes in my enumeration of the fifteen Shakespearean Globe plays, 209 remain to be accounted for.[3]

Is it true, as William Archer, Harley Granville-Barker, and George F. Reynolds have pointed out, that much localization was vague, that place faded elusively like a mirage before a traveler, and that often the Elizabethans treated the stage as stage? "Scene after scene," asserts Granville-Barker, "might pass with the actors moving to all intents merely in the ambit of the play's story and of their own emotions: unless, the spell broken, they were suddenly and incongruously seen to be upon a stage."[4] Many a scene gives just such an impression, and yet, in almost every scene that is not unlocalized, the characters do not actually act in a dislocated void but are known to be in some more or less specific region. Even when attention is directly called to the stage-as-stage, stage-as-fictional-world still remains. In such moments the audience experiences a double image.

It is a commonplace that the public stages of the Elizabethan period contained "Asia of the one side, and Affricke of the other." Though contemptuous in intent, in effect this phrase of Sidney's isolates one of the characteristics of Elizabethan scene setting. Perhaps, as some scholars have thought, the Elizabethans utilized place cards to inform the audience of the general location of a scene. But whether they did or not, they were in the habit of specifying a place at large but not a particular section of it. In such cases the stage stands for rather than represents the fictional locale, the confines of which cannot be reasonably encompassed within the limits of the stage. In this type of locale, placement is general rather than precise—for example, the city of Troy in *Troilus and Cressida,* not a particular part of it. Rome as a whole rather than some portion of it is often the setting in *Coriolanus* (I, i; IV, ii; IV, vi). Free movement within such a locale occurs readily as in *Julius Caesar* (III, i), where action takes place first in the street and then in the Capitol. Sequences of action which would be incongruous in a localized setting assume dramatic power in a generalized setting. In the very same place, Othello's castle, occur the private conflict of Othello and Desdemona and the public encounter of Cassio and Bianca (III, iv). Actually, in this type of setting, dramatic impact proceeds from the general rather than the specific nature of the locale. Without a doubt we know when the scene is Rome and when Egypt in *Antony and Cleopatra.* Dramatically that is all we need to know. To endeavor to isolate the whereabouts of Octavius' meeting with Antony (II, ii) would reduce the stature of that meeting. All of Rome is their stage just as in medieval practice all of paradise might be the setting for Adam and Eve. Among the 345 scenes of Shakespeare's Globe plays, 142 are clearly of this sort and 67 tend toward this sort, accounting together for fully 60 per cent of the scenes.

A. H. Thorndike described three types of localization too: the definitely localized, the vaguely localized, and the unlocalized.[5] At first my analysis may seem to repeat his. However, there is a fundamental difference. The generalized locale is not vague; it is extensive, it is symbolic, and dramatically it is concrete. The audience is not expected to identify the stage with a particular location but to understand that it functions as a token of Troy or the Danish palace or the Forest of Arden. Regularly editors have been reducing the generalized location to a localized setting congruent with realistic dimensions. This practice merely betrays the scope of Elizabethan drama. The real distinction between scene *loci* was not, as others have assumed, a separation of interior from exterior or realistic from conventional but a gradation from the unlocalized through the generalized to the localized setting.

Before investigating whether or not the Globe stage utilized stage decor to set these scenes, it is advisable to consider to what degree and by what methods location was conveyed by the playwright himself. It might be well to state at the outset that in extremely few cases is place projected through properties or other decor. Of all the scenes in Shakespeare's Globe plays I count only seventeen in which this occurs, a mere 5 per cent. The most frequently recurring methods used by Shakespeare to indicate location are by announcement: a character tells us where he is ("This is the forest of Arden," *As You Like It*, II, iv); by foreshadowing a location: a character in one scene tells us where he or others will be next ("To the Monument," *Antony and Cleopatra*, IV, xiv); and by identifying a character with a place (early in *All's Well*, the Countess becomes identified with Rossillion; whenever she appears thereafter, the scene, we know, is Rossillion). Some of these methods are used in combination. For example, we learn in the second scene of *Othello* that the Duke is in council, to whose presence Othello, Brabantio, and others are summoned. This is foreshadowing. In the next scene when we see a meeting in progress between the Duke and Senators, we can guess we are at the council, and when Othello and Brabantio enter shortly, we are sure of it. Of course, there are other methods employed to indicate place, but these three are the principal ones. Announcements help to locate 129 of the scenes (37.3 per cent), presence of characters,

128 of the scenes (37.1 per cent), and foreshadowing, 61 of the
scenes (17.7 per cent).

Though the chorus is used only occasionally to indicate place,
it tells us most about Elizabethan playwrights' attitudes toward
setting the scenes. Fortunately, the Globe plays include two
examples of this technique, one from the beginning and one
from the end of the decade. In *Every Man Out of His Humour*
Ben Jonson introduces three choral figures, Asper, Mitis, and
Cordatus. At the end of the induction Asper leaves the stage to
assume the role of Macilente; Mitis and Cordatus remain to
comment upon the action. Cordatus, who knows the play, is able
to inform Mitis where the action takes place. For some scenes
he indicates a generalized locale. "The Scene is the country
still," he remarks to Mitis (Chorus to II, i) or "Onely transferre
your thoughts to the city, with the Scene; where, suppose they
speake" (Chorus to II, iv). Sometimes he is more specific. Upon
the entrance of Cavaliere Shift (III, i), Mitis asks,

> What new *Mute* is this, that walkes so suspiciously?
> CORD.   O, mary this is one, for whose better illustration;
> we must desire you to presuppose the stage, the
> middle isle in Paules; and that, the west end of it.

At one time, where the presence of characters identifies the
location, Cordatus queries Mitis, "You understand where the
Scene is?" (Chorus to IV, i). Jonson, desirous of specifying particular London sites despite the fiction of Italian-named characters, is experimenting along the lines of Shakespeare who
shortly before tried a similar method in *Henry V*. Shakespeare
returned to this device in *Pericles*. Gower, the chorus, relates
portions of Pericles' adventures directly and in accompaniment
to several dumb shows. In passing he often sets the locale. The
first scene, he tells us, is "this Antioch . . . this city" (17–
18). Preparatory to the commencement of III, i, Gower asks
the audience,

> In your imagination hold
> This stage the ship, upon whose deck
> The sea-tost Pericles appears to speak.

Imagine! Suppose! Both Jonson and Shakespeare call upon the
audience to visualize the place of action. Clearly neither conventional nor realistic setting is introduced. Only words, in
these instances delivered directly, in most instances conveyed
in the midst of dramatic action, are the means for informing
the audience where the scene takes place.

II. THE PARTS OF THE STAGE

What the Choruses make evident is that the stage was not
altered for individual scenes. As a consequence, the stage structure itself, not scenery, served as the frame for the action. What
this structure was and how it was used has been debated for
years, and yet despite the lively and continuous debate, there
actually exists a broad band of agreement. About the size of the
stage, for instance, there is little dispute. It is deduced from
the Fortune contract. Without a doubt the platform, one side
of which was attached to the stage wall or façade, was large, probably about 25 by 45 feet, and bare. Whether or not the supporting trestles were seen by the audience, as Hodges claims, matters
little in a consideration of the use of the stage. What is important is that the stage extended to the middle of the yard, that
consequently a large portion of the audience stood or sat on
either side of the actors, and that the actors had to master the
techniques of playing on this open stage. Some disagreement
exists concerning the shape of the stage which, according to
John C. Adams, was not rectangular but tapered inward toward
the front. However, the weight of the evidence is against this
theory, and most scholars are inclined to accept the rectangular
shape.

Upon what other points is there general agreement? For one,
that there were two pillars, located halfway between the stage
wall and the front edge of the platform, which supported a
shadow or cover over part of the stage. For another, that at platform level the stage wall contained two doors at least and
probably a third entry or enclosed space and on an upper level,
some sort of acting area. Where there are disputes, they arise
over three matters: (1) what details complete this generally

accepted scheme, (2) how the parts of the stage were employed, and (3) what temporary structures, if any, supplemented the basic façade. To examine these issues, it will be necessary to review each part of the stage in the light of the Globe repertory.

The Globe plays confirm the presence of at least two entrance doors at some distance from each other. On several occasions there is need for two characters to enter simultaneously from separate entrances and after some conversation come together. For the existence of a third entry the Globe plays offer no conclusive proof. No stage direction specifying an entry from a middle door, such as can be found in non-Globe plays, appears. However, certain scenes do suggest the use of a third entrance. In *Macbeth* (V, vii) Malcolm, who has presumably come through one door *(A)*, is invited into the castle of Dunsinane by Siward. At his exit (through *B* presumably) Macbeth enters. Either he can come from the door *(A)* through which Malcolm entered, which is dramatically unconvincing, or from the door *(B)* of Dunsinane, which is awkward, or from a third entrance, evidence for which is not conclusive. Still, another sort of evidence does occur, which supports the idea of a third entry. In all cases, save one, where simultaneous entrances take place, the stage direction either reads "Enter *A* at one door, and enter *B* at another" or "at another door" or "Enter *A* and *B* severally," or "at several doors." In all the Globe plays, Shakespearean and non-Shakespearean, there are twenty-two instances of such stage directions.[6] The only exception is *Pericles* (IV, iv), "Enter Pericles at one doore, with all his trayne, Cleon and Dioniza at *the* other. Cleon shewes Pericles the tombe, whereat, Pericles makes lamentatton [*sic*]." The explanation for the article, "the" other door, if a third did exist, may be that the third entry was used to display the tomb. The presence of a word such as "another" in all other stage directions implies that when one door was used, more than one other entrance remained, and that, therefore, a third mode of entry was regularly employed on the Globe stage.

Regarding the position of the main entrance doors on either side of the stage, the Globe plays are equally unhelpful. Authority for oblique doors partly facing each other rests on three items of evidence that have been set forth. (1) The phrase "Enter *A* and *B* at opposite doors," which appears in some of the Jacobean plays, proves, according to W. J. Lawrence, that the doors faced each other.[7] (2) Certain plays need facing doors in the action.[8] (3) The historical development of the play-houses explains the genesis of the oblique doors.[9] Concerning the first item, I need only point out that in no stage direction in the Globe plays does the phrase "at opposite doors" appear. Nor does it appear in any pre-Globe Shakespearean play. The second item invites subjective judgment. Lawrence insists that the last scene of *The Merry Devil of Edmonton*, a Globe play, could not be played unless the doors were oblique. However, cross-observation in that scene concerns the exchange of signs over the doors to two inns in Waltham.

> SIR ARTHUR. Mine host, mine host, we lay all night at the George in Waltham, but whether the George be your fee-simple or no, tis a doubt-full question, looke upon your signe.
>
> HOST. Body of Saint George, this is mine over-thwart neighbour hath done this to seduce my blind customers.
>
> [Sig. F2^r]

Signs extending over a door would be readily seen from the opposite end of the stage whether or not the doors were oblique. What this interpretation comes down to is that insistence on opposite doors reveals a realistic conception of staging. Out of oblique doors characters emerge already facing each other or the action. They can respond "naturally" and "realistically." But, if the doors are flush with the façade, an "unnatural" formal entrance results.

The last argument for oblique doors is historical. Lawrence claims that they were introduced into the Globe from the second Blackfriars theater (1598–1600). Adams argues that they were developed when the Theatre's frame was adapted for the Globe. Neither offers sufficiently convincing proof to counterbalance the evidence of the Swan drawing which clearly shows flush doors. Therefore, though either oblique or flush doors could accommodate the Globe plays, flush doors were more likely to have been employed.

We can also dismiss the notion occasionally put forth that the doors consistently represented entrances from particular places, such as Olivia's house in *Twelfth Night* or Page's and Ford's houses in *The Merry Wives of Windsor*. The difficulty of maintaining a continuing identification of one place with one entrance is obvious in the latter play. The comedy opens with the entrance of Justice Shallow, Sir Hugh Evans, and Slender. Their point of entry (marked *A* for identification) is unspecified and therefore might be in the center. Having been insulted by Falstaff, whom he expects to find at Page's house, Shallow calls upon the Windsor worthy who emerges from his house (entry *B*). The remaining entrances and exits in scene i and in the brief scene ii maintain these associations. Scene iii occurs at the Garter. It is possible to confine all in-goings and out-goings to one door (entry *C*). But with scene iv all previous associations are shattered. The place is Dr. Caius' house. Entry *A, B,* or *C* must represent Caius' house. The neutral entry *A* can be selected. But in the course of the scene Simple is forced to hide from Caius. He cannot exit at *A*, for Caius is about to enter at that point. Thus he must choose *B* (Page's house) or *C* (the Garter). A continuation of this analysis would only confirm how hopeless it is to expect any correlation between an entry and a specific locality for more than one scene. Further evidence exists in *Twelfth Night* that the doors did not have locational significance. At the conclusion of Act I, scene v, Olivia sends Malvolio after Cesario to tell "him" that she'll have none of "his" ring. After an intervening scene, Malvolio encounters Cesario. His first line is, "Were not you ev'n now with the Countess Olivia?" Simple realism would demand that Malvolio, endeavoring to catch Cesario, would follow "him" on stage. That is how the scene is frequently staged. However, the stage direction specifies, "Enter Viola and Malvolio at several doors" (II, ii). Professor Reynolds has reconstructed the staging of *Troilus and Cressida* so that one stage door represents Troy, the other the Grecian camp.[10] An enclosed recess, with the curtain drawn, becomes Cressida's home and with the curtain closed, Achilles' tent. But, as Irwin Smith has reminded me privately, this arrangement is "proved wrong by the stage direction to Act IV, scene i, which specifies entrance at two doors," although the location of the scene is wholly within Troy. The fact is that every other Globe play lacks that neat division of place which enables us to assign one location to one door and another to the other door. Too often there is a major shift in location during the course of a play, such as, from the court to the forest in *As You Like It,* from Venice to Cyprus in *Othello,* from the castle to the field in *Lear.* Such a shift prevents the localizing of the stage door for any appreciable period.

As good evidence as that of Reynolds can be offered for a theory that actors almost always obeyed the convention of entering at one door and leaving at the other, regardless of location. In *Hamlet,* for instance, there are only three instances when such a convention would be violated: when Polonius is sent for the ambassadors and players in II, ii, and when the Prologue leaves to usher in the players in III, ii. I offer this suggestion not as a theory but as a warning against such reconstructed staging as Reynolds proposes.

The critical part of any study of an Elizabethan playhouse concerns the "third entry," "the place in the middle," "the booth," "the inner stage," "the discovery-space." The abundance of terms testifies to the uncertainty concerning this area. Every aspect of it is open to controversy: function, dimensions in all directions, the presence of curtains, and location. But that there is some space between the stage doors, capable of being enclosed or secluded, is granted by all scholars. Objection has been raised to calling this area an "inner stage," first because the term never appeared in Elizabethan texts, and secondly because it suggests a purpose that it did not have, namely, to house entire scenes. Increasingly the term "discovery-space" has been utilized, notably by Richard Hosley, but this has the disadvantage of suggesting too limited a function for the space. Since the area we are concerned with, whether recessed or not, had to be enclosed, almost certainly by curtains, I have chosen to refer to the "enclosure" of the Globe stage.

Any investigation of the enclosure is obliged to include an investigation of Elizabethan stage properties. For a long time it was suggested that a principal purpose of the enclosure was to mask the placement of furniture and other properties. While it is becoming increasingly evident that we must regard such a presumption with skepticism, nevertheless, the presence of a property has so often been cited as evidence for the use of an enclosure that it is necessary to review the handling of stage properties at the Globe before considering the enclosure directly. Aside from their connection with the problem of the enclosure, furthermore, stage properties deserve attention, for their appearance in a play can be more readily ascertained than any other element of production and as a result can provide clues to the methods of staging.

Anyone who has had occasion to produce a Shakespearean play realizes how few properties are needed for any single play. Yet even when we are cautious, we tend to overproperty a play. Even properties clearly alluded to may not exist on stage. Several times in *Julius Caesar* characters speak of Caesar having been struck down at the base of Pompey's statue (III, i, 115; III, ii, 193), even in the very scene where the action takes place. Yet the description is merely a paraphrase of Plutarch.[11] The Romans are beaten back to their trenches in their first assault against Corioles (I, iv). Once more the trenches are not on-stage but in Plutarch.

Consequently, in examining the Globe plays, I have tried to guard against seeing a stage property where none exists. Only when use is clearly demonstrable in action or stage direction can we assume that a property was introduced. Some instances exist where smaller properties were added to give verisimilitude to a scene, as Fabell's necromantic instruments in *The Merry Devil of Edmonton*, prologue, and Horace's papers in *Satiromastix* (I, iii), but larger properties which require placement or setting were charily employed. It is to these set properties that I shall refer.

In the fifteen Globe plays written by Shakespeare I count

sixty-five uses of properties, in the twelve non-Shakespearean plays, sixty-eight.[12] In the former plays the presence of fifteen of these "props" is difficult to verify. Such a property would be the "hedge-corner" around which the soldiers hide before pouncing on Parolles (*All's Well*, IV, i) or the "tree" upon which Orlando hangs his verses (*As You Like It*, III, ii). Since the hedge and the tree might very well be represented by the stage posts, I must omit consideration of them. In the twelve non-Shakespearean plays there are seventeen such properties. Consequently, in one category we are left with fifty properties and in the other with fifty-one, or one hundred and one altogether, an average of almost four properties a play. That this is not a slim list for a ten-year period is supported by the few properties inventoried by Henslowe in 1598. The heading of the inventory claims that *all* the properties are listed. Of set properties there are only twenty-one.[13] To these we may add chairs and tables which are not included. Nor are curtains mentioned unless "the cloth of the Sone & Mone" is a hanging of some sort rather than rudimentary scenery, as Malone suggested. In any case the list substantiates the conclusion that Elizabethan stage production employed few properties and reinforces the warning that we should not insist upon finding others where they do not appear.

How were the properties introduced onto the stage? Some were discovered. When Lychorida bids Pericles look upon his dead bride, she probably draws a curtain to reveal Thaisa on the bitter "child-bed" of which Pericles speaks (III, i). Other properties were brought on. For the fencing match between Hamlet and Laertes, though the 1604 Quarto stage direction notes, "A table prepared . . .," the Folio specifies that following the King, Queen, and others, there enter "other Attendants with Foyles, and Gauntlets, a Table and Flagons of wine on it" (V, ii). But many instances are not so clear, instances where at most we can assume that a property was *probably* brought on stage or *probably* discovered. Another small category exists. There are several instances where properties are taken off stage, although there is no evidence to indicate how they came to be on stage. Caesar, at the finale of *Antony and Cleopatra*, commands his soldiers to "Take up [Cleopatra's] bed,/and bear

her women from the monument" (V, ii, 359–360). To my mind
this suggests that the prop had been previously brought on.

I have carefully examined the one hundred and one properties for evidence of method of introduction. The chart below
summarizes my analysis.

How Props Are Introduced	In Shakespearean Plays		In Non-Shakespearean Plays		Total	
	No.	%	No.	%	No.	%
Brought on	12	24.	18	35.3	30	29.7
Probably brought on	11	22.	8	15.7	19	18.8
Taken off	2	4.	2	3.9	4	4.
Total	25	50.	28	54.9	53	52.5
Discovered	2	4.	8	15.7	10	9.9
Probably discovered	7	14.	1	1.9	8	7.9
Total	9	18.	9	17.6	18	17.8
Undetermined	16	32.	14	27.5	30	29.7
Grand Total	50		51		101	

In both Shakespearean and non-Shakespearean plays the percentages are about the same. Clearly the number of properties
brought on greatly outnumber those which are discovered. Yet
enough properties are discovered to make the presence of an enclosure certain.

Tables are usually brought out. In all the Globe plays tables
are used seventeen times. Ten of these are banquet tables, seven
of which are specifically directed to be brought out.[14] Of the rest
two are probably brought out, and one may or may not have
been brought out.[15] Since it was customary in Elizabethan life
for banquet tables to be portable, it has been objected that the
use of an enclosure is not disproved by such evidence. Instead
we are asked to regard the practice as a bit of realistic business.
This objection, however, does not explain why, as in *Macbeth*,
III, iv, a banquet is sometimes prepared in front of the audience
before the arrival of the principal characters. In any case the evidence concerning the table as stage property shows that the introduction of banquet tables does not depend upon an enclosure.

Of the other seven tables, four are definitely brought out, one is probably brought out, the introduction of one is undetermined, and one seems to have been discovered.[16] This last property is referred to in the stage direction in *Othello*, I, iii, "Enter Duke and Senators, set at a Table with lights and Attendants." The Quarto (1622) for this play is late, so that the discovery may depict a later method. In contrast to all other cases in the Globe plays, this is the sole instance where a table is discovered.

Tracing the introduction of seats is more difficult. There are infrequent references to chairs in stage directions. Only occasionally is a chair, or more usually a stool, named in the dialogue. More often there is the invitation of one character to another to sit down. Twenty-two instances of seating occur in Shakespeare's Globe plays, twenty-one in the non-Shakespearean plays. One type of seat is always brought in, that is the chair for an invalid. Two such chairs are definitely introduced by Shakespeare, one for Lear, the other for Cassio when wounded. A third might be intended for the King of France when he calls, "Give me some help here, ho!" (*All's Well*, II, i). One such chair containing the Wife, is brought in in *A Yorkshire Tragedy;* a similar type, a sedan chair apparently, is introduced in *Volpone* (V, ii).

An entire category of seats is represented by the simple jointstool. It appears for Goneril in Lear's arraignment of his daughters (III, vi), it serves for Volumnia and Virgilia as they sew (*Coriolanus*, I, iii), and it holds the Ghost of Banquo (*Macbeth*, III, iv). These stools are elusive though. Seldom are they specifically directed to be brought on. An illuminating instance occurs in *The Devil's Charter*. Lucretia Borgia is plotting the death of her husband, Gismond. The stage direction at the beginning of Act I, scene v, reads, "Enter Lucretia alone in her nightgowne untired bringing in a chaire, which she planteth upon the Stage." She prepares the trap-chair for her husband, and when he arrives "Gismond sitteth downe in a Chaire, Lucretia on a stoole beside him." But where did the "stoole" come from? If an attendant had accompanied her, why did Lucretia have to carry the chair? Obviously she must have entered alone. Therefore, unless one suggests that she also carried on a stool, hitherto unmentioned, the only possibility left is to suppose that the stool was already on the stage. Once one grants that stools may have been left on the stage, many scenes and directions become clear. When banquets are brought on stage, no mention is made of accompanying seats. Furthermore, when the type of seat at banquets is named, it turns out to be a stool. In various plays the actors sit in places that in reality would be devoid of seats, for example, on the watch in *Hamlet* (I, i), at the city gates in *Measure for Measure* (V, i), Antony somewhere after a defeat (*Antony and Cleopatra*, III, x). It is not too far a leap to assume that it was regular practice at the Globe playhouse to have stools distributed about the stage for the use of the actors.

Two other types of seats appear in the Shakespearean plays: the "chair" and the state. The chair is only mentioned once. It is the one to which Gloucester is bound before he is blinded. There is no indication whether it is brought on or discovered, one's decision in the matter being determined by where one places the scene on the stage. The state too is mentioned specifically only once. After the banquet is brought out, Macbeth tells the assembled guests, "Our hostesse keeps her state, but in best time/ We will require her welcome." (III, iv). This implies that Lady Macbeth sits apart from the company, perhaps in the enclosure. The state may have been placed there when the banquet was prepared or it may have been discovered. Significantly no action takes place at the state. Several other scenes would permit the use of a state. In each case there is evidence that the scenes proper take place on the stage platform. Though a curtain could be utilized to reveal the state in these cases, I incline to the theory that the state was brought or thrust out.

Of all properties beds are most frequently discovered. There are eleven instances in the Globe plays where beds or cushions for sleeping are introduced. In three the bed is definitely and in three others probably discovered, but in only two of these scenes is action sustained around the beds. The other scenes merely contain references to them or display someone reclining. Three other instances afford insufficient evidence to judge whether the beds are discovered or not and the remaining two provide curious evidence. *The Devil's Charter* and *Antony and Cleopatra* were written about the same time. In both plays people die from the bite of an asp; in the former play they are murdered (IV, v), in the latter they commit suicide (V, ii), but in both cases the scenes conclude with the order to take up the beds and bear in the bodies. Extended action takes place about the beds, perhaps offering the explanation for the beds being forward on the platform.[17]

The question of whether or not heavy properties were discovered is answered by a type of property which keeps recurring in the Globe plays. This may very well be the counterpart of "a payre of stayres for Fayeton" in Henslowe's inventory. In a well reasoned article Warren Smith has demonstrated the likelihood that scaffolding of some sort was introduced as a property on the Globe stage.[18] Not the upper level of the stage façade, but such a scaffold, he contends, was the pulpit in *Julius Caesar* (III, ii), a place to see the warriors in *Troilus and Cressida* (I, ii), the monument in *Antony and Cleopatra* (IV, xvi), the platform in *Hamlet* (I, i). Though his argument does not fit *Hamlet* or completely explain *Antony and Cleopatra*, its basic premise is verified by two non-Shakespearean Globe plays.

In the last scene of *Fair Maid of Bristow*, Vallenger, the prodigal, is about to be executed for the supposed murder of Sentloe. By this point in the play Vallenger has been spiritually redeemed from sin. About to die, he delivers a brief speech,

> Ere I ascend this stage where I must act,
> The latest period of this life of mine,
> First let me do my deuty to my prince.
> Next unto you, to much by me offended,
> Now step, by step, as I ascend this place,
> Mount thou my soule into the throwne of grace.
>
> [Sig. E4ʳ]

Presumably he reaches the top, as do his alleged accomplices, for shortly thereafter the King calls, "Dispatch them executioner: dispatch." Clearly some scaffold has been revealed or brought out for this scene. It is one which the actors can mount before an audience. It also had to be large enough to accommodate four people. From other evidence Smith suggests a platform of this sort would be three or four steps high. Despite its size a subsequent line indicates that it was moved about in front of the audience.

Before the execution can take place, Sentloe reveals that he is not really dead, but has pretended to be in order to subject Vallenger to a rigorous trial of soul and thus force him to purge his offenses. Amidst the joyful reunion of Vallenger and his wife, the King commands,

> Away with that same tradgike monument.
> [Sig. F2ᵛ]

Presumably the scaffold is withdrawn from the stage. In all likelihood a scaffold large enough to hold four people was too large to fit through a doorway. Therefore, we must assume that it was removed through the enclosure.

The forward placement of the scaffold is attested by another Globe play. Enamored of Corvino's wife, Volpone disguised as a mountebank mounts his bank under the window where he might glimpse the lady (II, ii). Dramatically and physically his bank could only be placed on the platform. That he has actually gone up on some structure which, however, is lower than window height, is proved, first, when "Celia at the windo' throwes downe her handkerchiefe," and secondly, when Corvino, the jealous husband, rushes out of his door and shouts to Volpone to "Come downe" (II, iii). Here too there is no stage direction for the setting up and taking down of a scaffold, but the reiteration of Corvino's "will you downe, sir? downe?" establishes its existence. Perhaps, in this case too, actors or attendants erected or thrust out some frame. Once it is established that such a scaffold was brought out upon the Globe stage, it becomes clear that it appears in some of the scenes cited by Smith. How its use affected staging is properly reserved for a later chapter.

Out of the total properties of one hundred and one, I have already accounted for seventy-six. The remaining twenty-five are divided amongst miscellaneous properties such as tombs, tents, greenery of some sort, and others. Only two scenes require tombs, a dumb show in *Pericles* (IV, iv) and the discovery of Timon's body (V, iii). How the tombs were revealed to the audience is not readily determined so that this subject had best be deferred to a consideration of the enclosure.

Tents are even more difficult to treat. Even when the action calls for a tent, it is uncertain whether a property or merely the enclosure is being employed. Frequent allusions to tents can be found in *Troilus and Cressida,* but there is no scene where more than one tent must be used. But how was that represented? When Ulysses says of Achilles, "We saw him at the opening of his tent" (II, iii), did the audience see a property tent or the flap of the enclosure curtain turned back? No interior is required in any of these scenes so that we are not dealing with a discovery proper. Some evidence for a property tent can be found in *The Devil's Charter.* Caesar Borgia leads an army against the town of Furly whose defense is led by the Countess Katherine (IV, iv). Unless she surrenders, Caesar will slay her two young boys, whom he has captured; when she refuses, he orders the children to execution. Then, after having scaled the walls and taken Katherine prisoner, Caesar "discovereth his Tent where her two sonnes were at Cardes," and says, "Behold thy children living in my Tent." But where is the tent? In the enclosure? A difficulty arises, if we suppose so, for it places the tent under the very walls which Caesar attempted and finally overran. Moreover, since the dumb show which opens the play requires two property tents, it is likely that Caesar's tent was brought in by his soldiers and set up on stage.

Similarly, it is difficult to distinguish when prop trees are used and when stage posts. Although property trees were regularly employed on the Elizabethan stage, no tree definitely appears on the Globe stage. In *A Warning for Fair Women,* a Lord Chamberlain's play published in 1599, a tree springs up in the midst of the stage (Sig. E3^v). But whether or not this was the normal method for introducing the tree prop is uncertain. The rest of the properties must be considered individually.

Some are discovered, most brought on. But the study of any one of these properties, if necessary, can be more profitably undertaken in connection with staging methods.

Two inferences can be drawn from this survey of properties on the Globe stage. One is that more often than not properties, even heavy ones, were carried onto the stage. As a consequence, it was not one of the functions of the enclosure to permit the setting of furniture or other properties.[19] The other is that the same class of properties is often introduced in the same way. Beds are likely to be discovered. Tables, scaffolds, and invalid chairs are brought out. These habits may have stemmed from solid theatrical necessity. On the other hand it is possible that they may have embodied a symbolic significance.

Therefore, since the presence of stage properties cannot guide us in deciding when the enclosure was used, some other means must be discovered. References to an interior setting, Richard Hosley has shown, are not reliable. Fortunately, however, several Globe plays contain scenes in which stage directions or incontestable stage business establishes the use of an enclosure. One of these, *The Devil's Charter,* supplies unusually valuable evidence.

Barnabe Barnes prepared his text of *The Devil's Charter* for the printer with much care. He supplied full stage directions, which show theatrical, not literary marks, and seems to have described an actual production, for the epilogue directly addresses spectators, albeit not of the public playhouse (Sig. M3ᵛ). The enclosure, or study, as he terms the area, is employed three times in his play. It will pay to examine these scenes minutely. In two scenes a stage direction opens the scene with the words, "Alexander in his study (or studie) . . . ," "with bookes, coffers, his triple Crown upon a cushion before him" (I, iv); "beholding a Magicall glasse with other observations" (IV, i). Alexander speaks a long soliloquy in the first scene, then his two sons enter, later a servant. At the most there are four characters in the scene. Whether Alexander remains in the study throughout the first scene is not indicated. In the second scene Alexander also delivers an extended soliloquy, but here a direction specifies after his sixth line, "Alexander commeth upon the Stage out

of his study with a booke in his hand." He conjures forth a devil
in order to discover who killed his son Candie. He is shown a
symbol of the murder: his other son, Caesar, pursuing the ghost
of Candie. The specters enter at one door and "vanish in at another doore" (G2ʳ19). On the heels of the apparition of Caesar,
Caesar himself arrives, outfaces his father, and parts reconciled
to him. The last direction is, "Exit Alexander into the studie."
Clearly the study supplied a novel scene opening and provided
access to the platform or stage, but was not utilized for extended
presentation.

The third study scene, in this instance containing two dis-
closures, occurs at the end of the play. Alexander is about to
face the consequences of his charter with the devil. The scene
commences, "Alexander unbraced betwixt two Cardinalls in his
study looking upon a booke, whilst a groome draweth the Curtaine" (V, vi). Alexander speaks eight lines, then "They [the
two Cardinals] place him in a chayre upon the stage, a groome
setteth a Table before him." After chastising himself, "Alexander draweth the Curtaine of his studie [the one which the
groom opened and presumably closed] where hee discovereth
the divill sitting in his pontificals." He disputes with the devil,
and later "They sit together," where is not indicated, and finally
Alexander's soul is carried down. In two of the scenes there is
incontestable evidence that the action is brought out of the
enclosure early in the scene. Furthermore, these three are the
only study scenes in a play of twenty-two scenes.

Yet the study is mentioned at one other time. At one point
Alexander plots the death of two young men, with one of whom
he has had a homosexual affair. The murder scene (IV, v)
begins with the direction, "Enter Alexander out of his studie."
After he has his servant Bernardo prepare a soporific for the
young men, he departs with the injunction that when the intended victims are asleep, Bernardo give him notice "at [his]
study doore." The young men come in from tennis, have a rub-
down by barbers, call for refreshment. The soporific takes effect,
and they lie down to nap both upon one bed. Bernardo
"knocketh at the study," at which Alexander comes forth "upon
the stage" with his asp to slay his paramour. After the act is

completed and the murderer has departed, Bernardo summons two Cardinals to see the dead youths who, he asserts, expired from drinking too much when overexerted. Bemoaning the fate of these two hopes of "Phaenza," the Cardinals bid Bernardo "Beare them in."

Several characteristics should be noted. First, the enclosure or study, when it is actually used, is revealed by the drawing of a curtain. But if a curtain hangs before the enclosure, upon what does Bernardo knock? Either upon the side wall, and then Alexander enters from behind the curtain, or upon a door, and a new area is presumed to represent the study. Hosley has suggested that one of the two side doorways, with the doors fully opened, might have served as the enclosure. This possibility must be excluded, however, for Act IV, scene i requires two doors for the passage of the specters of Caesar and Candie at a time when the enclosure or study is in use.[20]

Second, the direction that Alexander "commeth upon the Stage out of his study" indicates that the enclosure is recessed. With this conclusion most of the scenes utilizing the enclosure would agree. One complication is raised by *Volpone*, V, ii. Here Volpone must be behind a curtain, yet be able to "peepe over." There may be any one of three explanations. Perhaps the curtains did not reach the top of the recess. Richard Southern refers to such an arrangement at a booth theater in Brussels in 1660.[21] Another possibility is that the enclosure projected from the stage façade. Lastly, the curtain, called a "traverse" in the Folio, may have been hung especially for this scene and thus may not be the enclosure curtain. Of all the choices the last seems to accord best with the evidence.

Altogether thirteen or fourteen instances of discovery can be found in the non-Shakespearean Globe plays. To what degree do they substantiate Hosley's contention that the enclosure was used to disclose "a player or object invested with some special interest or significance"?[22] So many persons and things of interest, not so disclosed, appear in the Globe plays, that it is impossible to use such a yardstick. True, of the total thirteen or fourteen discoveries, six involve the sudden display of a figure or figures or, in one instance, of a striking object, Volpone's wealth. But among the other discoveries are mundane representations of a person reading, casting accounts, lying asleep. Yet, a certain pattern becomes apparent. For the moment let us consider twelve instances, excluding the two that occur in Jonson's plays. In the twelve instances of discovery, six reveal a person writing or studying or reading; in four scenes the person is alone; in two, a subordinate or two attends upon the central figure.[23] Three of the remaining discoveries reveal a person or persons sleeping.[24] Two discoveries reveal dead bodies.[25] There remains one discovery to be accounted for, that already described in *The Devil's Charter,* where Alexander draws the curtain to find the devil sitting "in his pontificals." Just before revealing the devil, Alexander cries,

> Once more I will with powrefull exorcismes,
> Invoke those Angells of eternall darkenesse
> To shew me now the manner of death.
> [Sig. L3ᵛ 18–20]

If one of the conventional uses of the enclosure was to discover corpses, then the Globe audiences would have well appreciated the irony of Alexander's last line, for when he draws the curtain, he does discover "the manner of death." Thus, in all preceding examples discovery reveals persons studying, sleeping, or dead. To what extent does Shakespeare follow the same practice?

In determining which scenes in Shakespeare's Globe plays employed the enclosure, it is necessary to allow reasonable latitude. At least three instances are fairly certain, *Pericles,* III, i; V, i, and *Othello,* V, ii. I am inclined to believe that there may be four others: *Pericles,* I, i; *Timon of Athens,* V, iii; *Lear,* III, vi; *Othello,* I, iii. Let us examine the definite instances of discovery.

The two which occur in *Pericles* are similar in character. In the first (III, i), Pericles is on a storm-tossed ship's deck. His newborn babe has just been placed in his arms. The sailors insist that the body of his queen, who has but now died in childbirth, be cast overboard. Pericles answers,

> As you thinke meet; for she must over board straight:
> Most wretched Queene.
>
> LYCHORIDA. Heere she lyes sir.
> PERICLES. A terrible Child-bed hast thou had my deare,
> . . . nor have I time . . . but straight,
> Must cast thee scarcly Coffind.
>
> [III, i, 54–61. Quarto copy]

At the end of the scene, Pericles sends one of the sailors out to prepare the "cauḷkt and bittumed" chest for the body, which we do not see removed, for the scene ends when Pericles says, "I'le bring the body presently."

In the second scene, again on the deck of a ship, Lysimachus is told of Pericles' trance out of which no one can stir him.

> HELICANUS. hee will not speake to any
> LYSIMACHUS. yet let me obtaine my wish [to see Pericles]
> HELICANUS. Behold him, this was a goodly person.
>
> [V, i, 34–36. Q.]

Presumably a curtain is drawn to reveal Pericles on a couch. Subsequently, Marina is brought to rouse him, and little by little the two discover they are father and daughter. The lines indicate some shifting in and out of the enclosure during this scene.

Because of the stage direction in the Folio, "Enter Othello, and Desdemona in her bed," this last scene of *Othello* probably employs the enclosure. If it is continued in the enclosure throughout, it is the only illustration that we have of extended action in this space. Only one other instance occurs in the Globe plays where "enter" precedes the discovery of a sleeping person (*A Yorkshire Tragedy*, scene v). As yet no one has explained convincingly the appearance of "enter" in such a context. In contemporary diction and common usage "enter" is not a synonym for "discover." Yet such stage directions clearly intend "enter" to bear a special significance. Therefore, until further light can be thrown upon such usage, it is best for us to accept stage directions reading "Enter *A* in a bed" or "Enter *B* asleep" as evidence of discovery.

A similarity between the three Shakespearean scenes and the non-Shakespearean scenes will be seen immediately. Two of the Shakespearean scenes involve the display of sleepers, one of a seeming corpse. When we return to the remaining possible uses of the enclosure, we find that they include the discovery of a conference (*Othello*, I, iii: "Enter Duke and Senators set at a Table with lights and Attendants." Q. 1622. The Folio s.d. is "Enter Duke, Senators, and Officers"); concealment of a sleeper (*Lear*, III, vi: "draw the curtains"); and the discovery of dead bodies (*Timon*, V, iii: a soldier finds Timon's body, and *Pericles*, I, i). In *Pericles*, I, i, Antiochus seeks to dissuade Pericles from endeavoring to win the hand of Antiochus' daughter by answering a fateful riddle. He points to the bodies of "sometimes famous Princes" who failed to answer the riddle and were put to death. These bodies may be discovered.

Once one puts all the evidence together, the degree of uniformity is amazing. Considering all these discoveries, in Shakespearean and non-Shakespearean plays, we find twenty-one examples, six of which involve sleepers, seven of which involve study or conference, five of which involve corpses. One, the devil as pope, is a slight variant of the last category. The final two variants appear in Jonson's plays. In *Volpone* gold is displayed, the only time an object is the center of revelation. It is possible that a chest rather than the enclosure contains the wealth. In *Every Man Out of His Humour*, the evidence for the use of the enclosure is slight.[26]

This theory, that the enclosure was reserved for certain kinds of display, augments the present theory that the enclosure was used infrequently and briefly. Both theories lead inevitably to the question: was the enclosure a permanent part of the stage, and if it was, why was it not used more frequently? Though I tend to believe that the enclosure was permanent, it could very well have been temporary, provided there were hidden access to it. To the second half of the question, the answer is that the enclosure *was* used more frequently, not to effect discovery, however, but to permit concealment. Lear, as I suggested, may have utilized the enclosure for that purpose, the enclosure which often served as a study. In Q. 1603 of *Hamlet*, Corambis advises the King:

> The Princes walke is here in the galery,
> There let Ofelia, walke untill hee comes:
> Your selfe and I will stand close in the study.
>
> [Sig. D4ᵛ]

At the corresponding point in the Folio version, Polonius says, "Be you and I behinde an Arras then." Naturally Corambis would think of the place behind the arras as the study. It was the enclosure to which he referred, the enclosure which served the double purpose, to reveal and to conceal. Of the fifteen Shakespearean Globe plays seven contain scenes of concealment and ten contain scenes of discovery or concealment or both. If, in addition, the enclosure was employed as the front of a tent in those instances where the interior was not revealed, then twelve of the fifteen Shakespearean plays made some use of the enclosure for other purposes than entry.[27]

One word about chronology remains to be said. The plays in which discovery takes place, *Pericles, The Devil's Charter, Othello,* tend to come late in the Globe period. The use of the enclosure for concealment, however, occurs throughout the period. Recognizing that discovery scenes can be found throughout the Elizabethan period, I should still like to suggest that the use of the enclosure for discovery was an extension of its use for entrance, concealment, and possibly introduction of properties. In popular plays of the pre-Globe period occur scenes where properties are brought forth from what must be the enclosure. Although none of the Globe plays contains evidence of similar practice, it is not unlikely that scaffolds, states, and pulpits were introduced from the enclosure.[28] If the origin of the Elizabethan stage truly lies in the booth theater erected in an inn yard, then the hangings of the booth first had to conceal the actors dressing, then permit entrance of actors and properties, and lastly, when the stage façade became permanent, allow discovery.

Among the parts of the Globe there was, all scholars concede, an upper level attached to the stage façade. Variously termed a "chamber" by Adams and a "gallery" by Hosley, it is referred to as a "window," "walls," or "above," in the Globe texts. To avoid any preconceptions about its nature, we might best refer to the upper level as it is usually called, "the above."

The nature of evidence for the above is of two sorts. First and surest is the category where a stage direction reads "Enter above" or the action involves two levels. The second is where characters refer to being above without actually performing actions which show them to be above, for example, when Bardolph informs Falstaff that "there's a woman below" (*The Merry Wives of Windsor*, III, v). Both categories of evidence occur in the Globe plays. The first involves scenes where the above is related to the platform below; the second involves scenes, if the lines can be taken literally, which would continue at length independent of the lower stage.

To begin with the second kind of evidence first. Eight scenes in the Globe plays contain references to people or action below without directly relating to any action below.[29] Three of these occur in one play, *A Yorkshire Tragedy*. All the other five take place in taverns, and supposedly the characters are in upper rooms. Since the scenes in *A Yorkshire Tragedy* cast an interesting light on these references, I shall examine them first. In scene iii a servant announces to the Husband that "a gentleman from the University staies below to speake with you." For the moment, we can imagine the scene is above. At the news the Husband leaves his wife to greet the visitor. The wife remains alone to deliver a soliloquy. In scene iv, after conversing with the gentleman, the Master of the College, the Husband suggests that the guest "spend but a fewe minuts in a walke/about my grounds below, my man heere shall attend you." Presumably the scene is still above. After the departure of the guest, the Husband kills one of his children and, crying that he will kill the other, he exits with the bloody child.

Scene v commences with the direction, already referred to, "Enter a maide with a child in her armes, the mother by her a sleepe." The Husband rushes in and endeavors to snatch the babe from the maid's arms. When she resists, he assaults her.

> Are you gossiping, prating sturdy queane, Ile breake
> your clamor with your neck down staires:
> Tumble, tumble, headlong.
>
> Throws her down.
[Sig. C3^r]

Thus, three consecutive scenes purport to be upstairs though certainly scenes iv and v must be in different parts of the "house." Adams places scene v in the "chamber." [30] What then becomes of the previous scene which, according to the dialogue, also took place upstairs? Somewhere an allusion to "below" does not reflect physical facts. Or is it that all the scenes fail to reflect physical facts and merely reflect the convention that most domestic and tavern rooms were situated in an upper story? None of the other scenes mentioned demands the actual use of an above, and in the tavern scene of *Miseries of Enforced Marriage* the scene concludes with one of the characters calling on all his friends to follow him to another room in the tavern, an unnecessary exit if a curtain in the above could close upon them. One is forced to conclude, therefore, that though a scene may contain references to being above, it was played below unless the action proves otherwise.

Of scenes upon the walls there are five.[31] Here the stage directions are straightforward. Action takes place between those on the walls and those below, in two cases involving sizable groups and much interchange. In *The Devil's Charter* (IV, iv) a sustained assault upon the walls, involving ladders, takes place.

All window scenes—there are four [32]—contain a reference to "window" or "casement" in a stage direction. All of them involve interchanges by one person with characters below. However, the shape of the window, whether bay or otherwise, is not disclosed.

Only one scene, scene x in *Miseries of Enforced Marriage*, is continued for an extended time above. Complicated though the scene is, the demands that it makes on the stage are somewhat

uncommon and well worth detailed consideration. Preceding
the scene in question, three sharpers, Ilford, Bartley, and Wentloe, have bilked Butler's master, Scarborrow. Consequently,
Butler has devised a way in which to turn the tables on them, in
particular, Ilford. He pretends, separately to Ilford and then to
the other two, that he has access to a rich heiress, and promises
each of them to arrange a match. In reality the "heiress" is the
impoverished sister of Scarborrow. Having appointed a place to
meet the sharpers, he sends them off. At that point, two of Scarborrow's brothers, privy to the plot, enter. Without a change of
scene, the action shifts to the "place appointed" previously.
After being assured that the brothers know how to handle their
task, Butler exits. The brothers commend him for his devotion.
Then occurs a curious stage direction, "Betwixt this Butler leads
Ilford in." The brothers finish their eulogy when another direction is inserted, "Enter Butler and Ilford above." Butler pretends that the heiress' uncles have arrived, and he urges Ilford
to overhear their conversation while he goes below to the girl.
It is interesting to note that Butler says, "stay you heere in this
upper chamber" to listen to the uncles, not at the window. Butler leaves. Ilford listens to the brothers who, pretending to be
concerned about finding a suitable husband for their niece,
describe the vast wealth of the "heiress." Butler returns to an
exultant Ilford. Light-headed with visions of playing the courtier, Ilford swears to love and be true to the girl. She comes in.
Butler leaves them alone to swear their mutual faith. At this
point

> Enter Wentloe, and Bartley beneath.
> BART.   Here about is the house sure.
> WENTLOE. We cannot mistake it, for heres the signe of the
>   Wolfe and the Bay-window.
>   Enter Butler above.
> BUT.   [to the lovers] What so close? Tis well, I ha shifted
>   away your Vncles Mistris, but see the spight Sir
>   Francis, if yon same couple of Smel-smockes,
>   Wentloe and Bartley, ha not sented after us.
>   [Sig. G4]

Under the stimulus of competition, Ilford is willing to rush into marriage without seeing the dowry of his wife-to-be. After sending the couple "below," Butler calls to Bartley and Wentloe to arrange to meet them below, timing matters so that they will arrive after the marriage ceremony is completed.

Location is here treated very loosely. In the course of the scene, action shifts from one place to another. Sometimes the characters seem to be at a window, sometimes in an upper chamber, but there is no exact indication where they are at any one time. Indeed this is a generalized setting, for we know that we are at Scarborrow's house. The scene clearly shows that an extended action could be played above, but only when related to action below.

Altogether there are twelve scenes in ten Globe plays that utilize the above. Ten have been cited. The other two, the monument scene in *Antony and Cleopatra* (IV, xiv) and the observation scene in *Julius Caesar* (V, iii) where Pindarus witnesses the distant battle, are discussed in Appendix B, chart iii. To sum up the evidence for the above, the limited study of the Globe plays substantiates Richard Hosley's broader studies of the plays of Shakespeare, Kyd, Marlowe, and others as well as of the Red Bull plays.[33] He shows that 46 per cent of all the plays examined do not employ a raised production area. At the Globe 66 per cent do not employ such an area. Wherever, in the remaining 34 per cent of the plays, action is set above, invariably it is related to action below, either through actual communication or through persons on one level observing persons on the other.

Several stage facilities remain to be considered: the traps, the heavens, and the pillars. Upon these subjects, there is less disagreement amongst scholars. Both J. C. Adams and George Reynolds, opponents in many matters of Elizabethan staging, agree that Elizabethan stages contained more than one trap.[34] In the Globe plays traps are used seven times. From this list I exclude the use of a trap for the Ghost in the first act in *Hamlet*.[35] Of the seven instances four occur in one play, *The Devil's Charter*. Three of these can be definitely placed at a trap near the front of the platform (prologue; IV, i; V, vi), for preceding each use of the trap a stage direction specifies movement forward. The other scene in *The Devil's Charter* (III, v) is similar to one in *A Larum for London* (sc. xii). In each case a figure peering into a river or a vault respectively is pushed down into the void. The two remaining instances of trap use occur in *Macbeth* (the cauldron scene, IV, i) and *Hamlet* (the grave-diggers scene, V, i). In light of the character of the enclosure, these too must have been played forward. Confirmation of this assumption can be found in *Hamlet*. Stage productions often begin the gravediggers scene with one or both of the diggers already in a half-dug grave. However, a close reading of the first part of the text rules out such a beginning. Early in the Folio text, the second gravedigger advises the first to make the grave straight. But a little later the first calls to the other, "Come, my Spade." If he has been digging all along, this remark is unnecessary. Only after the two clowns come in, chat, and then the one calls to the other, "Come, my Spade," does the digging begin. This action occurs forward on the platform. To summarize, it is certain that the Globe plays require a trap, a trap of sufficient size to raise and lower a cauldron or a man on a property dragon (*The Devil's Charter*, IV, i), but at no time do they demand more than one trap located on the platform.

About the machinery in the heavens the Globe plays offer no evidence whatsoever. No hint exists from which one can surmise that either actors or properties were dropped from above. Nor is there any evidence for such action from the pre-Globe plays of the Lord Chamberlain's company. This may be coincidental. Plays containing flying scenes may have perished. But a suggestion that this finding for the Globe may have a more general application comes from two sources. Jonson's contempt for the "creaking thrones" which come down "the boys to please" is expressed in the prologue to the Folio version of *Every Man In His Humour* (1616). Although the prologue does not appear in the Quarto of 1601, scholars have assumed that the scornful attack refers to stage devices of that period. But Jonson revised *Every Man In His Humour* thoroughly, recasting the entire setting of the play. The addition of the prologue is certain, for it is in keeping with the Anglicized setting. Furthermore, the first use of flying in the King's men's repertory is recorded in the dream sequence in *Cymbeline* (V, iv), immediately after the company began to play at Blackfriars. It is pertinent that a dream scene, very similar to the one in *Cymbeline*, occurs in *Pericles* (V, i), one of the last plays to be produced before the King's men took over Blackfriars. Instead of Jupiter, Diana appears but does not descend. Nor did the god Hymen in the last scene of *As You Like It*. Could it have been that the company lacked means for flying actors until it moved to Blackfriars? Actually the history of flying apparatuses in the Elizabethan theater needs further study. For the Globe, at least so far as the plays demonstrate, no machinery for flying existed.

It is generally conceded that the posts supporting the heavens not only did exist, but were introduced into the action. Against the evidence of the Fortune and Hope contracts and the DeWitt drawing, there is no effective argument. Assuming, therefore, the presence of the two pillars, a number of scenes do exist where one was probably employed in the story, either as a post or a tree. However, to suppose that a pillar is used, let us say, for the tree upon which Orlando hangs his verse, reduces the likelihood that property trees were placed on stage for incidental action. Our old friend, the ubiquitous Butler, climbs a tree in *Miseries of Enforced Marriage*. J. C. Adams suggests that what he climbed was a stage pillar. Hodges doubts that an actor could climb a main pillar, but he suggests that a decorative pillar might have been used. So far as staging practice is concerned, it matters little which pillar serves as a tree. The principle is the same. When the actors could use a ready-to-hand stage post instead of a prop, they did so. Inconclusive but provocative is a hint we have that prop trees were introduced when they had symbolic meaning. The tree that arises in *A Warning for Fair Women* represents the life of Sanders which has been hewn down. And the titles of the trees in Henslowe's inventory, such as "j tree of gowlden apelles," and "Tantelouse tre," support this possibility.

Although we have covered all those structural parts of the stage which are required by the Globe plays, we must deal with the theory that in addition to or in place of the enclosure, mansions, that is, free-standing wooden frames, curtained on one or more sides, usually removable, were employed to suggest specific locations in Elizabethan plays. Except for the tents in *The Devil's Charter*, no evidence exists for such units on the Globe stage. Even the tents are in a special class, for they may be similar to a property such as a scaffold rather than to stage scenery. Reynolds has found instances for removable structures on the Red Bull stage and Hotson would place mansions on all stages, but there is no warrant for supposing that they were used at the Globe. Henslowe, who claims to include *all* the properties belonging to the Lord Admiral's men in his inventory of 1598, lists nothing that can be construed as a mansion, and though evidence for the Lord Admiral's men is not necessarily evidence for the Lord Chamberlain's men, nevertheless, it indicates that one playhouse at least seems not to have used temporary structures. For the Globe company not only the absence of evidence but also the system of localization rules out such a method of staging.

A unique theory combining the presence of mansions with the rearrangement of the spectators has been devised by Leslie Hotson. Not content to modify current thinking about Elizabethan staging, he reveals, messiah-like, that after two hundred years of bafflement, the world will be able "now for the first time to understand and visualize the stage of the Globe" because of his discoveries.[36] Citing a compote of evidence from the English and Spanish theaters, he asserts that the essential relationship between actor and audience maintained at Court, playhouse, and college, was one in which the actor performed between two masses of audience, with the privileged audience sitting on one side. In the Globe this privileged audience sat in the gallery over the stage and on the stage between the stage doors. The tiring house, contrary to accepted thought, was below the stage. At either end of the stage two-tiered wooden frames with transparent curtains served as mansions. Actors entered through trap doors into these mansions and from thence onto the stage. Masked attendants drew the curtains as the action required.

By the extravagance of his assertions and the evangelical tone of his arguments, Hotson has made a cause of what is a matter for scholarly examination. His daring views and the insights they afford usually deserve careful consideration. Here, however, it is only necessary to evaluate those theories which directly affect staging at the Globe.

Hotson's early attempts to prove the existence of "Shakespeare's Arena Stage" at Whitehall Palace, contrary to what he chooses to believe, have not met with general approbation. Alois Nagler, for example, has shown that Hotson's reading of *atorno atorno*, a phrase which appears in a description of a Court performance written by Virginio Orsino, Duke of Bracciano, does not mean, as Hotson contends, "completely around on every side," but on three sides.[37] Nevertheless, extending his interpretation to the public playhouse, Hotson announces that persons of quality "customarily graced" the Globe's stage. In fact, it was the outstanding characteristic of Elizabethan staging to locate the best seats on the stage and in the gallery over the stage. In establishing his proof, Hotson unfortunately neglects to mention the Induction to *The Malcontent*. This play, it will be remembered, was presented by the Globe company presumably in retaliation for the theft of one of their plays, *Jeronimo*, by the Children at Blackfriars. No other piece of evidence so surely reflects conditions at the Globe as this Induction, written by John Webster especially to justify the appearance of Marston's satire at this public playhouse. To give the justification indisputable authority, Webster introduces the leading actors of the company, Dick Burbage, Henry Condell, and John Lowin, in their own persons, to explain the matter.

The Induction commences.

> Enter W. Sly, a Tire-man following him with a stool.
> TIRE-MAN. Sir, the gentlemen will be angry if you sit here.
> SLY. [as a gallant]. Why, we may sit upon the stage at the
>   private house.

Immediately it is apparent that, contrary to Hotson's fancy, sitting on the stage was not the custom and its introduction was not happily countenanced by the "gentlemen." Since the tire-man still holds the stool as he refers to the "gentlemen," the word "here" must mean the stage as a whole and therefore the "gentlemen" are the actors. The one time Sly refers to any spectators, he does it in such terms that he clearly intends the groundlings. Otherwise, no mention is made of other spectators on the stage. Toward the end of the Induction, Lowin succeeds in ushering Sly out by offering to lead him to a "private room."

Thomas Platter, who supposedly attended one of the opening performances at the Globe, in his enumeration of possible seats for the audience, makes no mention of seats on the stage. Dekker, in the widely known passage from *The Gull's Hornbook*, does refer to sitting on the stage at the public playhouse, but Hotson takes seriously what is patently a satiric description of a fool intruding where he does not belong. Throughout the passage the stage sitter is referred to in the most derogatory terms, and what sharply contradicts Hotson's contention is the injunction to the gallant that "though the Scar-scrows in the yard, hoot at you, hisse at you, spit at you, yea throw durt even in your teeth: tis most Gentlemanlike patience to endure all this." [38] Were all those gentlemen who "customarily graced" the Globe stage treated in this fashion? Obviously the thrust of Dekker's wit, coming as it did in 1609, was a vain endeavor to resist the press of gallants who sought to impose upon the public playhouse the privileges they enjoyed at the private.

Hotson also claims that the gentlemen sat "over the stage, i' the lords roome." For this claim he enjoys considerably more support. In and out of plays references to sitting "over the stage" suggest the employment in some way of the area I have called the above. But "over the stage" is not specific. Does "over" mean directly over, or to one side? Does it include the entire length of the stage wall, as Hosley asserts, so that actors in order to play their scenes above were obliged to thrust themselves into the midst of the auditors? [39]

However, the case for sitters in a gallery which runs the length of the stage wall depends not merely upon words, but more effectively upon graphic representation. Four interior views of Elizabethan and Jacobean theaters are extant: the Swan drawing (1596), the engraving on the *Roxana* title page

(1632), the drawing on the *Messalina* title page (1640), and the frontispiece to *The Wits* (1672). Only one, the first and most important, is Elizabethan. Three of the representations, the Swan, the *Roxana,* and *The Wits,* depict figures in the gallery above the stage.

In each drawing the figures appear to be looking at the action on the stage below, particularly in the *Roxana* print. The frontispiece to *The Wits,* obviously depicting an interior, shows solemn-faced puritans in the gallery. Dressed as they are like the figures grouped around the platform, they certainly seem to be members of the audience. Less certain but of a similar character is the evidence from the *Roxana* title page. Both of these representations come late, it is true. But because they seem to echo the same conditions as those in the Swan playhouse of 1596, they have been cited as authority. About the figures in the Swan drawing it is difficult to tell. They appear to be drawn in positions that connote listening and seeing a play. But they are small and indistinct. Two or possibly three persons are wearing hats. Quite clearly all are related in some way to the action taking place below them. To a certain extent all these representations verify the theory that spectators sat over-looking the playing area.

The investigation is complicated as soon as we inquire about the numbers and disposition of the spectators. Examining these prints again, all four of them this time, we discover some significant disparities. The Swan drawing shows a long gallery divided by five posts into six sections. Each section is wide enough for two people. No architectural treatment of the gallery is delineated. The frontispiece of *The Wits* has some things in common with the Swan drawing. A gallery divided into six sections runs across the back of the stage. Four of the sections apparently are cut in half, but from the appearance of the other two, each section seems to be able to accommodate two persons side by side. One difference does exist. In the center of the upper level, there hangs a striped curtain, somewhat like an awning. The flap is parted so that two balusters may be seen, indicating some architectural structure behind the curtain. It is possible, but not certain, that the structure is cantilevered and thus protrudes. Some lines behind the balusters may have been intended to represent an actor waiting for his cue. The *Roxana* title page shows an upper level divided into two sections by a column. The framing about each section conveys the impression of two windows. Two figures occupy each section. Finally the *Messalina* title page, showing a bare stage, depicts a curtained window placed high in a brick wall. Thus, each of the views presents a different physical arrangement. Aside from the Swan drawing there is no support for a long, unadorned, uncurtained gallery in theaters of this period.

Since its discovery in 1888, repeated attempts have been made to prove that a particular occasion is represented by the Swan drawing. Nagler, among the latest to repeat the attempt, believes "that a rehearsal was in progress. DeWitt seems to have visited the theater in the morning and sketched the interior while the actors were rehearsing a scene." [40] He asserts that the persons in the gallery were actors or "at any rate, theater personnel." Without quarreling with the last comment, I believe that we must discount the theory that a rehearsal was in progress or, in actuality, that any specific moment is recorded in the sketch. One internal contradiction has been noted often. Why are there people in the gallery, but not in the auditorium? Because a rehearsal is in progress, says Nagler. Because DeWitt did not trouble to sketch all the details, says Hosley. But another contradiction exists in the drawing. At the head of the sketch, flying from a staff at the top of the huts, is the ensign of the playhouse, a flag emblazoned with a Swan. The flag was a sign that a performance was in progress. Below the flag is a figure who is blowing a trumpet. Either he is summoning the audience or he is announcing the commencement of the play. Customarily the play began after the third sounding of the trumpet. But, in the sketch, a scene is already under way. Consequently, if a rehearsal was in progress, why is the flag flying, the trumpeter calling the audience? If a performance was in progress, why at the beginning are we in the midst of the action? Could it be that the sketch reflects no particular instance but a composite impression of the Swan and that the rendition of such an impression was likely to have been made after DeWitt had left the playhouse? The text which accompanies the sketch, starting with a general discussion of London playhouses and proceeding to a description of the Swan, indicates that DeWitt set down a summary of experiences either after he had visited various theaters or after he had had them described to him.

It may be well at this time to consider the reliability of the Swan drawing in other respects. Currently it is the fashion to adhere to the sketch closely. However, one fact must be faced, insofar as the Globe is concerned. Granted that the original drawing, as well as Arend van Buchell's copy that has come down to the present, were both trustworthy, nevertheless we are still forced to amend the sketch in order to have it accord with other, indisputable evidence. All sorts of ingenious explanations, that the hangings were not in place or that a stage-width curtain was added for performance, have been offered, but the fact remains: the Swan, as it is depicted in the drawing, unaltered, could not have accommodated the Globe plays. However plausible the suggestions for additions may be, they cannot still the doubt with which one is obliged to regard the sketch, and though DeWitt's testimony cannot be ignored, it cannot be accepted without corroboration.

From the preceding material two conclusions emerge. First, there was no single form for the above. Therefore, in developing an image of the Globe, we cannot rely on the Swan drawing. Yet even if we do, we discover that such an unrelieved gallery as it shows is simply not characteristic of the Renaissance design which presumably DeWitt sought to catch. A glance at prints of various continental stages will illustrate this point.[41] What is suggested by the later views and what accords with the needs of the Globe playhouse is an above which, regardless of the presence of auditors, could be differentiated structurally from the rest of the gallery. Architecturally this might have been accomplished by separating and emphasizing a central, probably uncurtained, section in the balcony, reserved for the actors. On either side of this area, auditors might have overlooked the stage.

Second, all the views agree that the maximum number of

spectators in each section was two. Keeping literally to the evidence, we must conclude that twelve persons could be accommodated in the Swan gallery. We could, of course, indulge in the fascinating game of using the dimensions of the Fortune to calculate the capacity of the Swan. But this is unnecessary. DeWitt tells us the Swan could hold three thousand people. Whether twelve or twenty or a few more could sit above, their proportion to the total would be small. Could the actors have directed their performance to such a minority? It is certain that they did not, for in one other respect the extant views are in complete agreement. Where performers are shown in action on stage, they play, not toward the "spectators" in the gallery, but toward the auditors listening "round about." In short, they turn their backs to the stage wall and play front.

III. THE DESIGN OF THE STAGE

Until now the discussion of the Globe playhouse has proceeded from dramatic function to theatrical realization. But inevitably the reader is bound to wonder, if only inwardly, what the Globe looked like. No one knows. Startling as it may seem, no one really can reconstruct the design of the Globe playhouse. The reader may remonstrate: what about the various reconstructions of Walter Godfrey, John C. Adams, C. Walter Hodges, Richard Southern? What about their sketches and models? All hypotheses, some reasonable, some farfetched. Each scholar, selecting for his palette certain scraps of evidence, has painted a hypothetical image of the Elizabethan playhouse. Each realizes, of course, that his image is conjectural. The damage occurs when the image is realized in drawings and the drawings are reproduced with such frequency that what was conjecture comes to be regarded as historical fact by the general reader. Acknowledging that "the hard facts available [for the reconstruction of Elizabethan playhouses] are insufficient in themselves," Hodges admits that each scholar interprets the evidence according to "influences of taste" of which he may not even be aware.[42] The result has been that equally reputable scholars have produced widely divergent images of the Globe playhouse. In recent times the once prevailing Tudor image has yielded to Renaissance design.

The leading advocate of Tudor style is John Cranford Adams. He affirms that it was a "tendency of [Elizabethan] stage design to imitate contemporary London houses," and therefore, that "the façade of the tiring-house differed from its model, a short row of London houses, mainly in having upper and lower curtains suspended in the middle." Each reference to a contemporary urban structural feature of the stage is considered to be a description of a realistic detail. "It was the habit of Elizabethan dramatists to accept the equipment of their stage rather literally and to refer to that equipment in dialogue." [43] He cites construction methods of the period for support. The building contract for the Fortune calls for wooden frames "sufficiently enclosed withoute [outside] with lathe, lyme & Haire." This specification suggests a half-timbered-and-plaster building of Tudor design, a type of construction which continued to appear through the early part of the seventeenth century. In contrast, buildings in the newer Renaissance style were largely built of stone or brick.[44] Since its completion in 1950, Adams' model of the Globe, now at the Folger Library, has impressed itself upon the imagination of lovers of Shakespeare, particularly in America.

In 1953 C. Walter Hodges presented an opposing image of the Globe.[45] Adhering closely to the Swan drawing, which Adams rejects, and deriving the Elizabethan stage from market place booth stages and *tableaux vivants,* Hodges developed a series of sketches in Renaissance style. Doors and galleries in the stage façade are flanked by columns of one of the three regular orders; obelisks and statuary appear above the cornices of the Fortune sketch; and in his drawing of the Hope, carved busts support the gallery ends of the heavens. To avoid contradicting the Swan drawing, which shows no enclosure, he devised one to project from the stage façade.

The contribution of the *tableaux vivants* to the design of the Elizabethan stage was first explored by George Kernodle. His thesis is that "The greatest problem of the Renaissance stage was the organization of a number of divergent scenic elements into some principle of spatial unity." Medieval art bequeathed three forms to the theater: the side arches leaving the center clear, the center arch or pavilion with subordinate side accents, the flat arcade screen. While the Italian theater, later to be imitated by Inigo Jones in England, utilized the form of side arches in combination with central perspective to create illusion, the northern theaters of England and Flanders developed the central pavilion into a theater of architectural symbolism. The immediate predecessors of these stages were the *tableaux vivants,* or street pageants, erected to signalize the entry of a royal or civic personage into a city. It was "from the *tableaux vivants* (whose conventions they took over)" that the Flemish and English stages derived "the power to suggest, by decoration and remembered associations, the places they symbolized." The conventions of medieval art, which persisted throughout the early Renaissance, were passed on to the street theaters where they were interwoven with Renaissance forms. Prints of the Flemish stages illustrate the conventional architecture which resulted from these influences. In parallel fashion, the English theater was subject to the same influences. "Most of the new buildings erected in England in the latter half of the sixteenth century were of the newer Renaissance architecture." Yearly the Londoner could witness the pageants in the Lord Mayor's Show. "A comparison [of street shows and stage drama] will make clear," Kernodle believes, "not only that many particular scenes of Elizabethan drama were derived from the *tableaux vivants* but that they provided the basic pattern of the English stage façade." [46] This basic pattern involved a central arch which conventionally represented an interior, and side arches or doors which conventionally represented an exterior. Architectural symbols as throne, arbor, arras, by general recognition could transform the façade into the symbols of palace, garden, room.

For the design of the English stage, Kernodle's theory is provocative rather than proved. There is no clear flow of Flemish theatrical influence into Elizabethan England, and even in art, though we know many Flemish craftsmen were in London, there is no certain influence.[47] Furthermore, the medieval tradition in art, which Kernodle has shown to have persisted on the continent, was abruptly terminated in England. "The year 1531, in which the convocation of Canterbury recognized Henry VIII as the Supreme Head of the Church of England, can be conveniently taken to mark the close of the medieval period of art in England [and the severance of] what had been the most fruitful field of subject-matter for artists in Europe for a thousand years." [48] What followed was a court art of portraiture which does not readily yield demonstration of Kernodle's thesis. Even in the popular forms of art, which he recommends for study, the formal medieval elements are absent. For example, the woodcuts of Wynken de Worde show no consistent use of conventional devices.

As for the street pageants, continental experience cannot be readily applied to Tudor practice. For the last half of the sixteenth century the royal entries were virtually abandoned by Elizabeth, and it was not until the coronation of James that the magnificence of the royal entry returned to London. When it did, it had all the characteristics of the flamboyant Renaissance style described by Kernodle. Until then, from 1558 to 1603, the Londoner could witness the Lord Mayor's Show, an annual event to honor the installation of the new Lord Mayor. The central device was a single pageant supplied by the Company of which the Lord Mayor was a member.[49] Featuring child orators, it was usually carried along in the procession by porters, though from time to time we hear of frames being built to support the pageants.[50] It appears that the pageant was stored in the company hall from which it was removed when needed, with or without redecoration, though occasionally a new pageant would be ordered.[51] The fact that the pageant remained on permanent view in the company halls suggests that it may have been similar to the figures of saints carried even today in religious processions.

Allegorical in nature, the pageant depicted a theme apt for the new Lord Mayor and his company. In 1561, for example, five ancient harpers, David, Orpheus, Amphion, Arion, and Iopas, were displayed in a pageant to honor the new Lord

Mayor, Sir William Harper. Often the themes of the pageants represented the trade rather than the man, the Ship, for instance, being deemed appropriate for the Merchant Tailors Company.[52] At an appropriate point in the procession, the figures in the pageant would speak commendatory verses to the Lord Mayor. From the extant texts, it is quite clear that the presentations were brief and rhetorical; they did not involve dramatic action. In fact, the very people being honored were those who most assiduously sought to destroy the public playhouses.[53]

No sketch of a sixteenth century pageant exists. The presence of mythical figures encourages the notion that Renaissance design characterized these pageants, but there is no graphic or thoroughly descriptive evidence for assuming so. Nor do the symbols which Kernodle enumerates appear prominently in these pageants. Instead the companies relied on those trade-or-personal symbols which held special significance for them. For one company the lion appears in pageant because a lion is part of the company's coat of arms; [54] for another, a Moor rides on a lynx, which animal is deemed appropriate for the Skinners' company.[55]

What is substantiated by these pageants and reinforced by the royal entries of the seventeenth century is the mode of presentation. Perhaps the particular symbols which Kernodle emphasizes did not have significance for the Londoner of the 1590's, but he was familiar with presenting and interpreting theatrical forms in a symbolic manner, and I believe that to this extent the pageants may have influenced the design of the public playhouse.

In conclusion, then, one can not verify whether the Elizabethan playhouse reflected the outgoing Tudor or the incoming Renaissance style. Roughed up by a master carpenter, such as James Burbage, Peter Streete, or Gilbert Katherens, the structure could have retained the traditions of design familiar to these men or it could have responded to the new fashions. These new fashions, however, were principally decorative; classical forms were applied to Tudor-Gothic foundations.[56] I tend to think that the pragmatic attitude of Elizabethan builders led them to erect a fundamentally Tudor structure to which they attached classical ornaments more or less at random. In such a structure the stage would certainly be the focus of such adornment.

Based solely on the evidence of the Globe plays, what then is the picture of the Globe stage? The principal part of the stage was a large rectangular platform upon which rested two pillars. At the rear of the platform two doors and a curtained recess between them provided access to the stage. The recess, which was an integral part of the tiring house, had to accommodate less than half a dozen people. Above the recess and/or doors was an upper level principally required where characters related themselves to others below. In the floor of the outer stage there was at least one substantial trap. No machinery for flying either actors or properties existed. In over-all design the stage, which was Renaissance in surface details, emphasized formal rather than realistic decoration. Altogether it was a theater that presented itself as a show place rather than as an imitation of London.

In a review once Granville-Barker remonstrated against overemphasis on the physical aspects of the stage at the expense of the imaginative. Such overemphasis has too frequently resulted. In their zeal to reconstruct the Elizabethan stage, theorists have given the impression that the theater of that day was constantly using traps, heavens, upper level, and enclosure. However, a comparison of the number of scenes which use some stage facility, be it merely a stool, with the number which use no stage facility whatsoever, neither property nor stage machinery, save merely a means to get on and off, shows that of the 345 scenes in the Shakespearean Globe plays, only 20 per cent require any facility. Fully 80 per cent need nothing but a bare space and an audience, not so much as a stool.

As a result, Shakespearean drama depends a great deal upon the vigorous movement of the actors coming on and off the stage. The actors themselves, rather than the stage equipment, provide the impetus for a play's progression. We are all familiar with the conclusion of a Shakespearean scene. More often than not, a character will say, "Come along with me," and off will go the actors. I have checked every scene in the Globe plays and found a startlingly high percentage of such exits. For purposes of computation I divide the scene conclusions into four categories.

First, there is the explicit exit line.

> ORL.   Come, I will bear thee to some shelter,
> and thou shalt not die for lack of a
> dinner if there live any thing in this
> desert. Cheerly, good Adam. Exeunt.
> [*As You Like It*, II, vi, 16–19]

Next, there is the implicit exit line.

> ANT.   [musing upon Sebastian's departure]
> But come what may, I do adore thee so
> That danger shall seem sport, and I will go. Exit.
> [*Twelfth Night*, II, i, 48–49]

Thirdly, there is the scene which ends with no exit line implying motion.

> To.   [to the dancing Sir Andrew] Let me see
> thee caper. Ha, higher! ha, ha, excellent! Exeunt.
> [*Twelfth Night*, I, iii, 149–150]

Lastly, there is the scene which ends in a soliloquy or an aside. Although the playwright occasionally inserts an exit line in such a conclusion, his opportunity to do so is slight. Below I have enumerated the scene endings that conclude with explicit and implicit exit lines, with no exit lines, and as a solo exit.

	Explicit Exit lines	Implicit Exit lines	No. Exit lines	Solo Exits
Shakespeare	192 57.2%	74 22%	35 10.4%	35 10.4%
Non-Shakes.	88 48.4%	37 20.3%	23 12.6%	34 18.7%

Only 9 to 13 per cent of the scenes fail to indicate that the characters end a scene by leaving the stage. Although the soliloquies may or may not imply that the actors leave the stage, the majority of the scene endings clearly demonstrate that it was the physical departure of the actors which gave fluency to the action. When a stage direction reads "exeunt" at the end of a scene, it means exactly that: "they go out."

It is time to revive an old cry. The pendulum has swung too far. It is time to reassert that the Globe stage *was* bare. Sumptuous and gorgeous as this playhouse may have appeared, the decoration was largely permanent and passive. In brief, the Globe was constructed and employed to tell a story as vigorously and as excitingly and as intensely as possible. Though spectators were usually informed where a scene took place, they were informed by the words they heard, not the sights they saw. Instead, place was given specific emphasis only when and to the degree the narrative required. Otherwise, the audience gazed upon a splendid symbol of the universe before which all sorts of human actions could be unfolded.

Chapter Four

THE ACTING

SINCE 1939 the debate over the style of acting in the Elizabethan theater has been argued on the grounds defined by Alfred Harbage. One of two styles could have existed, he wrote. Acting was either formal or natural.

Natural acting strives to create an illusion of reality by consistency on the part of the actor who remains in character and tends to imitate the behavior of an actual human being placed in his imagined circumstances. He portrays where the formal actor symbolizes. He impersonates where the formal actor represents. He engages in real conversation where the formal actor recites. His acting is subjective and "imaginative" where that of the formal actor is objective and traditional. Whether he sinks his personality in his part or shapes the part to his personality, in either case he remains the natural actor.[1]

Professor Harbage then, and a succession of writers subsequently,[2] have endeavored to prove that formal acting prevailed on the Elizabethan stage.

When we have sifted the various arguments presented over the years by this school of thought, we discover these common points. Oratory and acting utilized similar techniques of voice and gesture so that "whoever knows today exactly what was taught to the Renaissance orator cannot be far from knowing at the same time what was done by the actor on the Elizabethan stage."[3] Contemporary allusions which compare the orator to the actor establish this correspondence without a doubt. This system depended upon conventional gesture, "as in a sorrowfull parte, yᵉ head must hange down; in a proud, yᵉ head must bee lofty." [4] By learning these conventional gestures, the actors could readily symbolize all emotional states. Such symbolization was necessary since the speed of Elizabethan playing left little room for interpolated action. The result was that the actor did not so much interpret his part as recite it. His personality did not intrude, for his attention was devoted to rendering the literary qualities of the script. Although the emotions expressed in the play were usually violent, the actor projected them "by declaiming his lines with the action fit for every word and sentence." [5] In this way he properly stressed the significant figures of speech. He played to the audience, not to his fellow actors. The final effect, several writers have concluded, was more like that of opera or ballet than modern drama.

Rejecting this theory of formal acting, a smaller but equally fervent group of scholars is sure that Elizabethan acting was "natural." [6] Denying that oratory and acting were similar, they maintain that style was dynamic, that an older formalism gave way to a newer naturalism. Since Renaissance art sought to imitate life, the actors in harmony with this aim thought that they imitated life. To grasp how their style emerged from such a view, it is necessary first to comprehend what was the Elizabethan conception of reality. Admittedly, natural acting then was different from natural acting today in some respects, yet the intention was very much the same. "What can be said is that Elizabethan acting was thought at the time to be lifelike . . . [which would suggest] a range of acting capable of greater extremes of passion, of much action, which would now seem forced or grotesque, but realistic within a framework of 'reality' that coincides to a large extent with ours." [7]

Some attempt has been made to reconcile these contradictory views. Generally the reconciliation has taken the line that Elizabethan acting was mixed, partly formal, partly natural. Some have thought of the mixture as a blend: a unified style midway between the rigidity of formalism and the fluidity of naturalism. It has also been thought of as an oscillation: certain scenes played in a formal manner, such as longer verse passages delivered in a rhetorical style; other scenes, such as brief exchanges of dialogue, acted in an informal manner. The scholars who have proposed this reconciliation, despite the fact that they arrive at slightly different conclusions from those of the proponents of formal or natural acting, accept the fundamental premise that Elizabethan acting can be discussed only in terms of formal or natural styles.

Until now, it is true, the research and discussion that have gone into this debate have produced careful studies of contemporary allusions to acting. But it seems unlikely that further progress can be made by considering Elizabethan acting in relation to these fixed poles of formality and reality. Brown and Foakes have undertaken a new approach by urging an evaluation of Elizabethan acting in terms of the Elizabethan conception of reality. But neither has followed through. They have merely redefined what is meant by natural acting. Much of what the formalists consider conventional, they argue, represented reality to the Elizabethan. Do sudden insubstantially motivated emotional changes in *Othello* or *Measure for Measure* seem forced? They occurred in life and therefore were natural to the period, is their answer. The result has been confusion. The formalists describe the means at the actor's disposal, the techniques of voice and gesture; the naturalists, the effect at which he aimed, the imitation of life.

This confusion is inherent in the original proposition. Harbage wrote about both aims and means, but without sufficiently discriminating between the two. I think that it is necessary to clarify our understanding of the aims and methods of the actor's art in general before returning to a consideration of the Elizabethan actor's art in particular.

At the heart of dramatic presentation stands the actor, imitating a person in a fictional situation in such a way as to hold the continuous attention of the audience in the unfolding circumstances. This holding of attention is dramatic illusion. Whether that illusion is an imitation of contemporary life, historical life, or mythical life, the action and characters must achieve a level of reality sufficient to involve us. For the children who say, "I believe in fairies," Tinkerbell has become real. The means may be conventional and symbolic or contextual and descriptive;

the effect must be an "illusion of reality." Ultimately, we must reconstruct what that "illusion" signified and how it was achieved in order to visualize the acting of a period.

The understanding that the actor has with the audience about the relation of dramatic experience to life will determine the significance of the illusion. The common understanding that they, actor and audience, have about the characters and stories will affect the means at the actor's disposal for creating the illusion. Consider a simple stage movement. An actor turns his back on the audience. In the context of the Théâtre-Libre or the Moscow Art Theatre this movement emphasizes the convention of the fourth wall and the illusion of the unpresent audience. The same movement employed in Molière's *Le Bourgeois Gentilhomme* is a deliberate artifice introduced for comic effect. Not the fixed forms, but their function and context shape the illusion of reality. Not the intent, but the created image, determines the significance of that illusion. The aim may be one, but the manifestations are many.

When an illusion of reality becomes differentiated sharply, it eventuates in a style. Not being an arithmetic total of absolute qualities, style does not remain constant. It is a dynamic interplay of many impulses brought to a point of crystallization by the creative genius of the actor. Such a complex, if distinctive and appealing enough, itself becomes an impulse for further creative activity. What we often term "formal acting" is a previous means of creating illusion which has coalesced into a fixed form imitable by later generations. Some of the impulses that led the commedia dell'arte to create a Harlequin, a Francatrippa, and a Dottore were "realistic"; that is, the activities of Italian daily life helped to refine the stage figure. Gradually the types became stock and finally ossified so that they responded less to the impulses of contemporary life and more to the tradition from which they were derived. Perfection and variation of old roles rather than the invention of new devices and characteristics became the custom. By the time these figures came to the hand of Marivaux they had, through the loss of much of their original force, become somewhat precious and self-conscious. Illusion of reality was still achieved, but it was a new kind of illusion, less robust, more sophisticated, less aware of the cry of the street, more attuned to the repartee of the drawing room. Then the acting became "formal," that is, traditional, conventional, "objective." But from the germination of the improvised drama to the "decadence" of Marivaux, commedia acting went through several styles. To visualize the style of any single period we have to study a cross section of its theatrical and social conditions.

Of these conditions there are five which provide the principal clues to an understanding of the Globe acting style. First, there are general intellectual tendencies reflected in the theory and practice of Elizabethan rhetoric. Next, there is the theatrical tradition handed down to the Lord Chamberlain's men. Thirdly, and continuing the foregoing material, there are the playing conditions under which the company operated. Fourthly, there is the conception of human character and behavior held by society. Lastly, and perhaps most important, there are the playing materials themselves, the characters and actions with which the actors were provided. Cumulatively, the study of these conditions supplies an understanding of the means at the Globe actors' disposal for creating their "illusion of reality" and, through it, offers an insight into the significance of that illusion.

I. THE RELATION OF TUDOR RHETORIC TO ELIZABETHAN ACTING

Rhetoric played a vital role in the education and life of the Elizabethan man. From its study he could learn all that was known of the art and techniques of oral and written communication. Scholars of the school of formal acting have insisted that seventeenth century works on rhetorical delivery reflect an image of Elizabethan acting. Usually the actor is considered the transmitter, the rhetorician the receiver of influence. This contention has been disputed, as I have pointed out. For the moment, however, let us suppose that there was some connection between oratory and acting. What then does rhetoric teach us of Elizabethan acting? To answer this question Bertram Joseph relies principally upon Bulwer's double study *Chirologia* and *Chironomia* (1644), a late work. But, since we have been considering acting as a dynamic art, it would be well to examine the evidence of sixteenth and early seventeenth century manuals of rhetoric.

Compassed under the heading of rhetoric in the sixteenth century were three of the five parts of classical rhetoric. *Inventio* and *dispositio* had been transferred to logic, particularly in the Ramist scheme. *Elocutio, memoria,* and *pronuntiatio* remained. However, *memoria* or the art of memory was generally, though not entirely, ignored. Of the two remaining parts that made up sixteenth century rhetoric, *elocutio,* or the art of eloquence, and *pronuntiatio,* or the art of speech and gesture, the former received the almost undivided attention of Elizabethan writers.

Before 1610 only Thomas Wilson in *The Art of Rhetorique* (1553) and Abraham Fraunce in *The Arcadian Rhetorike* (1588) treat the art of pronunciation separately. The other writers,[8] except for occasionally defining the term or citing an example, or describing the qualities of a good voice, omit the subject entirely. Even Wilson and Fraunce treat it in summary fashion.

Wilson defines the two parts of the subject, voice and gesture. A praiseworthy voice is "audible, strong, and easie, & apte to order as we liste." Before an audience orators should start speaking softly, "use meete pausying, and being somewhat heated, rise with their voice, as the tyme & cause shal best require" (Sig. Gg1ʳ). For those with poor voices, attention to diet, practice in singing, and imitation of good speakers are the means of improvement. Gesture, which is a "comely moderacion of the countenaunce, and al other partes of mans body," should agree with the voice. Altogether, the orator should be cheerful, poised, and moderate in deportment (Sig. Gg2ʳ).

The entire section sets up standards for good pronunciation, but it does not specifically show how they are met. The standards place emphasis on comeliness and grace, on a harmony of speech, gesture, and matter. The actual manner of delivery shall be "as the tyme & cause shal best require."

Fraunce is both fuller and more specific in his treatment of pronunciation, although, like Wilson, he devotes the smaller portion of his book, *The Arcadian Rhetorike*, to it. Generally he reiterates the points made by Wilson: the voice must be pleasing, the speaker should begin softly and rise "as occasion serveth," the delivery should follow the meaning. Fraunce goes further than Wilson, however, in equating a kind of voice with appropriate rhetorical form.

> In figures of words which altogether consist in sweete repetitions and dimensions, is chiefly conversant that pleasant and delicate tuning of the voyce, which resembleth the consent and harmonie of some well ordred song: In other figures of affections, the voyce is more manly, yet diversly, according to the varietie of passions that are to bee expressed.[9]

His specific suggestions depend upon the equation of voice and affection, for example, "in pitie and lamentation, the voyce must be full, sobbing, flexible, interrupted." Largely there is an association of tone of voice with a particular passion. For "feare and anger" there are additional injunctions concerning rhythm. Otherwise, these "rules" seem suggestive and general rather than imperative and specific.

In writing of gesture, Fraunce once again supplements the standards of Wilson with illustrations of his own. The truism of the age that "gesture must followe the change and varietie of the voyce," is conditioned by the warning that it should not be done "parasiticallie as stage plaiers use, but gravelie and decentlie as becommeth men of greater calling." This implies that the attitude may have been similar but the resulting manner different. Actual suggestions are made for the portrayal of affections; for example, "the holding downe of the head, and casting downe of the eyes betokeneth modestie." Forbidding gesture with the head alone, Fraunce notes that its chiefest force is the countenance, and of the countenance the eyes "which expres livelilie even anie conceit or passion of the mind." How to use the eyes is not explained. The particular ordering of the lips, nose, chin, and shoulders is "left to everie mans discretion."

Concerning the arms and hands Fraunce writes little. The right arm in being extended reinforces the flow of the speech.

This action is supplemented by the moderate use of the hands and fingers which rather "follow than goe before and expresse the words." Since the left hand alone is not used in gesture, it is joined with the right in expressing doubt, objection, and prayer. The fingers in various combinations express distinct significance.

For the body as a whole Fraunce warns against unseemliness. He associates striking the breast with grief and lamentation, striking the thigh with indignation, striking the ground with the foot with vehemency. By and large the speaker should not move more than a step or two.

In substance this is the written material on pronunciation in English before 1610. Fraunce alone shows any indication that there was a conventional system of vocal delivery and physical gesture. As early as 1531 Elyot in *The Governour* (fol. 49) had included "the voyce and gesture of them that can pronounce comedies" in the attributes of a fine orator. This Ciceronian tradition is probably reflected in *The Arcadian Rhetorike* so that Fraunce may be following the custom of the players except where he specifically notes a difference. But do the "rules" of Fraunce demonstrate the presence of an accepted system of convention in voice and gesture, or are they personal observations organized into a system? Writing of the affections and speech, Fraunce indicates that the correspondence *must* be followed. In writing of the affections and gesture, he is less sure. Some matters are left to the discretion of the speaker, others must adhere to a certain convention. About the body he is suggestive. Striking the breast to express grief "is not unusuall," but striking the thigh to express indignation "was usuall" as was stamping. Usual where? On the stage? In the law courts? In the pulpit? He does not specify. Keeping in mind that Fraunce alone has detailed such "conventions of voice and gesture," it is apparent that he is regularizing the general habit current in sixteenth century England of finding external means of expression for internal conceits or passions of the mind.

A habit is not a convention, however. The gestures described by Fraunce reinforce the speech, lending harmony and vigor to the vocal expression. But there is little evidence that they were raised to the level of symbolism, that particular gestures came widely to represent particular meanings. That this was the case is supported by a comparison of the supposed meanings of several gestures. As quoted above, Fraunce claimed that "the holding downe of the head, and casting downe of the eyes betokeneth modestie." But the author of *The Cyprian Conqueror* (1633), cited by Professor Harbage, asserts that "in a sorrowfull parte, ye head must hang downe." Lest we think that two affections were expressed by the same gesture, we must note how sorrow was expressed according to Fraunce. "The shaking of the head noteth griefe and indignation." Obviously there was not complete agreement about the significance of a particular gesture. Nor could there be since forms of expression are usually left to the speaker's judgment in the rhetorics.

Nevertheless, although an exact pattern of conventions cannot be discovered in Elizabethan rhetoric, general attitudes toward speech can be discerned. Wilson and Fraunce call for a pleasant voice, neither too high nor too low, but mean, capable of expressing nuances of thought. The ideal blending of speech and movement for the Elizabethan age is well presented in Baldassare Castiglione's *Courtier*, translated by Thomas Hoby in 1561.

[What is requisite in speaking is] a good voice, not too subtill or soft, as in a woman: nor yet so boistrous and rough, as in one of the countrie, but shril, cleare, sweete, and well framed with a prompt pronunciation, and with fit maners, and gestures, which (in my minde) consist in certaine motions of all the bodie, not affected nor forced, but tempred with a manerly countenance and with a moving of the eyes that may give grace and accorde with the wordes, and (as much as he can) signifie also with gestures, the intent and affection of the speaker.[10]

Grace, dignity, and spontaneity, in short, beauty of expression, was the accepted aim of the age.

In addition to speaking pleasantly, the educated man was expected to speak meaningfully. His vocal delivery should express figures of eloquence effectively.

The consideration of voyce is to be had either in severed words, or in the whole sentence. In the particular applying of the voyce to severall words, wee make tropes that bee most excellent plainly appeare. For without this change of voyce, neither anie Ironia, nor lively Metaphore can well bee discerned.[11]

Nor must this attention to the figures of speech be lavished only upon the formal speech. In his informal *Direction for Speech and Style* (c. 1590), John Hoskins applies the same consideration to social occasion. Included in his discussion of Agnomination, or repetition of sounds in sentence, such as "Our paradise is a pair of dice, our almes-deeds are turned into all misdeeds," is a suggestion that "that kind of breaking words into another meaning is pretty to play with among gentlewomen, as, *you will have but a bare gain of this bargain.*" Sensitivity to the figures of eloquence was widespread; we may expect the actors to have been particularly attentive to their rendition.

Though scanty, indications exist that the speaker was not thought to deliver his speech by rote. As Hamlet compares his behavior with the player's, he describes the man's tears, distraction and broken voice,

> and his whole function suiting
> With forms to his conceit.
> [II, ii, 582–583]

"The conceits of the mind are pictures of things and the tongue is interpreter of those pictures," wrote John Hoskins to his student.[12] Just as eloquence contained figures of sentence encompassing an extended thought as well as figures of words expressing a turn of a phrase, so did delivery require an understanding of the conceit and passion as a whole as well as the appreciation of the particular literary form.

Among the figures listed by Henry Peacham in *The Garden of Eloquence* (1593) is Mimesis:

Mimesis is an imitation of speech whereby the orator counter-faitheth not onely what one said, but also his utterance, pronunciation and gesture, imitating everything as it was, which is alwaies well performed, and naturally represented in an apt and skilfull actor.[13]

Since imitation is confined to a single figure, it probably was not expected in delivery except in special situations. But this applies to the rendering of character types, for the projection of passion in oratory was generally accepted and encouraged. Fraunce, as we have seen, describes the kinds of tones to be employed in terms of the affections to be conveyed. Sir Thomas Elyot in 1531 writes that whereas "the sterring of affections of the minde in this realme was never used, therefore ther lacketh Eloqution and pronunciation, two of the princypall parts of Rethorike." [14] Wilson explicitly states not only the desirability of stirring affections but the necessity for the speaker to feel those affections himself.

He that will stirre affeccions to other, muste first be moved him-self.
Neither can any good be doen at all, when we have saied all that ever we can, except we brying the same affeccions in owr owne harte whiche wee would the Judges should beare towardes our awne matter . . . a wepying iye causeth muche moysture, and provoketh teares. Neither is it any mervaile: for such men bothe in their counte-naunce, tongue, iyes, gesture, and in all their body els, declare an outwarde grief, and with wordes so vehemently and unfeinedly, settes it forward, that thei will force a man to be sory with them, and take part with their teares, even against his will. [Sig. T1 ᵛ]

Not only Elyot's comment but also Peacham's changes in *The Garden of Eloquence* for the second edition in 1593 show that increased attention to stirring the emotions occurred in the last half of the sixteenth century in England.

Peacham's omission in 1593 of the grammatical schemes he had included in the first edition of *The Garden of Eloquence* and his addition of many figures based on appeal to the emotions may be taken as indications of a shift which had taken place in rhetoric in England between 1577 and 1593. . . . During these years, too, the rhetorical theories of Petrus Ramus and Audomarus Talaeus, with their emphasis on those rhetorical devices which directed their appeal to the emotions, flourished in England.[15]

In such a context, if rhetoric influenced or reflected acting, it emphasized the already present stimulation of emotion and encouraged the actor who wished to move his audience to "bryng the same affeccions" in his own heart to the stage.

That it is misleading to apply the circumstances of later rhetorical study to this earlier period is evident on two scores. First, during the first half of the seventeenth century a shift from medieval rhetoric, of which sixteenth century English rhetoric is an extension, to classical rhetoric took place, principally through the influence of Francis Bacon and Ben Jonson. This meant the reentry of *inventio* and *dispositio* into the framework of rhetoric, bringing about the second change. In the scheme that Francis Bacon proposed for learning, rhetoric no longer should be directed at moving the affections:

> It is the business of rhetoric to make pictures of virtue and goodness, so that they may be seen. For since they cannot be showed to the sense in corporeal shape, the next degree is to show them to the imagination in as lively representation as possible, by ornament of words.

Actually, rhetoric should be brought into the attack against affections:

> Reason would become captive and servile, if eloquence of persuasions did not win the imagination from the affections' part, and contract a confederacy between the reason and imagination against them.[16]

To infer conclusions about the details of Elizabethan acting from Elizabethan rhetoric is, as we have seen, highly conjectural. Yet, in the intellectual atmosphere of which rhetoric was a part, we can discern several attitudes that probably shaped acting. Detailed study was expended on the figures of eloquence and loving care was devoted to models of fine tropes. The oral rendition of these forms was left to the judgment of the individual, for the most part. The few expositions of delivery stress grace of expression and stirring of affections. But no thoroughly accepted conventions of voice and gesture seem to have existed. Thus, although rhetorical theory was conducive to the growth of formal and traditional acting, rhetorical delivery had not solidified sufficiently by 1610 to provide a systematic method. In seeking external forms for their conceits, the orator, and probably actor, still responded more to invention than tradition.

II. THE INFLUENCE OF THEATRICAL TRADITIONS UPON ELIZABETHAN ACTING

Although Elizabethan rhetorical tradition was essentially continental, Elizabethan theatrical tradition was largely native. For the better part of a century, troupes of four men and a boy had crisscrossed the English countryside, bringing plays to village and court. Though the Queen's men, with twelve actors, at its formation in 1583 became the largest troupe, the smaller troupes continued to flourish. The English troupe that traveled to Denmark in 1586 numbered five men, and the various companies that are portrayed in *Sir Thomas More, Histrio-mastix,* and *Hamlet* all number either four or five. Naturally, when the theater became stabilized in London, increasingly so after 1575, the companies tended to grow larger. But periodic difficulties because of politics or plague caused frequent resort to the small troupe during the next twenty years.

Small companies required the actor to play several roles in one play. *Cambises* divides thirty-eight parts among eight men, with five of the men playing either six or seven parts each. Only the Vice had fewer than three parts. *Horestes* divides twenty-seven parts among five. Even actors of the larger companies had to play several roles. *Sir Clyomon and Sir Clamydes*, presented by the twelve men of the Queen's company, contained seventeen substantial roles, plus twenty-one for supernumeraries. This tradition of doubling gave the Elizabethan actor no opportunity to develop a specialty. He could not concentrate on a specific genre, for he was called upon to play courtly men and country men, villains and saints. Probably we should except the leading comic from this stricture. Usually he played fewer roles, and through the recurrence of the Vice figure and the practice of extemporal improvisation, he had the conditions necessary to the development of a distinctive type. But the other actors had to enact all sorts of roles. Unlike the Italian comedian who devoted himself to his forte, the Elizabethan tried to become flexible and varied in his abilities. It is evident that the attention of the actor had to be concentrated on telling the story, not developing the characters. Since the shift from one character to another necessitated some change in appearance or manner, readily discernible characteristics must have distinguished each type of part. As we shall see, this kind of acting was in harmony with the generic nature of Elizabethan characterization.

Systematic training of the popular players does not seem to have been the rule either. Stephen Gosson in *Playes Confuted in five Actions* (1582), describes three sources of recruitment:

Most of the Players have bene eyther men of occupations, which they have forsaken to lyve by playing, or common minstrels, or trayned up from theire childehood to this abhominable exercise.

But the latter group, for which we can reasonably assume careful training, does not seem to have supplied many actors to the professional companies before 1600. Of the six men in Leicester's company we know the background only of James Burbage, who had been a carpenter by trade. Of the twelve in the Queen's men, we know little more. John Dutton may have been a musician, since Lincoln's Inn paid him for musicians in 1567–1568. Richard Tarleton, the renowned clown, tended swine, according to Fuller. But his fellow, Robert Wilson, asserted that he had been an apprentice waterbearer whose native wit led him to the stage.

When we come to the actors of the Globe company, the information is somewhat fuller. Shakespeare himself did not leave Stratford before 1584, when he was over twenty years of age, so that we can assume that he went from some craft or from a schoolhouse to the theater. Besides Shakespeare, there were thirteen other sharers in the company between 1599 and 1609: Thomas Pope, John Heminges, Augustine Phillips, Richard Cowley, Richard Burbage, William Sly, Henry Condell, and Robert Armin, all members before 1603, and Laurence Fletcher, John Lowin, Alexander Cooke, Nicholas Tooley, and Robert Goffe, all of whom became members after 1603. Of the antecedents of most of the members we know little. Thomas Pope had been one of the English players in Denmark and Germany in 1586–1587. Heminges, in his will, calls himself "citizen and grocer," which may indicate that he, too, was an artisan turned player. Burbage presumably grew up in his father's theater. While quite young, he appeared in the *Seven Deadly Sins.* Armin was said to have been an apprentice to a goldsmith. Condell is conjectured to have been the "Harry" of *Seven Deadly Sins,* but the identification is inconclusive. Thus, of the earlier group of actors, several seem to have come from the trades. In the later group of five, three may have been apprentice actors and one, Lowin, had been an apprentice goldsmith. Fletcher seems to have been connected with a troupe in Scotland. The evidence, inconclusive as it is, indicates that with the increased stability of the theater and the alteration in theatrical taste the source of actors shifted from adults to trained boys.

The ready transfer of a man from trade to stage in the early period argues that an elaborate training, at least at the beginning, was not expected. The ready conversion of the tradesmen into actors in *Histrio-mastix* (Sig. B1ʳ), once a poet has been secured, further demonstrates that the possession of a story, not the cultivation of a manner, was requisite. What the details of early acting may have been, we do not know. The conditions of training and the methods of recruitment, however, were not conducive to the development of precisely executed conventions.

The actual skills of the early Elizabethan actors can be inferred in part from references to various actors. Tarleton and Robert Wilson were commended for their "extemporall wit." In letters dealing with English players on the Continent in the 1580's, acting is always linked with dancing, vaulting and tumbling. Thomas Pope and George Bryan, a Lord Chamberlain's man until the end of 1597, were among the five "instrumentister och springere" at the Danish court in 1586. These scattered allusions reinforce the opinion that simple characterization, rude playing, native wit, and physical vigor were the qualities of the early actor.

We must turn to the plays presented by the public companies before 1595 to round out the picture of the theatrical tradition. Character was not fully developed in the popular theater until Marlowe. Before his plays appeared, character had been barely differentiated from generic types, such as kings, vices, rustics, tyrants, etc. A word is necessary about generic types. Each of the generic types arises from a social class, and the characters within each type reflect their class. Differences between generic characters of the same type are not as great as similarities. Some distinctive habits of thought and behavior cluster about each type, but these are never rigidly fixed. Simple representatives of the generic type are the merchant and the potecary in John Heywood's interludes of *The Weather* and *The Four PP.* respectively. The generic type differs from the stock figure partly in source but mainly in definition. The stock figure tends to coalesce into a single perfect representative of each type: a Scapin, a Columbine, a Harlequin. The generic type encourages multiplicity. The stock figure, such as the doctor from Bologna, often has a regional origin. From the region of his birth he usually derives physical or social idiosyncracies, for example, a dialect, an item of apparel, or a distinctive manner. As the stock figure develops, additional external features become attached to him. Certain bits of stage business, quirks of personality, modes of dress, and style of playing, become his trade-marks. But the generic character seldom becomes fixed and traditional. Instead, he constantly undergoes change according to the demands of the story.

The early popular plays definitely show that the actors were used to playing generic characters. Thus, they were able to concentrate on the story, the sentiment, and the sententiousness of their plays. In limited ways they relied on dress to identify types of characters. Alan Downer has shown that there was some symbolism in costume. Hotson has traced the evolution of a distinctive garment for the Elizabethan "natural." [17] Henslowe lists certain costumes which were probably generic or symbolic. But features of dress remained generalized rather than becoming attached to a stock type. Whether habits of carriage or gesture corresponded with types of roles, we do not know. But it is certain, as we found in our study of rhetoric, that no traditional, systematic scheme of vocal and physical conventions developed.

Actually, in a rudimentary way, the early plays show tendencies toward the kind of structure described in the chapter on dramaturgy. In *Cambises*, it is not the discovery or death of Sisamnes which occupies our attention, but the responses of the son, Otian, to his father's execution. Affective display and rhetorical pronouncement occupied the center of the stage. Some time ago, Albert Walker demonstrated that the methods for expression of emotions in the pre-Shakespearean plays can be found in Shakespeare's plays. [18] Many of the ways of portraying grief, joy, anger, rage, could be and were handed down from one theatrical generation to another. For the actor, the projection of grief in the following speeches would not be very different in each case.

OTIAN.   O father dear, these words to hear
              —that you must die by force—
              Bedews my cheeks with stilled tears.
                  The king hath no remorse.
              The grievous griefs, and strained sighs
                  My heart doth break in twain,
              And I deplore, most woeful child, that I
                  should see you slain.

                                [*Cambises*, 445–448]

NERONIS.   Ah wofull sight, what is alas, with these mine
                eyes beheld,
            That to my loving Knight belongd, I view the
                Golden Sheeld:
            Ah heavens, this Herse doth signifie my Knight
                is slaine,
            Ah death no longer do delay, but rid the lives
                of twaine:

> Heart, hand, and everie sence prepare, unto the
>   Hearse draw nie:
> And thereupon submit your selves, disdaine not
>   for to die
> With him that was your mistresse ioy, her life
>   and death like case,
> And well I know in seeking me, he did his end
>   embrace.
>   [*Sir Clyomon and Sir Clamydes,* 1532–1539]

AGA.   What greater griefe had mournful Priamus,
        Then that he liv'd to see his Hector die,
        His citie burnt downe by revenging flames,
        And poor Polites slaine before his face?
        Aga, thy griefe is matchable to his,
        For I have liv'd to see my soveraignes death,
        Yet glad that I must breath my last with him.
                     [*Selimus,* 1863–1869]

QUEEN. A sweet children, when I am at rest my nightly
        dreames are dreadful. Me thinks as I lie in my
        bed, I see the league broken which was sworne at
        the death of your kingly father, tis this my
        children and many other causes of like importance,
        that makes your aged mother to lament as she doth.
           [*The True Tragedy of King Richard III,* 802–807]

Essentially the actors were provided with methods for making emotion explicit. In the first three illustrations the characters name their emotions outright, in the last the Queen describes it. Descriptions of external manifestations of grief, such as "strained sighs," and apostrophe, either to another ("O father dear") or to oneself ("Aga, thy griefe") or to abstract properties ("Ah wofull sight"), or to divinity ("Ah heavens, Ah death") are common. The later plays were subtler in the depiction of emotion. In *Selimus,* the similarity of his state to that of Priam conveys the overwhelming grief of Aga. In *The True Tragedy,* the Queen expresses the grief of the moment through the terror of a dream. By utilizing these various methods for years, the actor had become familiar with openly rendering the character's emotion. Furthermore, the quality of the emotion was not highly differentiated. In force and depth, the grief for the loss of a loved or revered one, in each of the instances cited, is fundamentally the same.

One major development in the acting conditions must be noted. In the plays of the 1560's and 1570's the verse was regular and conventional. The galloping fourteener left little opportunity for nuance. The rhythm and accent of the verse in *Cambises,* for example, intruded upon the character. It erected a barrier to the immediate impact of emotion upon the auditor. The actor who rendered such verse was encouraged in the conventional expression of emotion and the reliance upon rhythmic sweep for his success.

In the 1580's the verse became suppler. Rhyme was abandoned, rhythm because subtler and more varied. The total effect was less stentorian and more lyrical. It was possible to utilize the superior advantages of poetic drama without the artificiality to which it is liable. For the actor the change tore down a veil. Character portrayal could be more vivid. Contact between actor and actor was easier to achieve. In a word, the actor was able to make events more "real." At the same time, he had a more difficult task in rendering speech. Whether or not this change led to a realistic style of acting will be discussed in connection with the Globe plays. To these plays the early actor contributed experience in playing all kinds of roles before all kinds of audiences, portraying generic types through conventional means, emoting in extravagant and conventional fashion, speaking verse with vigor and sweep, and performing in the peripheral arts of dancing, tumbling, and vaulting. The picture he presents is of a rough-and-ready trouper, not a sophisticated and refined artist.

III. THE EFFECT OF PLAYING CONDITIONS UPON ELIZABETHAN ACTING

After 1592, stability and new theater construction, though continuing the earlier tradition in many respects, brought about new playing conditions, the third factor which contributed to the acting style at the Globe. Playing conditions include the structure of the theater, the arrangement of the repertory, and the organization of the company. The first two of these conditions have been discussed at length in previous chapters and the last has been treated in Professor T. W. Baldwin's *Organization and Personnel of the Shakespearean Company*.

With the opening of the Globe playhouse the company, for the first time since its organization, had its own building. Although the Theatre may not have been very different in form, it had never served as a permanent home. How much this affected the actors is difficult to know. We found in Chapter Three that only 20 per cent of the scenes in the Globe plays made use of stage facilities. For the larger part of the play, the actor needed only a bare platform. Thus the conditions that the plays required were no different from those he had known for years.

But if the physical conditions did not change greatly, the artistic conditions did. The splendor of the stage façade enhanced the actions of the player. The very sumptuousness of the stage elevated them to a level of grandeur, setting them off with elegance and opulence. In return it called for scope in delivery, grace in manner, and audacity in playing. Against a setting so dazzling only intensive and extensive action could hope to make an impression upon an audience.

Not only the design but also the plan of the stage conditioned the acting. The flat façade and the deeply projecting platform had a serious effect upon the physical movement of the actor. For the moment we can assume that the actor played many scenes at the front of the stage. To do so he had to come forward twenty-five feet. The modern director would motivate such a movement, that is, provide the actor with some internal or external impulse to cause him to move forward. In some instances this must have been the same at the Globe. Often we read scenes where characters on stage describe the entrance and approach of another actor. But there are many instances where such aid is not forthcoming. In those cases one of two effects was possible. Either the movement forward was treated as a conventional action which the audience expected, or it was treated as a ceremonial action which dignified the player. Further investigation of this matter is reserved for the next chapter. Here it is sufficient to point out that in either case the actor's entrance was theatricalized. Boldness was necessary to catch and hold attention on such a vast stage.

The sightlines of the theater also had an effect upon the acting. Essentially they were poor. We are dealing with an aural theater, not a visual one. Note how the author of *An Excellent Actor* (1615) expresses the relation of actor and spectator:

> Sit in a full Theater, and you will thinke you see so many lines drawne from the circumference of so many *eares*, whiles the Actor is the Center. [My italics.]

Gesture for specific communication rather than general reinforcement of the speech was not feasible. For example, the comic actor could not rely on a visual gag. A humorous walk or risible situation, such as the tavern scene in *I Henry IV*, could be managed. But the type of farcical routine represented by the commedia dell'arte *lazzi* would have been lost to a large part of the audience.

The sightlines not only prohibited certain types of gestures, they also required a certain orientation of the body. Today as much as possible the actor will try to maintain the illusion that he is facing a fellow actor and not facing the audience. The flat picture frame of our theater encourages this illusion. In the Elizabethan theater the actor had to turn out, that is, orient himself to the circumference of auditors, if he were to be seen at all. This condition reinforced the conventional or ceremonial manner in acting.

By turning out, the actor emphasized the stage as a setting behind him rather than as an environment around him. This was in accord with the demands of the plays. As I have pointed out, most of the scenes were set in a generalized locale. The actor did not have to maintain an illusion of place. He could concentrate wholly on the action and the passion of a scene.

To achieve verisimilitude it was not necessary that he project time and place. Standard practice in movement and delivery would fit every play, for they would never seem out of harmony with the conventional façade. The result was that the actor did not adapt himself to every environment, as the actor does now, but translated every environment into a theatrical form.

These tendencies towards simplification and systemization were reinforced by the conditions of repertory. In Chapter One I showed how many plays were maintained actively in the Globe repertory. A member of the company, who was likely to be in every play, had to learn a new role every other week. At the same time, he had to keep in mind thirty or forty others. We do know that the players were used to preparing a script rapidly. Augustine Phillips, in the course of testimony offered on the Essex conspiracy, reveals that the Lord Chamberlain's men had only a day or a day and a half to revive *Richard II,* a play long off the boards.[19] The fact that the play was actually presented at the Globe is proof of the actors' adaptability.

But the player's task was still more arduous. There was no opportunity for him to fix a role in his memory by repetition. Rarely would he play the same role two days in succession. Even in the most popular role he would not appear more than twice in one week, and then only in the first month or two of the play's stage life. The consequences of such a strenuous repertory were twofold. First, the actor had to cultivate a fabulous memory and devote much of his time to memorization; various plays testify to the scorn of the playwright for the actor who is out of his part. Secondly, the actor had to systematize his methods of portrayal and of working with his colleagues. How far this could be done will have to be considered below in light of the variety of roles the actor played.

If we could have a glimpse of an actual rehearsal, we should learn a great deal about Elizabethan acting. The closest that we can come to such a glimpse is to examine various players' scenes in the drama of the period. From *A Midsummer Night's Dream* (I, ii, 101 ff.), we learn that it was the practice to distribute the sides to the actors and, after these had been memorized, to rehearse the company. That this was normal pro-

cedure is indicated by the surviving part for Orlando from
Orlando Furioso.[20] Used by Edward Alleyn, it embodies the
system adopted by the professional companies. The part, in-
scribed on a narrow sheet of paper, was originally arranged on
a long roll. From this roll Alleyn studied his part and from it
we can learn some of his methods, particularly by comparing
the part to the extant copy of the play.

The part contains Orlando's speeches, together with the cues
for each speech and some stage directions. The cues are extremely brief, consisting of no more than two or three words of
the preceding actor's speech. If the speeches of more than one
actor separate two speeches of Orlando, only the last cue is
inserted. Of the presence of any other actors on stage there
is no indication. The stage directions, usually written in the
third person, are not as descriptive as in the text of the play.
Entrances of other actors are not noted. In effect, the part
is shorn of almost everything but the speeches of the character.

As Dr. Greg has pointed out, the part does not rely upon
quite the same text as the full copy of the play. Therefore,
a word-by-word comparison cannot be made. Yet there is some
evidence that short replies by the other actors were conventionalized in the part. Compare the following extract, for
example:

Part.
    stay villayne I tell
the/e/ Angelica is dead, nay she is in deed
. . . . .lord
but my Angelica is dead.
. . . . .my lord.
         [154–158]

Play.
ORL. O this it is, Angelica is dead.
ORG. Why then she shall be buried.
ORL. But my Angelica is dead.
ORG. Why it may be so.
        [856–859]

In several other places short lines of the other actor have been omitted.[21] There is one instance, in an otherwise satisfactory section, where a cue is omitted (after Part, 344, compare with Play, 1311–1312). Another set of omissions involves brief interchanges between Orlando and another character. The brevity of the speeches where the omissions occur indicates that they are not cuts in the script. Perhaps these lines were picked up by the actors in rehearsal.

The uncertainty governing the relationship of part to play makes it difficult to depend too much upon the evidence of the comparison. But a few tentative deductions can be made. We must remember the little time available for rehearsal. Nowadays when extensive rehearsals in the Moscow Art Theatre manner are the ideal, the few hours that were available to the Globe actors appear to be an insurmountable obstacle to dramatic art. However, long rehearsals of an entire dramatic company are a comparatively recent innovation. In the last century, for instance, a rehearsal or two was deemed sufficient. An actress who was asked by Edwin Booth to rehearse the closet scene in *Hamlet* was so insulted that she left the production. Concentration upon the individual player rather than the play, which this anecdote illustrates, is also reflected in the part of Orlando. It is trimmed to provide the actor with the information he needed as a solo performer, not as a member of a group. Since the full copy of the play was difficult to secure, the one copy being zealously guarded by the bookkeeper, the part was all the actor had to rely on. From it he got his familiarity with the play. In it he put the essentials of his role. The absence of more stage directions in the part than are in the play indicates that the acting was free from any but the most relevant business, an observation with which B. L. Joseph seems to agree. Altogether, the evidence points to a type of acting which emphasized the individual performer, minimized his relationship to the other actors, and placed great emphasis upon the delivery of speeches.

The organization of the Globe company may have somewhat mitigated the emphasis upon the individual. Between 1599 and 1609 the company became stabilized and won the prestige of a royal patent. From the opening of the Glòbe to the accession of James in 1603, the sharers, who were the principal actors, remained the same. They were Thomas Pope, John Heminges, Augustine Phillips, Richard Cowley, William Shakespeare, Richard Burbage, William Sly, Henry Condell, and Robert Armin. At the time the company received the royal patent in May, 1603, it was enlarged to twelve members. Entering at the same time was a replacement for the deceased Pope, Laurence Fletcher. The three new members were John Lowin, who had been a member of Worcester's men in 1602-1603, Alexander Cooke, who may have been the "sander" of the *Seven Deadly Sins* of 1592, and Nicholas Tooley, who spoke of Richard Burbage as "master." E. K. Chambers conjectures that the Samuel Grosse whose name appears in the Folio actor list preceded Tooley into the company, but that he probably died of the plague almost at once. This history is doubtful, but even if true, it made little difference. Since it is generally accepted that Fletcher did not act with the King's men, only three actors joined the company. One was clearly an outsider, one was probably an apprentice, who had grown up in the company, and one, Cooke, may have been an apprentice. On the death of Phillips in 1605 either Samuel Gilburne or Robert Goffe succeeded him. To account for Gilburne's name in the Folio actor list, Chambers places him after Phillips, to be followed by Goffe before 1611. Baldwin believes that Goffe, who was Phillips' brother-in-law, entered the company in 1605. He was possibly the "R. Go." of *Seven Deadly Sins*, and may have remained with the company as apprentice or hired man throughout. In 1608 William Ostler replaced Pope, who was buried August 16, and John Underwood replaced Fletcher, who was buried September 12. Both men came from the Revels company, where they had been boy actors. However, since they entered during the period when plans for placing the King's men at Blackfriars were under way, we can exclude them from our consideration. Thus, in the ten years we are treating, three new actors joined the company and one replaced a former actor. Two of the new actors had probably appeared with the company previously, another possibly had, but only one had been definitely associated with another group, and that one of the popular companies. The hired actors have not been considered, it is true, but the sharers who were the principal players made a tightly knit, relatively unchanging group.

Determination of the identity of the boys of the company who played the ladies is somewhat difficult. Baldwin lists seven names of boys who acted the female roles between 1599 and 1609.[22] In 1599 Samuel Gilburne, Ned (Shakespeare?), and Jack Wilson were boy actors. Samuel Grosse joined them in 1600, shortly after which Gilburne and Ned ceased playing women. In 1603 John Edmans, John Rich, and James Sands began playing women's parts. Grosse in 1604 and Wilson in 1605 in their turn ceased performing as women. This rapid turnover is to be expected, since the span of a boy's ability to play a feminine role was relatively short. However, since each of these boys was apprenticed to one of the members of the company, his training and performance would probably have harmonized with the adult acting.

What effect, then, did this closed and intimate group have upon the style of the acting? Baldwin proposed that each actor had a special character "line" to which he devoted himself and to which the playwrights, particularly Shakespeare, trimmed the roles. Baldwin points out that the same actors consistently took the major roles. In this I believe he is correct. Richard Burbage invariably played the leading role, Robert Armin the leading comic role, Robert Cowley played important secondary roles. Lowin seems to have come in to play leads or second leads just below the rank of Burbage: Baldwin gives him the role of Enobarbus to Burbage's Antony. Although this designation may not be strictly accurate, the relation it reflects is likely. It is apparent that a modified star system obtained in the Globe company. This arrangement had two advantages. On the one hand, it enabled the company to develop virtuoso acting. On the other, it ensured a high level of general competence throughout the production. The competitive conditions which drew actors away from the King's men after 1615 did not exist at this time, so that actors who received minor roles year after year had little opportunity to separate from the company.

The distribution of prominent roles to the same actors at all times, however, does not constitute a "line." By a "line" Professor Baldwin seems to mean the recurrent appearance of a type of role, requiring certain definite characteristics in the player. Although he applies the conception of "line" rigorously, he never defines the term clearly. The criteria which he apparently considers in establishing a line are prominence of role, physique, age, genre, temperament, and special skills. First, actors distinguished according to prominence of role was a fact of Globe organization as we have seen. But instead of aiding the formation of an actor's "line," it interfered with it, for a leading actor would assume a leading role regardless of its type or nature. Secondly, Shakespeare may well have kept the physiques and ages of the actors in mind as he wrote, but, though such a practice may have aided naturalism, it hardly affected the type of role. In effect, the practice is no different from the kind of casting that occurs today. Thirdly, Baldwin distinguished an actor's line according to the genre in which he specialized, comedy or tragedy. Probably the clown was a comic specialist who had to be given a role in most plays. But that there was any general tendency to specialize in one genre or the other is unlikely in view of the alternation of plays, some of which call for almost all comedians, others for almost all tragedians. *The Merry Wives of Windsor* was performed about the time of *Hamlet,* and *Volpone* about the time of *Lear.* Fourthly, special talents may be dismissed, for they involve such abilities as Kemp's dancing. Finally, we are left with one criterion for the actor's "line": his temperament. Baldwin links the temperament of the actor to the temperament of the "line" that he played. Sly was the player of jolly, roisterous roles; Lowin, the player of blunt, honest soldiers. Ultimately Baldwin rests his case for a "line" upon the playwright's adherence to distinct character types and his imitation of the actors' temperaments.[23]

The Elizabethan playwright, however, could not adhere to types, for the actor had no tradition of playing clear-cut types, as we have seen. The actor did not specialize, but he portrayed a wide range of characters. This practice persisted into the

Shakespearean era. For example, Dogberry may be regarded as a comic type, the bumbling constable. The character who most nearly approaches him in type is Elbow in *Measure for Measure*. He too is the inept comic constable, malapropisms and all. But the original actor of Dogberry, Will Kemp, was not in the company when *Measure for Measure* was presented. Obviously, in this case at least, the type was not shaped by the actor, that is Kemp, but the actor fitted the generic type.

Nor did the playwright imitate the actors' temperaments, for the host of different roles which a single actor was called upon to play could not have been shaped to one personality. The four Shakespearean roles that are assigned to Burbage upon reliable evidence are Richard III, Hamlet, Othello, and Lear. I think no one would care to describe the personality that could serve as a model for these four roles. Moreover, when we add to this repertory, Baldwin's assignments to Burbage of the parts of Claudio in *Much Ado,* Ford in *Merry Wives,* and Bertram in *All's Well,* we must give up any idea that these characters were fitted to a personality except that of a sensitive, capable actor. Instead, the Globe company seemed to have distributed roles without attention to personal traits of the actors. This is evident in *II The Return from Parnassus.* Philomusus, after he has been auditioned by Burbage and Kemp (IV, iii), is considered suitable for parts as different as a foolish justice and Richard III. The scene may be mockery, but it accurately reflects all we know about role distribution. In contrast to this method, Molière, in his public plays, kept the number and distribution of roles fairly constant, evidently to meet the needs of his company. But neither the number, distribution, nor type of role was consistently repeated by Shakespeare or any other writer for the Globe company. Consequently, I fear that Baldwin's "line" is a fiction which bears little relation to reality. His insistence upon it betrays an ignorance of histrionic method.

We must not, however, presume that the stability of the company and the absence of rigid types gave rise to ensemble acting in the naturalistic sense. The arrangement within the plays was suitable to individual playing. Most scenes in Shakespeare's plays involve less than five active players on stage at one time. Even where there are a large number of actors on stage, the action is confined to a scene between two or three. For example, only 24 per cent of the lines in *As You Like It* are spoken when more than three actors are active on stage. In *Twelfth Night* the percentage is higher, 34 per cent, but in *Hamlet* it is only 19 per cent and in *Lear*, 31 per cent. These percentages are as high as they are because the final scene in most plays is a formal resolution of the story involving a public revelation or judgment. In *Lear* half the lines involving more than three active players occur in the first and last scenes of the play. The actor generally had to play with one or two others. When on stage, he was involved in the action. When on stage and mute, which was rare, he was excluded from the immediate sphere of action. In most scenes, one or more of these actors were likely to be virtuosi performers, for though the Globe plays require large casts, they rely upon relatively few performers to carry the bulk of the play.

IV. ACTING AND THE ELIZABETHAN VIEW OF HUMAN BEHAVIOR

The dramatic tradition, however, affected the general type of character rather than its specific form. In evolving this form the actor was guided by two influences: his own understanding of behavior and thought and the poet's image of behavior and thought. In the first instance we must deduce the actor's understanding from the outlook of Elizabethan society as a whole. In the second we can analyze the poet's image in his plays. The poet's unique outlook, infused in his image, is still a part of society's conception of behavior and thought, and in the case of Shakespeare has come to represent the larger conception of the age. Together, age and poet present the psychological and philosophical foundation which the actors and audience took for granted and thus upon which the actors built their roles.

Study of characterization is complicated by the absence of decisive evidence. The literary practice of the time does not encourage a ready formulation of a poet's idea of character. As Hardin Craig says:

> One sees no evidence in the field of knowledge of the art of characterization as it is known in modern criticism. The art of characterization, as distinguished from simple biographical narrative, was there, but often not as a conscious factor.

Craig goes on to relate this lack of development to the Elizabethan idea of personality:

> Indeed, the conception of human character as set down in formal psychology, and often evident in literature, taught instability in the natures of men, taught that there was no such thing as consistency of character, except in so far as it might result from "complexion" or be super-induced by training.[24]

It is in the works of "formal psychology" that the most explicit statements of the Elizabethan conception of human character can be found. But in offering a detailed exposition of how Elizabethans thought man functioned, the works are inconsistent. Miss Louise Forest has pointed out the contradictions in the theories and definitions of the Elizabethan and Jacobean writers. Instead of a scientific system with which the dramatists were familiar, we find that "Elizabethan popular psychology was simply every man's private synthesis of observations of human behavior understood in the light of whatever selections from whatever authorities appealed to him." [25] Although her criticism has won general approbation as a healthy corrective for facile and mechanistic application of "psychological" theory to literature, it has not undermined the conviction of scholars that the evidence of Elizabethan psychology can prove illuminating in revealing not necessarily *what* the Elizabethans thought, but *how* they thought.

Mr. R. A. Foakes admits that although the disagreement in detail hinders the application of Elizabethan psychology to literature, it does not hinder an understanding of "the general habit of thought from which the detail springs." [26] The exposition of this "general habit of thought" has been set forth in part by

Theodore Spencer, Lily B. Campbell, E. M. W. Tillyard, and John W. Draper, and most fully by Hardin Craig in *The Enchanted Glass*.²⁷ Against the broad and deep background painted by them, I shall consider the "general habit of thought" as it affected three aspects of character: decorum, motivation, and passion.

a. Decorum

Classical decorum in literature sought to reflect a broader decorum in life. As it came down to the playwrights of the Renaissance, however, it implied little more than a trite correspondence between character type and nature. Edwardes in The Prologue to *Damon and Pithias* (1565–1571) refers the audience to Horace as his model in the observance of "decorum":

In Commedies, the greatest Skyll is this, rightly to touche
All thynges to the quicke: and eke to frame eche person so,
That by his common talke, you may his nature rightly know:
A Royster ought not preache, that were to straunge to heare,
But as from vertue he doth swerve, so ought his woordes appeare:
The olde man is sober, the yonge man rashe, the Lover triumphyng
    in ioyes,
The Matron grave, the Harlot wilde and full of wanton toyes.

[Prologue, 14–20]

George Whetstone seconds this propriety in his Epistle to William Fleetwood, prefixed to *Promos and Cassandra:*

For to worke a Commedie kindly, grave olde men, should instruct: yonge men, should showe the imperfections of youth: Strumpets should be lascivious: Boyes unhappy: and Clownes, should be disorderlye.

Both statements of the principle of decorum rigidly match character type with nature or behavior. By simplification of character, consistency could be assured. It is obvious that this view of dramatic character did not prevail in Elizabethan drama, but not because it was completely out of harmony with Elizabethan thought. When Timothy Bright approvingly noted that "butchers acquainted with slaughter, are accepted therby to be of a more cruell disposition: and therefore amongst us are discharged from iuries of life & death," [28] he was reflecting a type of thinking in keeping with the principle of decorum.

It is against such Idols of the Tribe that Bacon inveighs. But even when he attacks such habits of thought, he gives us a clear concept of them.

The spirit of man (being of an equal and uniform substance) pre-supposes and feigns in nature a greater equality and uniformity than really is. Hence the fancy of the mathematicians that the heavenly bodies move in perfect circles, rejecting spiral lines. Hence also it happens, that whereas there are many things in nature unique and full of dissimilarity, yet the cogitation of man still invents for them relatives, parallels, and conjugates. Hence sprang the introduction of an element of fire, to keep square with earth, water, and air. Hence the chemists have marshalled the universe in phalanx; conceiving, upon a most groundless fancy, that in those four elements of theirs (heaven, air, water, and earth,) each species in one has parallel and corresponding species in the others. . . . Man is as it were the common measure and mirror of nature. For it is not credible (if all particulars be gone through and noted) what a troop of fictions and idols the reduction of the operations of nature to the similitude of human actions has brought into natural philosophy; I mean, the fancy that nature acts as man does.[29]

For the Elizabethans, as Bacon laments, external and internal experiences were manifestations of a single spirit which had parallels in the natural and moral universe. Consequently, in depicting and understanding character, the Elizabethans looked for similarities, not differences. What made one man like another and like the macrocosm was a habitual way of estimating character.

However, instead of the simple formulae of "decorum," the Elizabethans employed a complex system of correspondences. For them, man was volatile. Potentially he was capable of absorbing concepts shared by other men. This reduced the possibility of matching thought and character. He was also capable of experiencing passions common to all mankind. This made it impossible to match nature and character. In so dynamic a philosophy the meaning of decorum had to change. Professor Lily B. Campbell has rightly pointed out that decorum in Elizabethan drama was "not a law of aesthetic theory but a law of moral philosophy." To extend her definition, it was also a law of social organization and political life.

In the highly stratified Elizabethan society, precepts and models of behavior were strictly developed. Bearing, speech, and dress reflected class status. Ceremony was not only appropriate but necessary, for, as Sir Thomas Elyot admonished:

> Lette it be also consydered, that wee bee men and not Aungelles: wherefore we know nothyng but by outwarde signification. [Honor is not everywhere perceived] but by some exterior signe, and that is eyther by lawdable reporte, or excellency in vesture, or other thing semblable.[20]

In this context ceremony is not unnatural, and in fact, to the Elizabethan, ceremony signified the natural order of the universe. Man constantly saw his corresponding reflections in the "outward signification" of society, nature, and morality.

That this central habit of thought was deeply ingrained in Elizabethan nature is reflected in Bacon himself. Despite his recognition of the fallacy of such thought, he still finds general similitude between feature and nature. He still thinks that the deformed person must be evil, although he tries to provide a scientific explanation of the causes of this correspondence. It is true that this form of logic was falling before the development of inductive thought, particularly in the sciences. Nevertheless, through most of the Renaissance and certainly in the period with which we are dealing, it prevailed.

Its effect on the decorum of character was twofold. First, character fitted into a group. Whatever his individuality might be, a man was a member of a class and his behavior conformed to the behavior of the class. Second, external features implied internal qualities. Man carried the mark of his class and his nature, in his walk, talk, features, and costume. The outer man was the inner man; therefore, the inner man tended the form and bearing of the outer man carefully. In these ways decorum still functioned in Elizabethan thought and served as a basis for the portrayal of character by the actor.

b. Motivation

The habit of generalized thinking operated also in the explanation of human motivation. Thinkers and writers were not concerned with the unique impulse that drove a man to certain ends but with the broad desires that all men experienced. This aspect of personality was understood in terms of the struggle between passion and reason which went on in each man.

It was an Elizabethan commonplace that reason allied man with God, passion with the beasts. Imagination, which receives images of experience and relays them, should be subordinate to reason. Unfortunately, since it is often allied with the affections, the affections rule man. As Bacon explained it:

> The affections themselves carry ever an appetite to apparent good, and have this in common with reason; but the difference is that affection beholds principally the good which is present: reason looks beyond and beholds likewise the future and sum of all. And therefore the present filling the imagination more, reason is commonly vanquished and overcome.[31]

This "good which is present" is often the satisfaction of the senses or passions without concern for the consequences. When the affections, like the imagination, are under the control of reason, all is well. When the passions lead man, they often lead to disaster.

Man, therefore, was moved either by his reason or his affection. If he were learned in or persuaded by a moral or politic course, he could measure the particular good in terms of the enduring good. Thus reason, moved by consideration of ethics or policy, obeyed objective and rational motivations which, individual though they might have been in particular circumstances, had in common with all cases the attainment of goodness or power. But if affection ruled, then man was moved to satisfy it. Although his personality might make him liable to cer-

tain passions more readily than to others, he could give way to
any of them. His past life did not accumulate motivations which
impelled him or influenced his reception of new motivations.
Instead, immediate and direct contact was effected between the
object of desire and the governing passion.

Functioning in such a way, man was moved by generalized
ends. The habit of seeing motivations in general terms is reflected in the titles of essays by such men as Bacon, Charron,
and Sir William Cornwallis: "Of Ambition," "Of Envy," "Of
Affections," etc. Although a physio-psychological theory in part
replaced temptation by the devil as an explanation of motivation, entities such as pride, lust, ambition, and envy, among
others, continued to be regarded as genuine temptations by the
Elizabethan. By and large the motives for man's actions were
taken for granted or symbolized. Often in the drama they are
never made explicit. Here too correspondence was observed.
Women were easily given to lust, unpromoted men to envy,
young men to prodigality, Italians to revenge. An Elizabethan
audience would assume or ignore the reasons for Iago's or
Antony's or Bertram's actions. They would be interested in
what they did and how they felt.

c. Passion

In concentrating on what happened to the characters, the
audience found its attention directed toward the passions that
the characters experienced. Passions were divided in kind and
number. They were either concupiscible or irascible, that is,
arose either from coveting or desiring some end, such as Love,
or from accomplishing or thwarting some end, such as Anger.
However, there was disagreement over the number of passions.
Coeffeteau lists more than fifteen, Bright only six, some writers
even fewer.[32] In the matter of detail there is no concurrence,
but the difference arises from the degree of subordination observed by the different writers. Behind all their thinking is the
habit of regarding a passion as an autonomous quality which
is either operative or not. An inclination toward or a repulsion
from an object induces physiological changes in the bodily
humors. These changes feed the passion so that it dominates

the individual entirely. But the passion is a fixed thing. It betrays external symptoms; for example, fear leads to trembling and love to sighing. It affects internal operation, such as the contraction of the heart and the acceleration of breathing. It alters the view of reality, for passions are like "greene spectacles, which make all thinges resemble the colour of greene; even so, hee that loveth, hateth, or by anie other passion is vehemently possessed, iudgeth all things that occure in favor of that passion, to bee good and agreeable with reason." [33]

Moreover, a particular passion was the same for all persons affected by it. Fear in one was the same as fear in another. Love in one man was not very much different from love in another. One man was not distinguished from another by the quality of a passion, but by his propensity toward it. Man was thought to have a dominant temperament or complexion. It might fall into one of four principal categories: the sanguine, the choleric, the phlegmatic, or the melancholic. The Elizabethan physiologists developed a series of correspondences, of course disagreeing among themselves, between temperament and physique, intellect and passion. Supposedly each type was liable to certain passions more readily than others. Yet, when a man is carried away by a passion uncongenial to his temperament, he assumes the quality of the passion fully. "Each passion alters the complexion of the entire body, which assumes, at least temporarily, the very qualities which excite the emotion." [34] Thus, in Elizabethan thinking, there was a range of distinct passions and a range of distinct temperaments. Although there was a tendency for certain passions to cluster about a certain temperament, any passion could enter into any temperament. When it did, it transformed the temperament into its quality.

Some disagreement existed over the completeness and ease with which a temperament could be transformed. Bright considers the complexion strictly fixed. Other writers believe that there is a strong tendency toward a specific temperament, but that an uncongenial passion could overpower natural resistance to it. As Forest has observed of these discrepancies in the Elizabethan views about complexion, it is difficult to establish any firm conclusions about the details of the subject. Generally, it can be said that each man was thought to have some definable central temperament which arose from the disposition of humors in his system, that his external and internal faculties corresponded in a broad sense with his temperament, and that he was liable to passions which were sympathetic to his temperament. And yet it was accepted that his natural temperament could be overpowered by passions in disharmony with it, that one passion could drive out another, and that the nature of the passion was not affected by his temperament. These two groups of concepts are at bottom mutually contradictory; the first visualizes relative stability and consistency in character, the second, virtually complete subordination of the individual to immediate impulses. These views reflect the desire for similitude and order on one hand and the awareness of the power of passion on the other. Without reconciliation they continued as habits of thought throughout the English Renaissance.

Both views acknowledged the swiftness with which passion could overwhelm an individual. Professor Craig explains sudden changes in Bellafront in *The Honest Whore I* and in Hamlet by reference to "the theory that one emotion or passion drives out another, and that the substitution is immediately operative." [35] One passion yields readily to another, the concupiscible passion often giving way to the irascible, as hatred may give way to anger or grief to despair. Love at first sight, as R. A. Foakes points out, is a convention based on a reality and the "common and ancient thought-habit that the sight is the chief and most powerful of the senses." Sudden emotional changes were either the daily acts of Elizabethan behavior or the usual explanation of more gradual alterations. In either case, the potential for such immediate transformation was thought to be ingrained in every man, just as at present the potential for repressed infantile conflicts is thought to exist in every man.

Furthermore, the ability to suppress the mounting passions within oneself was thought to be very slight. Once a passion subdued the reason, the reason was virtually powerless to control the passion. It coursed through the entire body, expressing itself in external signs. An individual of extraordinary will could suppress these signs, but the vast majority of people was helpless to hide the play of passion within their souls. A correspondence between the passions and the external signs was assumed, but as we found in the study of rhetoric, there was no clear codification of passions and symptoms. Instead, the habit of expecting an expression of emotion in recognizable symptoms rather than the repression of emotion in enigmatic behavior marked the Elizabethan age. The volatile and pervasive nature of passion, then, was one of the crucial assumptions of the Elizabethan period.

Thus, the Elizabethan conception of how human beings function and feel shows two principal tendencies. In a strictly regulated society such as the Elizabethan, the members were keenly aware of degree and order. So urgent was the impulse to find order in the universe, that an elaborate series of correspondences was observed between man and all other forces in nature as well as between man and all forces within himself. It was natural for the Elizabethan to look for correspondences, no matter how farfetched, and to insist on decorum, no matter how trifling. In conflict with this tendency toward order was the recognition of the tendency toward disorder. Largely, this was thought to arise from man yielding to passion. The orderly arrangement of the moral and political world could be destroyed by the unrestrained passions of man. As a result, the description and analysis of passion became a central function of Elizabethan psychology and philosophy. Bacon carries the condemnation of passion to such an extreme that he condemns love almost entirely. It is a weak passion, it is a "child of folly." As we turn to a consideration of the plays themselves, we shall find that by and large the tendency toward order subsumed the actions, and the depiction of passion occupied the forefront of the Globe stage.

V. THE EFFECT OF THE GLOBE PLAYS UPON THE ACTING

The drama that appeared on its stage is the single most important witness to the acting style of the Globe company. Through this drama the general style of acting, which was a product of the conditions I have outlined heretofore, became refined into the specific style of the company. The wide gap between the quality of the Shakespearean and non-Shakespearean plays in the repertory makes the delineation of this style extremely difficult. The differences are those of subtlety, insight, and penetration. Probably the acting wavered between the more obvious requirements of the non-Shakespearean plays and the modulations of the Shakespearean.

For the actor an important part of the drama was the distancing of the action. Almost every popular pre-Globe play is distanced in time or place or both. Plays such as *Orlando Furioso* and *A Knack to Know an Honest Man* are set in France and Italy respectively. The *Troublesome Reign of King John* and *Fair Em* are set back in English history, the latter to the days of William the Conqueror. Plays such as *Selimus* and *The Battle of Alcazar* are set back in time and place, to Islamic Turkey and Moorish Africa. Sometimes the action was placed in a mythical or semimythical land. But only three of the pre-Globe plays are set in London. Two are moralities of Robert Wilson, *Three Ladies of London* and *The Three Lords and Three Ladies of London*. In these the allegory distances the action. Only *A Warning for Fair Women* is placed in contemporary England. Its realism, however, is somewhat removed by a morality framework in which Tragedy as a presenter moralizes upon the sins of lust.

This practice is followed by the Globe plays. Of the Shakespearean plays *The Merry Wives of Windsor* is usually thought to picture contemporary England. However that may be, the action is actually placed in the days of Henry IV or Henry V. Falstaff's presence and Page's references to Fenton's escapades with the young prince identify the period. The compliment bestowed at the end of the play upon the worthy owner of Windsor Castle is anachronistic. Of the non-Shakespearean plays, four may be considered as taking place in contemporary England. Three of these are prodigal son plays, still close to the morality theme. The fourth, *Every Man Out of His Humour*, is clearly set in England, as the scene at Paul's shows. But the characters have Italianate names. The effect is one of a double image, a removed intimacy.

The characters who are distanced are also typed. Most of them fall into one of several categories: the tyrant, the tyrant-father, the gull, the beloved, the lover, and so on. Usually they stem from generic types. Unlike the practices in the commedia dell'arte where the characteristics of the stock figures dictated the plot, in the English drama, as I have shown in Chapter Two, the story dictated the handling of character. The types that existed were a function of the story. That is why the generic types did not develop into stock characters. As long as the story could wrench a character as it required, the stock type could not become solidified.

In Shakespeare the generic types are blended and enriched. An examination of all the characters in the Globe Shakespearean plays reveals the presence of a definite group of related characters. They are more than the repeated figures of any author's art, for they hark back to the traditional types. The most frequently recurring and most sharply marked are the lovers, villains, clowns, gulls, loyal advisers, faithful friends, chaste maids, faithful wives, tyrant fathers, tyrant princes, and politic princes. One could go on multiplying subsidiary classes of characters as Polonius does classes of drama. Though certain types, such as the faithful servant (Adam, Provost in *Measure for Measure,* Corin in *As You Like It*), recur with some frequency, many do not. One type, the elderly *grande dame,* has only two representatives: the Countess in *All's Well,* and Volumnia in *Coriolanus.* Nor do the types recur in the same form. Horatio is the faithful friend in *Hamlet;* Kent is also the faithful friend, but he has something of the court adviser in him too. From this it follows that the types are not differentiated clearly. Antony in *Julius Caesar* has some of the faithful friend in him, but as his character develops, he reveals something of the Machiavellian politician, and in battle shows himself the honest soldier. Furthermore, the same generic type may show strong differences in temperament. Lafeu, the court adviser of *All's Well,* is a merry gentleman; Escalus, the same type of adviser in *Measure for Measure,* is sober and serious. They are both members of the same type whose quality is dictated by the function that it performs in the story. But the full range of the character does not remain within the confines of the types.

The combination of distanced action and generic type served to romanticize and symbolize the Shakespearean stage figures. No matter how reminiscent of a contemporary Londoner a character may have been, the audience reposed in the fiction that he was an Italian, a Roman, or an ancestor. With the Elizabethan's insularity, the fiction took on imaginative reality and tinted the action of the plays with romance. The characters of this romance, who had a generic base, were not only individuals but also symbols of the host of kings, lovers, and clowns who peopled the world. Again, this is a reflection of the Elizabethan habit of seeing similarities rather than differences in human behavior. The interaction of these two qualities alone would have elevated the action into a wondrous world of imagination, untouched by real experience. But, as we shall see, other elements were at work.

Within the broad boundaries of the generic type, individualization of character took place. But in what manner was this accomplished by the dramatists, particularly by Shakespeare? Today we place great stress on motivation. Our plays constantly search the past to explain the present. In *A Streetcar Named Desire* Blanche is revealed and drawn in terms of her tortured past and her unfulfilled desires. In the Elizabethan period, as we found, there was little awareness of specific motivation. The plays reflect this condition. The motivation is usually generalized. Viola wishes to love and be loved, and Sir Toby wants to have an easy life. Antony wishes to love Cleopatra, Coriolanus to satisfy his pride. But little attention is directed to probing or developing these motivations. At the conclusion of these plays we do not understand the motives of these characters one whit better. Motivation is often assumed, as in Lear's partition of his kingdom, or promised for the future, as in *Othello* when Iago persuades Roderigo to kill Cassio. In the same type of character there is little distinction in motivation. The motives for Horatio's loyalty to Hamlet are no different from the motives for Kent's loyalty to Lear. In the prodigal son plays, the motivations for the prodigality are barely noted. It is considered a condition to which all youth is liable. Motives for any act were so often assumed that they could not have demanded concentrated attention by the actors.

Another way in which the modern playwright individualizes character is through speech and gesture. This does not seem to have been a regular practice at the Globe playhouse. Here and there are hints that status may have been indicated by carriage and accent. In *As You Like It* Orlando questions "Ganymede" about his life.

ORL.   Your accent is something finer than you could purchase in so removed a dwelling.
Ros.   I have been told so of many. But indeed an old religious uncle of mine taught me to speak, who was in his youth an inland man.

[III, ii, 359–363]

In these externals the Elizabethans maintained a strict decorum. Yet the play does not reveal any difference between Rosalind's and Corin's speech insofar as breeding is concerned. References to fineness in speech, as in *Twelfth Night* (I, v, 311), place the character in a class rather than make him unique. Only in a few cases can we be certain that characteristic speech habits are used to individualize. The Hosts of *The Merry Wives of Windsor* and *The Merry Devil of Edmonton* have their tricks of speech; so does Corporal Nym. Edgar as Poor Tom alters his speech as an aid to his disguise. Other less certain instances are Osric in *Hamlet* and Thersites. But more important characters are not drawn in that way. Dogberry and Elbow both use malapropisms, but the characters are not distinguished by them. In fact, the linguistic twist tends to obscure the differences of character and emphasizes the likeness in type. The distinction between the two comes from Dogberry's fatuous self-confidence and condescension in contrast to Elbow's alternate deference to authority and scolding of Pompey.

If neither kind of motivation nor form of speech and gesture individualized the characters, perhaps the kind of action they performed did so. In modern drama this usually happens, for the action comes out of the character. But the narrative nature of Elizabethan drama, with its loose causation, makes this less possible. Plays based on the same narrative, for example, differ not so much in action as in character. *Lear* does contain a subplot, the Gloucester story, not present in *King Leir*. But this addition does not affect the character of Shakespeare's Lear very much. In a number of scenes both Lear and Leir perform the same action, but there is a world of difference in the characters. Lear proposes the division of his kingdom upon entering, and then immediately questions his daughters. At Cordelia's muteness his emotions mount in three stages: rejection of Cordelia, banishment of Kent, and dismissal of France. From the beginning Lear demonstrates authority and pride. Leir, however, reveals two reactions: delight at the flattery of Gonerill and Ragan, anger at the bluntness of Cordelia. But he does not have Lear's intensity of emotional expression.

In their first realization of rejection, the two men repeat these differences. Leir mourns, repenting his folly, regarding Gonerill's treatment as payment for his sins. This is the beginning in Leir of the grief that he shows throughout the play. Lear, on the other hand, demonstrates amazement, anger, scorn, all at a great height of intensity. This too is the beginning of the barely suppressed rage which finally drives him to madness. When, near the end, Leir's request for Cordelia's pardon emerges as grief, he is continuing the emotional quality he attained at the beginning. Lear, however, comes to that level of humility only after having passed through the fires of rage and madness. Of the central range of passion poured out by Lear on the heath, there is no sign in *King Leir*.

For it is mainly through the depiction of the passions that Shakespeare individualizes his characters. Just as the Elizabethan age envisions reason struggling with passion, so Shakespeare reveals the individual emerging through his passions. With the possible exception of Jonson, this was the general method of the other writers for the Globe company. By them too the generic type is rendered unique when passion is freshly portrayed.

A secondary means of individualization was the presentation of a character's mind. Many of Shakespeare's finest characters are distinguished by a profuse and keen wit. Rosalind, warm-hearted and merry, becomes the distinct figure she is through the play of her wit.[36] Octavius Caesar in *Antony and Cleopatra* is a man supremely guided by reason. In these cases wit or reason, rather than passion, controls the character. But in the gallery of Shakespeare's portraits such characters are in the minority. Prepared as the actor had to be to render thought vividly, his main efforts had to be devoted to painting the varied passions of man.

The application of this interpretation will be more evident in an examination of Globe plays. For example, the faithful wife type appears in them with some frequency. In the prodigal son plays she is probably closest to a pure type. Luce in *The London Prodigal* does not wish to marry Flowerdale, but she is forced to do so by her father. After the marriage, when Flowerdale is revealed as a wastrel, the father commands Luce to leave her husband. She replies:

LUCE. He is my husband, and hie heauen doth know,
   With what vnwillingnesse I went to Church,
   But you inforced me, you compelled me too it:
   The holy Church-man pronounced these words but now,
   I must not leaue my husband in distresse:
   Now I must comfort him, not goe with you.
LANCE. Comfort a cozoner? on my curse forsake him.
LUCE. This day you caused me on your curse to take him:
   Doe not I pray my greiued soule oppresse,
   God knowes my heart doth bleed at his distresse.

               [Sig. E1ʳ]

Her grief is conventional. It is echoed by the wife in *A Yorkshire Tragedy* and by Anabell in *Fair Maid of Bristow*. Shakespeare, however, assuming the conventional devotion, deepens the emotion of the wife. Virgilia in *Coriolanus* is the same type of character. Her only individualizing element is her readiness to weep at the slightest hint of her husband's danger. This sensibility serves as a strong contrast to Volumnia's Roman pride and honor. Portia and Calpurnia in *Julius Caesar* are other representatives of this type, yet they are distinguished from each other. Not through motivation: they both wish the well-being of their husbands. Not through action: they both try to persuade their husbands to another course of action. Portia demonstrates a stoicism, a suppression of fears, in order to persuade Brutus to reveal the reasons for his troubled state, only to give way later to her uneasiness. Calpurnia pours out her fears and forebodings, nagging and pleading in turn. Probably in manner, gait, speech, and gesture, this type would be played in the same way. Only the drawing of the different passions would transform them into distinct characters.

In many types this kind of differentiation occurs. Leonine and Thaliard are minor villains in *Pericles*. They are both commoners and servants, both are commanded to commit murder by their masters. Yet they differ from each other. In manner Thaliard is prompt, reflecting a cynical attitude toward his task. Leonine is reluctant, reflecting an innate gentleness. Dogberry and Elbow, as I have noted, are distinguished from each other by one being condescending, the other deferential. Kent and Enobarbus, faithful friends and advisers, have much in common: bluntness in speech, an unbreakable tie to their royal masters, loyalty in the face of disaster. Their abilities too are not so very different, though Enobarbus is a soldier. The distinction arises from their temperaments and passions. Enobarbus is critical and scornful, Kent is blunt and protective. But Enobarbus attains striking individuality only when he undergoes the pangs of shame for having abandoned Antony.

Implied emotion is not characteristic of the period. Today actors hint at unfathomed depths or suppressed drives which are ever on the verge of bursting forth. This was not the style of the Globe. Passions were immediately and directly presented. A character revealed the full extent of his passion at once. Our habit of seeing unplumbed depths in people may lead us to sense inner turmoil in Elizabethan plays where it does not exist. But this is in accord neither with Elizabethan thought habits nor with Elizabethan dramaturgy. Professor Albert Walker has shown that Shakespeare inherited conventional expressions of emotion and utilized them in a unique manner. A perusal of any of the Shakespearean plays will demonstrate the prevalence with which the overt expressions of emotion enumerated by Professor Walker are found.

One matter of the treatment of passion by Shakespeare remains to be considered, that of consistency. In analyzing the Elizabethan theory of passion, we discovered some dispute over the stability of temperament. Some writers believed that it was fixed and sympathetic to certain passions only. Other writers believed it was fairly flexible, that any passion could overwhelm the temperament. The same question arises in reference to the plays. Professor Draper, for example, has attempted, unsuccessfully, to prove that the Shakespearean characters fitted into one of six types of temperament. It seems to me that he attributes to a consistent temper what may only be the result of a dramatic type.[37]

Nevertheless, though it is unwise to press consistency of temperament too far, some characters seem to be controlled by a dominant passion. There is a distinction. Temperament differs from dominant passion by including a predisposition not only to a particular passion, but also to a specific physique, intellect, and morality. Malvolio is moved by self-love, a form of pride; Antony, by lust; Angelo, by self-righteousness. Malvolio's temper is never superseded by another passion; Antony often gives way to self-chastisement or grief, yet fundamentally obeys his passion; Angelo is transformed into another man by yielding to lust and still another by yielding to penitence at the conclusion. Thus the degree of consistency varies with the individuals, yet even with the most consistent characters, the interest is not directed to incidental characteristics such as physique, but to the passions to which they yield. Only here and there do we find a man of balanced temperament who does not yield to passion. As we might expect, such a man, of whom Horatio is the most famous example, shows very little individuality.

All of the foregoing conditions, verbal and physical expression, theatrical tradition, playing circumstances, thought habits, and acting roles shaped the Globe actor. As he took on a role, he had to work with dispatch. In less than two weeks the show was to go on the boards. While he was studying a new role he was playing from eight to twelve others. Given a copy of his part, he depended principally upon himself for working up the role. Shakespeare might advise him about the interpretation, but in the time available not much group rehearsal could take place. Since most of the scenes in which he appeared involved only one or two other characters, little time had to be spent in worrying about blocking out the movements or about grouping.

The role he had been given most likely fell into one of several general types to which had become attached some conventions of portrayal. But these conventions were suggestive rather than absolute since the period had not developed a rigid correspondence of passion and external expression. The actor could rely on these conventions or habits because the basic outline of his character would fit into some social group. He endeavored to impersonate a typical character of this group in his walk, manner, character relationship, speech. Acutely conscious of ceremony, he infused these elements with an artistry which imitated the ideal rather than the specific. With his voice he did not attempt to imitate particular persons, but expressed the meaning of the speeches by accenting the figures of language. In all this he obeyed the tendency of the age to find similarities rather than differences in behavior.

This ritualistic acting, however, contained within it specific passions which burst from these typical characters. Unto the portrayal of these passions the actor had to give himself fully. Audacity and vehemency were required. He knew he had to feel the emotions himself if he were to move his auditors. Overtly expressed, the emotions came forth without self-conscious restraint. Perhaps in other acting companies the actors relied on conventional expressions of emotions. But Shakespeare gave his actors too rich a variety of emotions of too fine a subtlety to permit them to rely upon a stock rendition of outworn conventions. Although the actor did not have to search for the emotion, as actors do now, he had to discriminate among the various emotions and individualize each of them in order to project an effective character. His conceit or idea of the passion had to be keen to make the character come to life; he knew that without a vivid comprehension, the external expression would be hollow.

On stage, he shared his experience directly with the audience. He was part of an elaborate pageant taking place in a far-off land against an opulent backdrop. Yet on an emotional level he communicated intimately and directly with the audience. In more or less unrestrained utterance he portrayed extremes of passion, passion which was so alive and real that the audience might wish to say about the Globe player what Polonius said about the player in *Hamlet:*

> Look, whe'r he has not turn'd his colour, and
> has tears in's eyes. Prithee no more!
> [II, ii, 542–543]

At the peak of his passion he might well have fitted Hamlet's description of the player who

> in a dream of passion,
> Could force his soul so to his own conceit
> That, from her working, all his visage wann'd,
> Tears in his eyes, distraction in's aspect,
> A broken voice, and his whole function suiting
> With forms to his conceit.
> [II, ii, 578–583]

To this type of ceremonious acting, the heart of which was overwhelming passion intensively portrayed, neither the adjective formal nor natural applies. I suggest that we accept the inevitable adjective and call it romantic acting, but romantic acting understood in the finest sense before decadence and extravagance set in. The Globe company brought this art to perfection.

Chapter Five

THE STAGING

I. STAGE ILLUSION AT THE GLOBE PLAYHOUSE

STAGING, like acting, is an art of illusion, but its illusion, unlike that of acting, deals not with being but with time and space. In the manipulation of time, it has long been recognized that Shakespeare is a master. An oft-cited example of his mastery occurs in the guard scene in *Othello* (II, iii). During the course of the action a night is made to pass. At the beginning of the scene, the time is not yet "ten o' the clock" (15). At the conclusion, Iago remarks, "By th' mass, 'tis morning!" (384). In the midst of the alarum, Othello speaks of night and Iago agrees that Cassio should see Desdemona "betimes in the morning" (335). Here, as elsewhere, Shakespeare creates his own illusion of time corresponding neither to actual chronology nor to agreed convention, but solely to narrative demands.

It has also been generally recognized that Shakespeare may utilize more than one time scheme within a single play. For example, after Edmund has shown "Edgar's" letter to his father, the Duke of Gloucester, he assures him that he will seek out Edgar as quickly as he can,

> convey the business as I shall find means, and
> acquaint you withal.
>
> [I, ii, 109–111]

In Act II, scene i, three scenes later, he expedites his plot, presumably without delay, for the action picks up where it had left off. In the intervening scenes, however, Lear spends sufficient time at Goneril's castle for her to complain to the Steward, "By day and night, he wrongs me!" (I, iii, 3). Certainly the spectator is to suppose that a good portion of a month has gone by.

Through a kind of illusion the author accelerates or decelerates the passage of time to fit the needs of his narrative. Thus, the time sequence varies during the course of the play. In some scenes time is extended, in others highly contracted. Antony is told, only a moment after the mob, which he has stirred to fury, rushes out to revenge Caesar's death, that Brutus and Cassius have fled before this same mob. The reference point, manifestly, is not the length of time that the events would require in actuality, or a fixed standard of time, such as the twenty-four-hour neoclassical day, or a symbolic dimension, such as the morality time scheme of man's life on earth, but the duration of time required to tell the story. This narrative ordering of time, moreover, has a parallel in a similar narrative ordering of space.

Simultaneous staging illustrates the operation of such ordering of space. By simultaneous staging is meant, in this instance, the practice of mounting more than one setting on stage at the same time so that during one scene the setting for another is already present. The degree to which it was employed by the popular companies is a matter of controversy.

In 1924 E. K. Chambers endeavored to distinguish between simultaneous staging in the private theaters and sequential staging in the public playhouses. But Professor George Reynolds has shown that at the Red Bull, some of the time at least, simultaneous staging was practiced. Later studies by George Kernodle and C. Walter Hodges have supported his position. In writing about simultaneous staging Reynolds, as well as Kernodle and Hodges, refers to the disposition of properties only. Reynolds argues that properties from one scene were occasionally left on-stage during the playing of another. Or he suggests that tents or shops, utilized much like the mansions of the medieval stage, were erected on-stage. He cites the tents scene in *Richard III* (V, iii), where both Richard's and Richmond's tents occupy the stage, as evidence that "theaters permitted violation of realistic distance and the use of simultaneous settings." Instances of such simultaneity, although not abundant, do occur among the Shakespearean Globe plays.

The disguised Kent is placed in stocks before Gloucester's castle where he is to remain all night (II, ii). The Quarto specifies that at the end of a soliloquy he "sleeps." A soliloquy by Edgar follows. After Edgar's exit, with the coming of morning, Lear arrives. Editors frequently treat the sleep and Edgar's exit as the conclusions of separate scenes, thus marking Edgar's soliloquy Act II, scene iii, and the scene commencing with Lear's arrival, Act II, scene iv. However, neither the Folio nor the Quarto texts have any divisions at these points, although the Folio text is otherwise divided. John C. Adams, in his proposed staging of *King Lear*, suggests that the "inner stage" curtain was closed while Kent sleeps in order to allow Edgar to deliver his soliloquy, and then reopened for the next scene. But the direction "sleeps" indicates that this was not the case. Edgar merely entered while Kent slept in the stocks. Whether he was supposed to be in the same part of the castle yard or another part does not much matter. In this instance an imaginative expansion of space occurs and he "does not" see Kent.

A similar instance occurs in *As You Like It*. While Amiens and Jaques are singing in the Forest of Arden, a banquet is brought out. Seeing the uncovered dishes, Amiens says,

> Sirs, cover the while; the Duke will drink under
> this tree.
>
> [II, v, 32–33]

After they sing some more, Jaques announces that he will go off to sleep and Amiens replies:

> And I'll go seek the Duke. His banquet is prepar'd.
> [64–65]

These definite exit lines spoken by Amiens, as well as those spoken by the Duke at the end of Act II, scene vii (where he is careful to have Adam supported off stage), indicate that discovery of the banquet is not intended in either scene. Between the setting and partaking of the banquet, there intervenes the scene in which Orlando and Adam enter the forest fainting from want of food. Here is demonstration of the blending of general localization with simultaneous staging.

However, such simultaneous staging did not set the style for an entire play. Nowhere is there evidence that mansions or properties were left on-stage throughout an entire play. Nor is this surprising. It is apparent by now that scenic materials appeared infrequently on the Globe stage. Therefore, if there were conventions of spatial order, they involved not merely the physical elements of staging but more especially the organic elements, namely, the actors.

A nonrealistic ordering of space becomes necessary when the demands of a dramatic story create a disparity between the actual dimensions of the stage and the spatial dimensions of the action. Utilizing the theatrical conventions of the age, illusion masks this disparity. Such illusion is a product of two factors: the extension and/or compression of space and the juxtaposition of actors and properties.

As in the case of temporal illusion, Elizabethan *spatial* illusion does not obey a fixed proportion between stage and reality. It employs neither the unity of place nor the cosmic range of medieval drama. Between property and actor and between actor and actor, space assumes whatever dimension the narrative requires. This is true not only of the compression of space, that is, how closely characters stand to one another, but of their dramatic relationship, that is, the quality of that proximity.

To illustrate how the Elizabethans employed narrative space relationships between actors, I turn to a striking, and, as far as I am aware, hitherto unnoticed instance of compression in one of the Globe plays, *Pericles.*

In the first scene of the play Pericles seeks the hand of the Daughter of Antiochus. To win her, he must successfully answer a riddle. To fail, as many princes before him have done, means death. After the Daughter appears before him in all her regal beauty, Pericles receives the text of the riddle which he reads aloud. Almost immediately he fathoms the meaning: Antiochus and his daughter have committed incest. Pericles expresses this

revelation in an aside, in the midst of which he addresses the
Daughter directly.

> Y'are a fair viol, and your sense the strings:
> Who, finger'd to make man his lawful music,
> Would draw heaven down, and all the gods, to hearken;
> But being play'd upon before your time,
> Hell only danceth at so harsh a chime.
> Good sooth, I care not for you.
>
> [I, i, 81–86]

We might assume that, since the character speaks an aside, the
actor was standing some distance from the Daughter in order
to give the illusion that he is not overheard. But the next line,
which Antiochus addresses to Pericles, shows that Pericles was
actually next to the Daughter.

> ANT. Prince Pericles, touch not, upon thy life,
>   For that's an article within our law,
>   As dangerous as the rest. Your time's expir'd.
>   Either expound now, or receive your sentence.
>   [I, i, 87–90]

Apparently, Pericles in his aside gestures toward the Daughter
on the line, "Good sooth, I care not for you." Antiochus mis-
interprets the meaning of the gesture and warns Pericles not
to touch his daughter. Thus, instead of speaking from afar,
Pericles delivers the aside in the midst of the other actors.

In analyzing the aside as a dramatic device, writers have accepted the convention but rejected a conventional delivery by
suggesting that in performance the platform stage enabled the
actor to render it realistically. Not only this scene in *Pericles*,
but equally significant instances of spatial compression contradict this theory. Many asides give the actor neither time nor
motivation for creating verisimilitude. When Othello meets
Desdemona, after Iago has awakened the "green-eyed monster"
within him, he is struggling to hide his conviction of her guilt.
Desdemona greets him.

DES. How is't with you, my lord?
OTH. Well, my good lady. O, hardness to dissemble!
How do you, Desdemona?

[III, iv, 33–35]

Today the actor mutters the aside, "O, hardness to dissemble," turns away, or in some other manner endeavors to give plausibility to the convention that Desdemona does not hear the remark. In final desperation, he may cut the line. The study of asides below shows that these were not the methods employed at the Globe.

Naturally, the high degree of spatial compression among the players caused a change in the quality of their relationships. When one actor comes closer to another than realistic action plausibly admits, as in the scene in *Pericles*, he destroys illusion, if it is one of reality, or he creates a new illusion, if it is one of convention. By standing near the defiled princess while he unravels the mystery, the actor of Pericles can convey his horror with maximum effectiveness, and by speaking his aside near her while he paints a word picture of her outer beauty and inner pollution, he can project his revulsion at her foul proximity. The Globe players, in the staging of asides, did not think in terms of creating an illusion of actuality but of relating the crucial elements of the narrative to each other. Within such a frame of reference the dilemma, folly, or scheme which gives rise to an aside is demonstrated more lucidly and more dramatically than it could be within a realistic frame of reference. What is true of the aside is equally true of observations, disguises, concealments, parleys, and other theatrical devices.

The conventions governing grouping of actors also governed the sequence of actions. From scene to scene, and within scenes, space had a fluidity which was accommodated to the narration. Generalization of locale required such fluidity, for locale was as broad or as narrow as occasion demanded. The picturing of locale, we must remember, was not accomplished with scenery. Nor was passage from one locale to another accomplished through physical changes in the stage façade, as some scholars have insisted. According to various views, the drawing of a curtain or a shift from one part of the stage to another or from one mansion to another was a conventional means of conveying a change of place to the audience. All these views assume in common that the establishment of space was dependent upon clues of a physical sort.

The application as well as the refutation of such an assumption can be illustrated in the assassination scene of *Julius Caesar*, which begins in the streets of Rome and moves to the Capitol (III, i). Ronald Watkins would express this sequence in a change in the stage itself. To mark the moment when the scene shifts into the Capitol, he would open the "inner stage" curtain to reveal a state for Caesar.[1] The possibility that the street and the Capitol were situated in the same imaginary area is never explored although there is no instance in a Globe play where a shift takes place like that which Watkins predicates. Before examining this scene in detail, it might be well to turn to another Globe scene which is unqualified evidence against Watkins' method of staging.

In scene x of *Miseries of Enforced Marriage*, it will be recalled, Butler has convinced Ilford, Bartley, and Wentloe that he can provide them with rich wives. Appointing a time to introduce them to their "brides-to-be," he arranges to meet first Ilford and then the other two "at the sign of the Wolfe against Gold-smiths row" (Sig. G1ᵛ). After these rakes depart, Butler soliloquizes upon the punishment that he will inflict upon them for their villainy. At the conclusion of this brief soliloquy, he does not exit. Instead, Thomas and John Scarborrow enter.

> BUT.   O, are you come. And fit as I appointed.
> [Sig. G2ʳ]

He bids them wait while he sets up the plot for Ilford. The scene with Ilford is played in continuous fashion. There is no indication that the scene has shifted to any other part of the stage, for Ilford observes the Scarborrows from a window. When Wentloe and Bartley appear, Wentloe points out the sign of the Wolfe. Through dialogue, the audience is made aware that a change of locale has occurred without either a clearing of the stage or a shift in area. Furthermore, the appearance of the sign suggests one of three possibilities: the sign was visible throughout the scene, thus creating a type of simultaneous setting; it was not employed physically and thus Wentloe's line is imaginative; or it was placed in position during the course of the scene. In any one of these instances the change of scene did not depend upon any change in the form or size of the stage space.

To return to *Julius Caesar*. It is possible to carry out the staging of the scene as Watkins suggests. But there is no instance in the Globe plays which clearly shows this to be Globe practice. A scene in *The Devil's Charter* (II, i, Sig. E1ʳ) contains a similar scene of procession, this time to a papal state. In the other stage directions of the play, Barnes has carefully indicated when the enclosure was employed, even within a scene, so that his failure to mention it in a stage direction for this scene argues against its use. In that event the state must have been thrust out. This method would serve equally well in *Julius Caesar* with the result that both street and Capitol would be simultaneously presented.

Essentially the stage was a fluid area that could represent whatever the author wished without the necessity for him to indicate a change in stage location. The actors did not regard the stage as a place but as a platform from which to project a story, and therefore they were unconscious of the discrepancy between real and dramatic space. How far behind Malvolio were the "box tree" and his tormentors? How far from Brutus and Cassius are Caesar and Antony when Caesar sneers at Cassius' "lean and hungry look"? Is the eye meant to take in both parties at once? In performing these scenes, the Globe players probably concentrated on making the observation of Malvolio and the scornful characterization of Cassius dramatically effective. That this frequently necessitated the substitution of imaginary for real distance must have passed unobserved both by the players and the audience.

Space, though flexible, was not amorphous. Principles of order in staging existed independently of the stage façade and machinery. As in Elizabethan graphic art during this period, the principles were simple and derivative. The "primitive" art of the medieval period had been suppressed by Henry VIII. No vital growth in a secular art appeared to take its place. Save for some painters who created original and masterly miniatures, among them the master Nicholas Hilliard, the Elizabethans failed to develop a school of graphic art and thus resorted to foreign artists or imitators. It is not surprising, therefore, that the stage which developed at this period was simple in composition and imitative in adornment. Massive and symmetrical, not easily varied in its fundamental appearance, its boards served any scene.

Evidence for fixing stage positions is scanty at best. The text of a drama, unless it is accompanied by detailed stage directions, does not contain the kind of evidence needed. Unfortunately, no one at the Globe thought of preparing a *regiebuch*. Furthermore, methods of rehearsal indicate that the pictorial arrangement of the actors received little attention. Considering the history of the Elizabethan acting company and the conditions of its repertory, it is not unlikely that traditional patterns of arrangement were retained and repeated. Novelty in the stage picture is a characteristic of the director's theater, not of the stock company's repertory. But, though the evidence for stage composition is scanty, what evidence there is is consistent.

The simplest order in art is symmetrical balance. It is this type of composition which one observes in the Globe plays from time to time. At a banquet in *The Devil's Charter*, Act V, scene iv, Pope Alexander enters with three cardinals and three soldiers. The stage direction reads,

> The Pope taketh his place, three Cardinals on one side and [three] captaines on the other. [Sig. L1ʳ]

Poisoned at this banquet by the Devil, Alexander rushes to his study,

> Alexander unbraced betwixt two Cardinalls in his study looking upon a booke, whilst a groome draweth the Curtaine. [Sig. L3ʳ]

This might be an echo of Richard III's position between the Bishops as he receives the Lord Mayor's embassy from London. A more dramatic use of symmetry can be found in the finale of *Miseries of Enforced Marriage*. At the last moment Scarborrow repents his wild courses. Surrounded by the brothers and sister he has ruined, the wife and children he has neglected, and the uncle he has abused, he is deeply shamed.

> Harke how their words like Bullets shoot me thorow
> And tel mee I have undone em, *this side* might say,
> We are in want and you are the cause of it,
> *This* points at me, yare shame unto your house,
> *This tung* saies nothing, but her lookes do tell,
> Shees married but as those that live in hel.
>
> [Sig. K4ʳ. My italics]

The demonstratives indicate brothers and sister on one hand, the uncle on the other, and his wife next to him.

This type of symmetry can be seen in Shakespearean plays also. At one point in *Antony and Cleopatra* Antony's soldiers, while on watch, hear the subterranean music which signifies, according to one of them, that "the god Hercules, whom Antony lov'd,/Now leaves him." For the setting of the watch occurs the stage direction, "They place themselves in every corner of the stage" (IV, iii, 7). What arrangement could be simpler? In the same play there is another example. Antony and Caesar are to meet to settle their dispute (II, ii). The scene opens with Lepidus urging Enobarbus to "entreat your captain/To soft and gentle speech." Then the two monarchs of the world enter from opposite sides of the stage. I quote at length to make the balance clear.

LEP.   Here comes
                        the noble Antony.
                        (Enter Antony and Ventidius.)
ENO.   And yonder, Caesar.
                        (Enter Caesar, Maecenas, and Agrippa.)
ANT.   If we compose well here, to Parthia.
                        Hark, Ventidius.
CAE.   I do not know,
                        Maecenas. Ask Agrippa.
LEP.   Noble friends,
                        That which combin'd us was most great, and
                                let not

A leaner action rend us. What's amiss,
May it be gently heard. When we debate
Our trivial difference loud, we do commit
Murther in healing wounds. Then, noble partners,
The rather for I earnestly beseech,
Touch you the sourest points with sweetest terms,
Nor curstness grow to th' matter.

ANT.   'Tis spoken well,
Were we before our armies, and to fight,
I should do thus.

                    (Flourish)
CAE.   Welcome to Rome.
ANT.   Thank you.
CAE.   Sit.
ANT.   Sit, sir.
CAE.   Nay then.

                                    [13–28]

And they sit, to discuss their grievances. From the entrance
to the final seating, the scene and dispositions are balanced.
At the end of this episode there is a formal symmetrical grouping: Caesar seated with his two supporters in attendance facing
Antony with his two supporters in attendance. Between them,
mediating the matter, is Lepidus.

Throughout the Shakespearean Globe plays instances of this
sort can be found, not only in the arrangement of the actors
but also in the writing of the scenes. An extended example of
verbal symmetry occurs in *As You Like It,* where Rosalind vows
to marry Phebe if she marries any woman (IV, ii, 90–118). Often
these symmetrical arrangements are taken for granted because
they seem dramatic and do not disturb the flow of narrative.
Yet occasionally we can discern dramatic logic sacrificed for
symmetrical arrangement. This "failing" can be more graphi-
cally observed in the buildings of the period and, therefore, I
digress for a moment. A feature of the great houses built as
show places during the Tudor age was the adherence to sym-
metrically balanced design. Usually a central structure would
be flanked by more or less elaborately developed ells or wings,
as at Wollaton Hall, Hatfield House, Charlton House, or Hard-

wick Hall. The main hall was in the center, naturally, and the quarters of the noblemen were in one wing. In the other wing the buttery, scullery, or otherwise menial part of the household was located. In both Wollaton and Hardwick Halls, the kitchen or scullery occupies the front chamber of only one wing to balance the opposite lordly wing.[2] From a functional point of view in planning, the symmetrical arrangement did not satisfy the living accommodations of the Tudor household. But from a visual point of view, it represented a dignity and order that relatively unsophisticated builders could create. Despite the obvious waste in space, the visual need determined the structural design.

This tendency can be observed on the stage. I have already cited the scene in *Twelfth Night,* when Malvolio "returns" Olivia's ring to Viola. Olivia had sent him to run after the "peevish" boy to tell him that she would not take "his" ring (I, v, 318–323). We should suppose that, in order to catch the boy, Malvolio would have followed Viola on the stage. Yet the stage direction clearly specifies that they enter "severally," that is, from opposite sides of the stage. The entrance is symmetrical but not logical.

The general thesis for symmetrical staging that I have advanced must be qualified in two respects. First, the reliance upon symmetrical arrangement was probably stronger in the earlier than in the later period. The plays themselves change from a more formal, balanced arrangement of speeches to a more colloquial, asymmetrical arrangement. The balanced dirges of the various queens in *Richard III* (IV, iv) and the measured laments of Blanch in *King John* (III, i, 326 ff.) begin to disappear. However, they do not wholly vanish during the Globe period.

Secondly, the principles of composition may not be readily perceived in scenes involving only a few characters. Therefore, in the Globe plays symmetry as an element of staging can be best studied in group scenes, for it is a simple way to arrange groups of actors. The nature of Elizabethan dramatic material made simple balance not only the most feasible but also the most meaningful method of composition.

II. STAGE GROUPING AT THE GLOBE PLAYHOUSE

In considering grouping on the Elizabethan stage, we should keep in mind the basic conditions of production. During its periods of rehearsal the Globe company was actively engaged in daily performance. Within two weeks customarily, the actors had to learn extensive parts and mount a multiscene play. In a certain proportion of these scenes many characters appeared on stage. Once presented the play was not repeated for some days. Furthermore, the stage on which the actors played had poor sightlines. The only area from which they could be seen by virtually all members of the audience was at the center of the platform in front of the pillars, at the very place where De-Witt's Swan drawing shows a scene in progress.

Although most scenes in the Shakespearean Globe plays require five people or less on the stage at any one time, there are still quite a number of scenes or sections of scenes in which more than five people appear. In the fifteen plays of Shakespeare in the Globe repertory, I count one hundred and sixty-six such scenes or episodes, or an average of more than ten in each play. The lowest proportion is 14 per cent in *Twelfth Night*, the highest 61 per cent in *Coriolanus*. Generally 20 to 30 per cent of a play consists of what I term "group" scenes or episodes.[3]

In terms of the problems of staging, these group scenes fall into four distinct categories. More than half of the group scenes, eighty-eight, fall into category one. These are scenes in which, though there are actually five or fewer speaking characters on the stage, the addition of one or more mute supernumeraries increases the size of the group to six or more. Almost all of these mute supers fall into one of several distinct generic types, easily recognizable and probably conventionally portrayed. The most frequently recurring types are soldiers in thirty scenes; attendants and servants in twenty-three scenes; and noblemen of one sort or another in twenty-one scenes. A small but important type consists of the crowds in *Julius Caesar* and *Coriolanus*. The rest of the supers come from various miscellaneous classes, such as ladies, musicians, sailors, and so on. It is probable that the stock-in-trade of the hired men and gatherers was a standardized portrayal of such types. Problems in grouping must have been solved as readily. The prevailing types, soldiers, attendants, and noblemen, contain in their ranks and duties the rationale for their positions upon the stage. Implied in the relationship of servant to master or nobleman to king is an attitude of service expressed in a characteristic manner. That this pattern was representative of Globe plays as a whole is borne out by the examination of the non-Shakespearean and non-Jonsonian plays in the Globe repertory. Although in proportion there are fewer group scenes in the non-Shakespearean plays than in the Shakespearean, in the separation into types of group scenes, the same divisions are evident.

A second category consists of group scenes which require more than five actors with speaking roles on-stage at one time. This numbers twenty-two. However, though there are more than five characters on-stage, no more than five of them are active. In effect, the others become mute observers, functioning much as the nobleman, soldier, or attendant type. For example, in the debate upon Grecian policy in *Troilus and Cressida,* Act I, scene iii, 1–212, three people speak: Agamemnon, Nestor, and Ulysses. During the utterance of these 212 lines neither Diomedes nor Menelaus speaks, although they are present throughout. In this scene they are mere supers. Donalbain is on-stage throughout *Macbeth,* Act I, scenes ii and iv, but he does not speak. He, too, functions as a mute nobleman. Once Lear faces Goneril and Regan before Gloucester's castle (II, iv, 129–298), Kent and the Fool, who have been prominent hitherto, drop into the background as mute attendants. This practice, not of subordinating characters but of reducing them to ciphers, facilitated the handling of large groups of characters. That this was the technique of the poet is evident when one considers those scenes where characters, who have every reason to be active, fail to respond to events in which they are immediately involved. When the Duke reveals to Isabella the brother whom she thought dead (*Measure for Measure,* V, i, 495–498), we might expect Isabella to say something, but she does not. Or when Cleopatra beats the messenger who brings the report of Antony's marriage to Octavia (II, v), we might expect the otherwise talkative Iras or Alexas to say something, but Charmian alone intervenes. In that scene the others play mute supers.

The third, and second most numerous, category of group scenes requires more than five active characters on-stage at one time *excluding* mute supers. There are forty-six instances of such scenes. What distinguishes them as a class is that all of them represent some type of situation which demands ceremonious grouping. Among others there are banquet scenes, single combats, council sessions, trials, parleys, processions, and greetings. In all of them the formal character is marked, attention is directed to one focal point, and the arrangement of the action is often symmetrical and ceremonial (see Appendix C, chart ii).

It is apparent from categories one, two, and three that in the case of 156 of the 166 group scenes, the organizing principle is ceremony or duty. Movement and arrangement, though formal, are not artificial. Rather, they reflect circumstances of Elizabethan life. In the group scenes the personage of greatest prestige is usually the one who directs the action and to whom the other characters relate themselves. The importance of this organizing principle is demonstrated by considering the plays of domestic life, such as *The Merry Wives of Windsor*. Without a ranking figure, another system of grouping had to be developed. In such a play, an object of ridicule, accusation, or pity serves as the focal point, as in the final scene of *Merry Wives*.

In the ceremonious scenes it happens sometimes that the focal figure is not a major character in the play, yet as the person of highest rank he is the one to whom all the characters address themselves. This is clearly the situation in *Othello* (I, iii), where Brabantio accuses Othello before the Duke and Senate. It is the Duke whom Othello answers.

Where no single figure serves as the point of reference in the grouping, a center of activity invariably does. The wrestling scene in *As You Like It* (I, iii) or the duel in *Hamlet* (V, ii) are examples of this kind of organization. Another method is the processional. Most processions pass over the stage with or without halting for brief speeches. Occasionally the procession might combine a focus of both activity and a central figure, as in *Julius Caesar* (I, ii). In some instances characters on-stage describe or discuss members of the procession (*All's Well*, III, v; *Pericles,* II, ii; *Troilus and Cressida*, I, ii). Given the free passage of the stage and a point of observation when needed, these scenes offer little problem in staging. In fact, the regular recurrence and similar arrangement of these scenes suggest the influence of standardized staging.

Even where more than five characters are active in the course of a group scene, more than five are rarely active during extended portions of the scene. The finale of *As You Like It* will serve as a succinct and relatively typical example. The scene opens with Orlando and Duke Senior briefly discussing Ganymede (1–4). Rosalind enters, still disguised, to make certain that the mutual pledges of marriage hold. She asks each interested person in turn for confirmation (5–25). Five speak, all but Phebe answering Rosalind with one line. She speaks two. Orlando and the Duke return to the discussion of Ganymede (26–34). Touchstone enters and engages in conversation with Jaques and the Duke while Rosalind has a chance, off-stage, to change into her maidenly garments (35–113). Hymen appears, leading in Rosalind; the pledges are finally confirmed in single-line refrains. Hymen blesses the marriages. Five speak (114–156). The Second Brother enters to tell the story of Duke Frederick's conversion. He is welcomed by the Duke only. In fact, his brothers, Orlando and Oliver, never speak to him. Jaques, in his own fashion, blesses each marriage. Three speak (157–204). Rosalind delivers the Epilogue. In scenes of this pattern there is no need for all the characters to be seen at all times. Instead, the actors could come forward when needed, to play where they could be heard and seen by everyone. At the conclusion of such a portion of the scene, as when Touchstone and Jaques finish speaking, the unneeded characters could retire to the rear until called for once again.

That this was indeed the practice is illustrated by the Globe play, *Every Man Out of His Humour.* Jonson's stage directions in Act II, scene iii, show that when Sordido and Fungoso are not needed, they "with-draw to the other part of the stage" and that when Puntarvolo has completed one part of his action he "falls in with Sordido, and his Sonne" while other action is in progress.

The last category of group scenes contains as did those already enumerated, more than five characters *excluding* supers. However, these scenes do not have a formal arrangement. Thus, the method of grouping these scenes is not quite so rigidly set as that of the previous category. Of this sort there are relatively few examples, only ten or about 6 per cent of the group scenes. Some of these verge on a formal arrangement without fully realizing it. The scene of choosing a husband in *All's Well* (II, iii) is a unique example in Shakespeare, although in the pattern of the writing there is a symmetry which tends to give the scene a schematic quality. The farewell scene in *Antony and Cleopatra* (III, ii) and the arrest scene in *Twelfth Night* (III, iv) also approach formality. What distinguishes these scenes from the rest of the formal group scenes is merely the degree of ceremony.

The presence of formal patterns in stage grouping enabled the Globe company to present large-cast plays with a minimum of rehearsal. The presence of sub-scenes within the larger scene enabled the essential action to be brought forward and viewed. Such a practice naturally reduced the importance of the stage façade as a frame for the stage picture, for the attending figures remained in the background, near the tiring house, and the active characters came forward to the front of the stage where they could be seen in the round. Nothing hindered the operation of such a stage procedure, for more than 80 per cent of all Globe scenes required no stage machinery or properties whatsoever. Everything favored it. The platform stage was not a gargantuan apron before a modern proscenium. It was *the* stage and the group scenes were played to make full use of its expanse and flexibility.

I have devoted this much attention to Elizabethan stage illusion and the group scenes in order to show that there were theatrical practices in operation which did not depend upon the stage façade or machinery. Yet the scholar of Elizabethan staging invariably approaches the subject by first considering the function of the stage and its properties in identifying the location of scenes. E. K. Chambers categorizes scenes according to what setting they need. Even Reynolds, who understands the necessity for considering scene situations rather than stage locations, uses the latter to determine the arrangement of his book. The result of such an approach has been that a drama, which in production relied almost wholly upon the voice and movement of the actor, has been studied in terms of its settings, its least pertinent part. When a modern character enters a scene, he enters a definitely indicated place. The audience or readers are made very conscious of that place, its odors, its atmosphere, its effect upon the characters. But in the Elizabethan drama, particularly in the Shakespearean, a character enters not *into* a place but *to* another character. Where he enters is of secondary importance—to whom he enters or with whom he enters is of primary interest.

Coordinately, the continuity of action from scene to scene was independent of the stage façade. This conclusion is a logical corollary of the evidence offered in Chapter Three. The enclosure, used for discovery or concealment, is introduced sometimes within scenes, sometimes with scenes, but not for the purpose of providing flow from scene to scene, as we saw. Neither the above nor the hell below ever serve the function of enabling one scene to follow another. Properties, even though they serve conventional uses, appear too infrequently and too irregularly to afford a means of scene connection. Consequently, these conclusions have led me to draw up five premises covering continuity in staging.

(1) The mention of place in the dialogue does not necessarily mean that either a part of the stage façade or a property is employed. Only actual use of the stage area or property confirms its employment or appearance on stage. (2) A new scene does not have to be played in a different part of the stage from the previous one. This premise is closely connected with the idea that (3) a change of location in the narrative is not neces-

sarily accompanied by a change in location on stage. Most scholars have recognized that the exit of one character and the entrance of another from a different door is enough to signify a change of location. Although this is generally true, there are exceptions even in these cases, for examples of scenes exist where a change of location is effected without the clearing of the stage (*Julius Caesar*, III, i; *Miseries of Enforced Marriage*, scene x; *Measure for Measure*, III, i–ii; *London Prodigal*, D3^r– E1^v). (4) No regular system of scene alternation occurs. Bröd-meier's simple theory of alternation, one scene in front of a curtain and one scene behind, has been discarded by scholars long ago. But more elaborate systems of alternation, employing the "inner" and "upper stages," are still advanced. Examples are available for examination in Watkins' book and Reynolds' reconstruction of *Troilus and Cressida*. (5) Evidence for the use of the enclosure in one scene of a play does not mean that the enclosure was used in other scenes for which there is no evidence. Many years ago Ashley Thorndike advocated the opposite premise. "Clear evidence of the curtained inner stage in one scene of a play must be taken as a presumptive evidence that it was used in others," he wrote.[4] Thorndike's presumption has been liberally interpreted by students of staging. Perhaps the absence of additional mention of the enclosure is the clearest proof of its limited use. After all, when the total evidence for a curtained space is gathered together, the bulk is fairly slim in comparison to the vast number of scenes which contain no such mention. Of the 519 scenes in the Globe plays, sixteen of them show fairly strong evidence of being partly placed in the enclosure. This is about 3 per cent of the total. Perhaps the texts of the non-Shakespearean plays offered by the Globe company reflect a truer percentage. Of their 182 scenes, twelve show evidence of enclosure use, or about 6½ per cent.[5] In either case the total percentage is low.

These premises arise from my conviction that the part which the stage façade played in the presentation of the plays has been greatly overestimated. Visually, the façade was always the formal background, but in the overwhelming number of cases the action took place before it, not within it. Instead of looking to the façade for the organizing principles of staging, it might be better to look to the patterns of the scenes themselves.

III. ACTORS' ENTRANCES UPON THE GLOBE STAGE

At one time, Sir Mark Hunter defined a scene as the action between clearances of the stage.[6] Since this definition is generally accepted, we can consider that the scene concludes with the exit of all characters and commences with the entrance of other characters. This so-called "law of reentry" operates in the overwhelming majority of scene changes. It is rare for a character who has left the stage in one scene to enter immediately in the very next. As C. M. Haines has pointed out, most of the exceptions occur in battle scenes. In those instances it is usual for an alarum or excursion to separate the two scenes. The other exceptions are in large measure suspect.[7]

Ready analogy to cinematic technique has led a number of scholars to minimize the scene markings. Emphasis has been placed on the flow of scene *to* scene, to the extent that the separation of scene *from* scene has had to be made by a shift from one stage area or mansion to another or by the opening or closing of a curtain. However, in deemphasizing the contribution of the stage façade to the continuity of the play, it is necessary to consider that the pointing of scene divisions was managed by the actors themselves. Overlapping of the exit and the entrance may not have been the habit of the Globe company; instead separation and pause may have been the method. The actors or stage attendants, on occasion, had to bring out properties. This necessitated a pause, however brief. Nor need this pause have been reflected in the text. For one entrance in *The Battle of Alcazar* the stage direction in the Quarto reads:

Enter the king of Portugall and his Lords, Lewes de Sylva, and the Embassadours of Spaine.

In the plot of the play, however, the corresponding direction reads:

Enter: 2 bringing in a chair of state (mr. Hunt) : w. Kendall Dab
& Harry enter at one dore: Sebastian: Duke of Avero; Stukeley: 1
Pages: Jeames Ionas: & Hercules (th) to them at another dore
Embassadors of Spaine mr Iones mr Charles: attendants George and
w. Cartwright: 8

Unfortunately, no similar parallel of stage direction and plot
exists for any of the Globe plays. In these same plots, we may
also notice, a line was drawn across the page to separate one
scene from another. Probably this was done to clarify the
sequence of scenes, but it had the added effect of fixing the
scene divisions firmly in the actor's mind. Together with the
rhyming couplet which concluded so many scenes, it may have
encouraged the insertion of a slight pause between the scenes.

In Chapter Three I fully examined the character of the
scene endings. The conclusions are relevant at this point although the evidence need not be reviewed. Seventy-nine per
cent of the scene endings indicate explicitly or implicitly that
the actors march off-stage. About ten and one-half per cent of
the scenes end with solo exits. About the same number of scenes
fail to indicate that the actors actually move out. It is obvious,
from this distribution, that at the ends of scenes the playwright
normally provided the actors with exit lines or movements.
These served a double purpose. They stressed the conclusion of
the scene, and they bridged the movement across the large platform.

The sufficiency of such simple movement to separate scenes
is reflected in what I call split entrances or exits. The split entrance or exit occurs when characters come together or go apart
through more than one entryway. Entrance of two or more characters "at several doors" or exit of two or more characters bidding farewell to one another are split. Of the 644 entrances and
exits which begin or end scenes in the Shakespearean Globe
plays, only 12.1 per cent are split scenes. Even of this low figure
only 6.4 per cent are definitely split scenes, the remaining number including probable cases. Thus nearly 90 per cent of the
scenes merely involve the exit of one actor or group at one door
and the entrance of another actor or group at another. The
split scenes are readily staged, if the third entry through the

center curtain is employed. Thus the burden of maintaining the continuity and clarifying the story is placed on the actors—not on the stage.

Shakespeare relies on few methods for opening a scene. In 339 entrances [9] in the Shakespearean Globe plays he employs eight methods for 88 per cent of the entrances. The most frequent type of entrance is that of the mid-speech, which accounts for over 40 per cent of the scene beginnings. In such an entrance two or more characters come on-stage engaged in a conversation the topic of which was begun off-stage. This type of entrance is best adapted to emphasize continuity of action. Among the seven other types is the processional entrance, 9½ per cent of the total; the inquiry, soliloquy, and commanding entrance, about 7 per cent each; and finally the salutation, summoning, and emotional entrances, between 5 and 6 per cent each. In the commanding entrance a character enters giving a command to someone already on-stage; in the summoning entrance the character summons someone who is off-stage, and in the emotional entrance a character enters disturbed by some emotional experience, as Julius Caesar is after the tempestuous night (II, ii).

Except for the processional and salutation entrances, the entrances plunge the audience into the midst of a new situation or a more highly developed stage of an earlier situation. In this respect the evidence would appear to contradict my suggestion that a hiatus may have defined the scenes. But considered in terms of the stage, the contradiction is more apparent than real. This can be seen by turning to the mid-speech entrance, 132 examples of which appear at the beginning of scenes. A typical example opens *Othello*. Roderigo and Iago enter, apparently after Iago has told Roderigo of Desdemona's marriage.

Rod.   Tush, never tell me! I take it much unkindly
   That thou, Iago, who hast had my purse
   As if the strings were thine, shouldst know
    of this.
Iago.   'Sblood, but you will not hear me!
   If ever I did dream of such a matter,
   Abhor me.

              [I, i, 1–6]

But where do the characters begin speaking? At a stage door?
The stage doors on either side of the stage are virtually behind
the stage pillars. No matter how narrow one supposes these
pillars to be, and they cannot be very narrow considering their
function of supporting the heavens and huts, they interfere with
action at the stage doors. Although the exact locations of the
doors in the back wall are uncertain, they must have been behind or nearly behind the pillars if one allows for the enclosure. Consequently, I doubt that the mid-speech, which usually
provides information vital to the narrative, was begun at a door,
and think it more likely that the characters took several paces
toward the center or forward before speaking. This action may
have provided a hiatus sufficient to mark a new scene. Presence
of such a hiatus is supported by the fact that the mid-speech
entrance seldom occurs within the body of a scene. Shakespeare
uses it almost exclusively to enable the actor to maintain continuity from scene to scene. For example, in *All's Well* and
Measure for Measure, fifteen and ten mid-speech entrances respectively all occur at the beginnings of scenes.

However, if the characters entered through the rear curtain,
they could engage in immediate conversation. Entrance of actors through the enclosure curtains was not unusual, and, in
fact, may have occurred more frequently than we usually assume. For instance, in *The Battle of Alcazar*, the Quarto stage
direction reads:

Enter the king of Portugall and the Moore, with all theyr traine.

For the same action, the plot reads:

Enter at one dore the Portingall Army with drom & Cullors:
Sebastian . . . att another dore Governor of Tanger . . . from behind the Curtaines to them muly mahamet & Calipolis in their
Charriott with moores one on each side & attending young mahamet. . . .

Behind the terse stage direction then, lies a more elaborate
entrance involving the curtain. Although definite evidence for
such entrances does not exist in the Globe plays, there is, on
the other hand, no evidence to exclude such entrances. More-

over, there are several situations which imply such use. At the conclusion of scene i in *Othello*, Brabantio and Roderigo exeunt to seek Othello. At line 160 Brabantio had come out one door, representing his house. At line 184 he and Roderigo go out, certainly not back into the house. Othello and Iago enter in mid-speech, surely upon the outer stage. But from where? Not from the door through which Brabantio and Roderigo just went out. Possibly from the door which only recently had been the entrance to Brabantio's house. Probably through the curtain in the center of the stage. Although the evidence is not conclusively applicable to the Globe plays, it may be pertinent to note that in the *Roxana* drawing, the flap of the curtain is partially open, and in the frontispiece to *The Wits* a character is shown coming through the curtain. In all likelihood, actors regularly entered through the center curtain, and when they did, they could begin speaking immediately upon entrance. But when the entrances were made through a stage door, I suggest that conversation was held back for the several seconds needed by the actors to move into the acting area proper and there to mark the beginning of a new scene.

That a need to focus attention upon an entrance existed is evident from a consideration of the entrances within the scenes. Many of these entrances are heralded by some form of announcement or question, such as "My lady comes," or "How now?" or "Who comes here?" Other means of emphasizing entrances were through action, such as a procession, or through music, such as the horn announcing Lear (I, iv), or through response to a previous command, such as Lucius' report of the Ides of March in *Julius Caesar* (II, i). In *As You Like It*, I count thirty-one intrascene entrances: twenty-one are announced, one is accompanied by action, three are responses to a previous command or scheme, and six are unprepared. In *Lear*, there are fifty-one intrascene entrances, of which twenty-five are announced, ten accompanied by action, three by music, and thirteen unprepared. The unprepared entrances in *Lear* are usually unannounced for dramatic purposes. Oswald's entering impertinently to Lear (I, iv), Lear's bearing in the body of Cordelia (V, iii), and Oswald's sighting "the proclaimed prize," Gloucester,. (IV, vi) depend upon suddenness for dramatic effect.

In addition to directing attention to an incoming actor, the announcement filled an awkward gap. The depth of the stage caused a dislocation between the actors already on stage and those coming on-stage. Frequently, the former would be at the front but the entrant would be at the rear. It was necessary to allow time for the entrant to come down stage. The full effect of these announcements was to formalize the entrances and enhance their ceremonial impression.

Just how conventional the entrance might have been can be seen by examining a particular group of entrance announce-. ments. About forty-three entrances in the Shakespearean Globe plays are accompanied by announcements of greater length than the brief, "Who's there?" These announcements run from two lines to sixteen lines in length. Most of them are short, two to four lines in length, but a few are longer than ten lines. In each of these instances a character or characters on-stage describe or comment upon someone who has just entered. Usually the entrant is aware of the others, but it is understood that he does not hear the description. Modern producers often try to cover these awkward entrances by giving the entrant some motivated business to account for the delay in speaking. But these scenes are frankly demonstrative, for the audience is supposed to be aware of both parties. In *Hamlet,* Polonius greets Hamlet, Rosencrantz, and Guildenstern. Hamlet, without answering, says:

Hark you, Guildenstern—and you too—at each ear a hearer!
That great baby you see there is not yet out of his swaddling clouts.
[II, ii, 398–401]

And so forth for another three and one-half lines. Polonius can "cover up" by waiting upon the prince, or by engaging in character business, but in essence he becomes an inert object for that period.

The longest delay in an entrance, sixteen lines, occurs in

Coriolanus (V, iii, 19 ff.) when Coriolanus describes the delega-
tion of Volumnia, Virgilia, young Marcius, and Valeria ap-
proaching him. By no means could it require a speech of that
length for the actors to reach him, no matter from what part of
the stage they may have entered or where he may have been
standing. During his speech they become the visible expression
of the inner struggle that he is about to undergo. If they move,
they must move very slowly; if they stand still, they compose a
picture. It is highly unlikely that the Globe company tried to
"naturalize" this entrance by giving the entrants business or
movement which would divert the attention of the audience
from the effect their entrance was having upon Coriolanus.

Essentially the plays were written to enable the actors to enter
effectively without the aid of the façade, to play intimately near
the audience, and to retire convincingly without loss of attention. When one takes into account the number of processions,
salutations, commands, summonses, and expressions of duty introduced to cover and emphasize the entrances, one realizes that
continuity from scene to scene was mannered rather than casual,
ceremonious rather than personal, conventional rather than
spontaneous. The effect was probably not too far removed from
the daily social manner of the Elizabethans, but on stage their
natural predilection for ceremony may have been more fully
systematized.

IV. RECURRENT PATTERNS OF STAGING

The patterns of continuity then do not lie in a play's use of
the stage façade but inhere in a play's structure. Chapter Two
traced the principal method of Shakespearean storytelling with
its apparent looseness of construction but its actual scheme of
central intensification and narrative finale. Within this framework abounds a tremendous variety of scenes which seem to
defy classification. Nevertheless, situations and devices do recur
in Shakespeare's plays. It is to those recurrent devices that I now
turn, for an examination of their patterns provides the best
means of envisioning the staging of Shakespeare's plays at the
Globe.

At one extreme there are those devices, such as the soliloquy, which are highly conventionalized and frequently employed. At the other extreme are the situations or episodes which are so individualized that they seem to rely upon no distinct dramatic convention, and therefore seem to be "a mirror of nature." Between the common theatrical device and the unique dramatic situation exist the many episodes and devices in Shakespeare which are more or less formal and which are repeated with greater or lesser frequency in play after play. Through the reconstruction of the staging of these recurrent devices and scenes, such as asides, disguises, and so forth, the practices of the Globe playhouse should become apparent.

I shall first consider the soliloquy, the aside, and the observation scene. These forms being readily imitable appear throughout the Globe repertory with frequency. For that reason comparisons in function and technique are plentiful. Although these devices compose a brief portion of a play, they contribute to the development of the action and represent the theatrical method employed to tell the story.

The soliloquy is probably the most characteristic theatrical device of the Elizabethan stage. In the great soliloquies of *Hamlet* and *Macbeth* Shakespeare perfected this form of expression. Unfortunately, these supreme examples have epitomized the content and atmosphere of all soliloquies. The result has been injurious both to the study of literature and the reconstruction of theatrical conventions.

In tone and character, the soliloquy displays great variation. Among the 144 soliloquies which I count in the Shakespearean Globe plays, I distinguish three main subdivisions. All of these represent some form of conscious thought brought to a point where it verges on speech. Broadly, the soliloquies can be divided into those which are essentially emotive in expression, those which are cerebral, and those which are invocative. The divisions are not hard and fast, however. The emotional release of Hamlet, after he castigates himself as a "dull and muddy mettled rascal," gives way to rational plotting to ensnare his uncle. For convenience, however, it is not inaccurate to speak of these three categories. The emotive soliloquies make up about

40 per cent of the total; the rational, containing philosophical comments, plotting, and moralizations, make up about 46 per cent of the total; and the invocative, such as Lady Macbeth's call to the spirits of evil, make up about 7 per cent. These figures are suggestive, not definitive, nor does it matter that they are so. The important thing to note is that the introspective soliloquy is rare. Among the emotive soliloquies, there are expressions of sheer emotion, such as Orlando's paean of love (*As You Like It*, III, ii, 1–10) and Angelo's cry of remorse (*Measure for Measure*, IV, iv, 22–36), Ophelia's lamentation over Hamlet (*Hamlet*, III, i, 158–169), and Thersites' railings (*Troilus and Cressida*, V, iv, 1–18). But there are few examples of the soliloquy of inner conflict, no more than 5 per cent of all the soliloquies.

Not only in character are the bulk of the soliloquies nonintrospective, but also in style they are extroverted. Shakespeare depends a great deal upon apostrophe to sustain the soliloquy. The character's address may be directed toward the gods (*Pericles*, III, i, 1–2: "Thou god of this great vast, rebuke these surges,/Which wash both heaven and hell") or to another person not on stage (Antony to Cleopatra, IV, xiv, 50–52: "I come my queen. . . . Stay for me."/Where souls do couch on flowers, we'll hand in hand/And with our sprightly port make the ghosts gaze") or to natural forces (*Timon*, IV, iii, 176–196, to Mother Earth) or to bodily organs (Claudius in *Hamlet*, III, iii, 70: "Bow, stubborn knees"). In fact, this form of address may be directed to anyone or anything. The effect of this literary figure was to substitute a listener for an absent actor. True, the listener was imaginative rather than actual, mute rather than responsive. But instead of directing the soliloquy inward, the apostrophe enabled the actor to direct it outward.

Other literary forms were also employed toward this end. Frequently the character makes himself the listener by self-interrogation. "Am I a coward? Who calls me villain?" asks Hamlet of himself (II, ii, 598–599). Often the emotive soliloquy is couched in a series of flat assertions or descriptions or comparisons, all of which are contained in Hamlet's soliloquy beginning, "How all occasions do inform against me" (IV, iv). However, because twentieth-century ears are acutely sensitive to psychological nuances suggested by a soliloquy, they very often hear a false echo of inner revelation. Only a few speeches of admittedly great soliloquies reveal profound conflicts of the mind (*Hamlet*, I, ii, 129–159; II, i, 56–89; *Macbeth*, I, vii, 1–28; II, i, 33–64; *Julius Caesar*, II, i, 10–69).

In line with the modern conception of the soliloquies as moments of the most intimate, intensive personal revelation has arisen the idea that the very front of the platform stage is the true province of the soliloquy. Surrounded by the audience, so close that he could almost touch the spectators, the actor is pictured as unveiling his soul. But this view of the soliloquy must be questioned. Although there is no evidence in the Shakespearean Globe plays concerning the actors' positions during the delivery of the soliloquies, in the non-Shakespearean Globe plays there are four instances where soliloquies are delivered from the enclosure, two each in *The Devil's Charter* and *Thomas Lord Cromwell*. Whether or not the speaker remained in the "study" throughout the speech is uncertain. In one case, *The Devil's Charter*, Act IV, scene i, a stage direction after the sixth line of the soliloquy specifies that Alexander "commeth upon the Stage out of his study" (Sig. G1ʳ). In *Cromwell* one soliloquy is six lines long (Sig. B1ʳ) and the other is ten lines long (Sig. E4ᵛ). None of the three soliloquies is introspective or intimate. Alexander expresses rage as he gazes into his magical glass. Cromwell and Gardiner in *Cromwell* are planning one thing or another. The remaining soliloquy in Act I, scene iv (Sig. B2ᵛ–3ʳ), of *The Devil's Charter*, is lengthy, running to thirty-two lines. In it Alexander reviews his covenant with the devil. He chastises himself, but moderately, as befits a man who benefits hugely from his compact with Lucifer. There is no indication that Alexander moves out of the "study." In the absence of a specific direction and in view of the stage direction in Act IV, scene i, it seems likely that Alexander remained in the study. Perhaps all that the evidence can demonstrate is that no special area of the stage seems either reserved for or barred to the soliloquy and that the actor took the stage as the temper of the scene prompted. In all likelihood the actor himself decided how and where he played the soliloquy.

In none of the Globe plays is there any certain indication that the audience was directly addressed in the soliloquy. A. C. Sprague has pointed out that some soliloquies lend themselves to such delivery.[10] When Falstaff says in *The Merry Wives of Windsor* (III, v, 12–13), "you may know by my size that I have a kind of alacrity in sinking" or Iago queries (*Othello*, II, iii, 342–343), "and what's he then that says I play the villain,/When this advice is free I give and honest," the actor could speak directly to the audience. In earlier popular plays actors undoubtedly did.[11] But the plays of the Globe company do not provide conclusive evidence on this point.

Two types of asides are usually recognized. In the first, something is said "by one of the dramatic characters to another (or others) not intended to be heard by all those present." I shall refer to this type as the "conversational aside." In the second, what is said is "very like a soliloquy (usually short) spoken while other characters are present—and known to be present by the speaker—but unheard by them."[12] I shall refer to this as the "solo aside." Warren Smith distinguished a third type of aside, composed of those speeches which "appear to be aimed at rather than addressed to, another character on stage—and the words are evidently not intended for his ears or any others."[13] For the purposes of examining the staging, the third type can be included with the second. It will be sufficient to treat only two types of asides.

Although, in a count of the two types of asides in all of Shakespeare's plays, Warren Smith finds that the conversational aside is more numerous than the solo aside, in a similar count in the Shakespearean Globe plays only, the reverse is true. There are fifty-six conversational asides and eighty solo asides.[14] Next to the soliloquy the two together make up the most frequently used device in these plays.

The conversational aside is usually introduced by some transitional phrase which enables the speaker to move away from the rest of the actors. When Brutus agrees to permit Antony to deliver a funeral address over the body of Caesar, Cassius interrupts.

> Brutus, a word with you.
> You know not what you do. Do not consent
> That Antony speak in his funeral.
>
> [III, i, 231–233]

Sometimes the transitional phrase enables the nonspeakers to retire. After Macbeth receives word from Ross and Angus that he has been made Thane of Cawdor, Banquo addresses them,

> Cousins, a word, I pray you.
> [I, iii, 127]

This leaves Macbeth free to muse upon "the imperial theme." Of course, not all conversational asides are so explicit. But in most cases some provision is made for enabling the speakers to separate themselves from the others. After the murder of Duncan, Lady Macbeth faints, drawing the other actors to her. This action leaves Malcolm and Donalbain free to converse (II, iii, 127–130). On occasion this type of aside may be delivered immediately upon entrance, before the newcomers have joined the other actors (*Measure for Measure*, IV, i, 8–9). In only a few cases is there no definite removal of the speaker from the rest of the action. Rosencrantz covertly says, "What say you?" to Guildenstern when Hamlet presses him to confess that the King sent for them (II, ii, 300) or Iago surreptitiously urges Roderigo to follow after the drunken Cassio, "How now, Roderigo?/I pray you after the Lieutenant, go!" (II, iii, 141–142). This sort of aside is flung by one character to another usually without drawing forth a response. In a few asides a single line is elicited, but only two instances occur where an extended conversation is conducted without previous separation having been indicated (*All's Well*, II, v, 22–29; *Julius Caesar*, I, ii, 178–214).

Comparison of these conversational asides with those in the non-Shakespearean Globe plays shows that the convention of separating speakers and nonspeakers was common to the playwrights of the company rather than peculiar to Shakespeare alone. To introduce extended conversational asides, the playwrights resort to such trite phrases as "A word in private Sir Raph Ierningham," (*The Merry Devil of Edmonton*, Sig. B3^r 10–18), "Sir Ralphe Sadler, pray a word with you" (*Fair Maid of Bristow*, Sig. A4^v 12–B1^r 10). Where oral evidence is missing, sufficient evidence is often present in the stage directions that the speakers and nonspeakers separate. In both the Shakespearean and non-Shakespearean plays the patterns of conversational asides are the same.

In the non-Shakespearean plays, fortunately, there are additional indications of how the asides were delivered. In two cases stage directions require the actors to move away from others. On meeting Astor Manfredy and Phillippo in *The Devil's Charter*, Bernardo addresses Astor alone. Then according to the stage direction, "They draw themselves aside" (Sig. E1^v). A similar instance occurs in *A Larum for London*. Egmont and the Marquis d'Harvuy are trying to convince Champaign, the Governor of Antwerp, to permit them to quarter their troops in the city. At one point, in the margin opposite the lines of the Marquis to Egmont, is a stage direction, "Take Egm. aside" (Sig. B3^v 25). The movement aside may have also been followed by whispering upon the part of the actors, for after Clare draws his wife aside, saying, "My daughter Milliecent must not over-heare," Millicent remarks aside, "I, whispering, pray God it tend my good" (*The Merry Devil of Edmonton*, Sig. B1^v 7). Such whispering may not have been a practice in all the conversational asides, but it seems plausible. As a whole the entire pattern of excuse, movement aside, and possible whispering seems intended to create an impression of reality. This evidence, therefore, strengthens the theory for realistic staging. However, the aside was by its very nature a conventional device. Although the staging of the conversational aside appears to minimize or hide its conventionality, I believe that there is another explanation, the exposition of which depends upon an inspection of the solo aside.

In the Shakespearean plays seventy-six of the solo asides may be divided into two types according to whether or not the author made some attempt to shield the aside of the actor from the attention of the other characters on stage. In one type the other characters are occupied in conversation or business so that it is reasonable for them not to hear the aside. They may actually turn away from the actor or they may be at some distance from him. Arranging the delivery of asides in this way shows some attention to creating an illusion of actuality. In the second type the other characters are fairly near the speaker; in fact, they may be actually speaking to the person who delivers the aside. It is understood, of course, that they do not hear the aside, even in certain cases when the aside is delivered directly to them. This kind of solo aside relies heavily upon the convention of unheard speech, for which presumably there were conventional means of delivery. Of these seventy-six solo asides, exactly half falls into each category.

There is a difference in the categories, however. The evidence for the realistic solo aside is negative, that for the latter positive. The scenes in the first group enable the actor to deliver the aside apart from the other actors, that is, neither immediately before nor after the aside is he directly involved with the other characters. When Othello greets Desdemona lovingly after the sea voyage, embracing her with passionate ardor, Iago remarks:

> O, you are well tun'd now!
> But I'll set down the pegs that make this music,
> As honest as I am.
>
> OTH.   Come, let us to the castle.
> [II, i, 201–203]

Iago may or may not be near Othello and Desdemona. Modern production prefers separation, but this type of aside neither confirms nor rejects such practice. In this sense such evidence is negative.

For the second group of asides, the evidence is positive. The asides are so inserted into the dialogue that the actor has no opportunity to separate himself from the other characters. I italicize the aside.

> FRIEND. [to Timon] The swallow follows not summer
>   more willing than we your lordship.
> TIMON.   *Nor more willingly leaves winter; such*
>   *summer birds are men.*—Gentlemen, our
>   dinner will not recompense this long stay.
>   [*Timon of Athens*, III, vi, 31–35]

In addition to instances of this sort of aside, there are examples of an aside within a speech of a character. Master Page plans with his wife, Master and Mistress Ford, and the Parson to trap Falstaff at Herne's Oak, where he will be assaulted by pinching fairies. Page offers to provide the material for the fairy garments.

> PAGE.   That silke will I go buy, *and in that time*
> *Shall M. Slender steale my Nan away,*
> *And marry her at Eaton:* go, send to
> Falstaffe straight.
> [*The Merry Wives of Windsor,* IV, iv, 73–75. F.]

In such speeches, the actor had no time realistically and credibly to leave the individual or group to whom he was speaking. A slight turn of the body or face or a change in voice had to suffice. But the evidence of *Pericles* indicates that the action may have been deliberate and emphatic rather than precipitous and surreptitious. The abundance of asides is sufficient testimony that their delivery was not slighted. However, instead of suggesting by the division of solo asides into two groups that there were two methods of delivery, I suggest that the first group, for which the evidence is negative, were staged in the same way as the second, that is, not realistically but conventionally.

The asides were spoken from all parts of the stage. Actors delivered them from the enclosure as well as from the very front of the stage. Both Marina and Pericles speak rather long asides from the cabin or tent of Pericles' ship, certainly a discovered setting (V, i, 95–97, 163–167). But there is no specific evidence that indicates the method of delivery. The traditional picture of the cliché aside being delivered by the actor out of the corner of his mouth or from behind the back of his hand as he leans toward the spectator did not originate in the Globe playhouse. Instead, as the following scene from *Troilus and Cressida* shows, the actor cultivated the irony or mockery of the aside quite overtly. Perhaps the other actors had to "freeze" during the aside, for there is no indication that they covered the solo aside with action as they did the conversational aside.

Occasionally, an elaborate pattern of asides is unfolded, often including conversational and solo asides in the same sequence. In these extended asides the formal character of staging at the Globe is readily perceptible. One particularly mannered example occurs in *Troilus and Cressida.* Ulysses has convinced the Grecian chiefs that they must pit Ajax against Achilles if they are to gain the services of the latter. Following this advice, Agamemnon flatters Ajax, stirring his pride and vanity. Ulysses seconds Agamemnon, asserting that Ajax should not be asked to go to Achilles as a messenger. I quote at length, italicizing the asides so that the pattern may be clear.

NEST.	*O, this is well! He rubs the vein of him.*
DIOM.	*And how his silence drinks up this applause!*
AJAX.	If I go to him, with my armed fist
	I'll pash him o'er the face.
AGAM.	O, no, you shall not go.
AJAX.	An 'a be proud with me, I'll pheese his pride.
	Let me go to him.
ULYS.	Not for the worth that hangs upon our quarrel.
AJAX.	A paltry insolent fellow!
NEST.	*How he describes himself!*
AJAX.	Can he not be sociable?
ULYS.	*The raven chides blackness.*
AJAX.	I'll let his humours blood.
AGAM.	*He will be the physician that should be the patient.*
AJAX.	An all men were o' my mind—
ULYS.	*Wit would be out of fashion.*
AJAX.	'A should not bear it so, 'a should eat swords first.
	Shall pride carry it?
NEST.	*An 'twould, you'ld carry half.*
ULYS.	*'A would have ten shares.*
AJAX.	I will knead him; I'll make him supple.
NEST.	*He's not yet through warm. Force him with praises.*
	Pour in, pour in; his ambition is dry.

[II, iii, 210–234]

This scene is a charade, not a realistic dramatic situation. Ajax talks at times as though no one else were present. Perhaps he turns away, but there is no need. It is far more likely that Nestor and Ulysses stand on one side, since they converse together and Nestor urges Ulysses on at the end, and Agamemnon and Diomedes on the other side. Ajax remains between them. There is no evidence for this arrangement, but it accords with the tendency toward symmetrical design previously discussed.

Within the limitations of the evidence, two apparently contradictory methods of staging emerge. The method of the conversational aside seems realistic, the method of the solo aside conventional. Does this mean that the Globe company practiced a mixed style of staging? I do not believe so. Although the conversational aside appears to strive for credibility in staging, it does not try to make the motivation for separating the speaker and nonspeaker credible. When Banquo calls to Angus and Ross, "Cousins, a word, I pray," he has no reason to do so other than to leave Macbeth free to speak. His comments upon Macbeth's reception of the new honors are hardly the reasons. Similarly, the phrase with which Hamlet draws Rosencrantz and Guildenstern to him, "at each ear a hearer," does not lead to a realistic scene, for Hamlet, speaking aside to them, mocks Polonius who stands before Hamlet but is not supposed to hear him. There is a genuine difference in the methods of staging the two types of asides, but its purpose, I suggest, was to differentiate the kinds of asides and to preserve a clear story line. In the conversational aside the speakers draw apart, for they have to indicate which actors are supposed to hear the conversation. In the solo aside the speaker remains where he is, for his delivery indicates that no one else hears him. Both were devices, equally conventional in form, and yet regularly staged in variant methods to further the narrative.

Closely allied to the aside in structure is the type of scene that I shall call the "observation" scene. In the observation scene one or more characters on-stage, unseen whether hidden or not, observe and usually overhear other characters on-stage. In the course of the observation the observer or observers may or may not comment. In essence, the situation is contrived, although the scene in which no comments are made is more plausible than that in which comments, unheard by the observed, are uttered. But the asides have already demonstrated the basic conventionality of Elizabethan theatrical devices. The observation scene is of the same nature.

The observation scenes can be most easily studied by dividing them into those in which the observers speak and those in which they do not. Where the observers do not speak, the problem of placement is greatly simplified. In several cases, for example, the observers actually go off-stage. The location of the exit used in such cases is revealed in *Hamlet*. Before going to the Queen, Polonius tells the King,

> Behind the arras I'll convey myself
> To hear the process.
> 　　　　　[III, iii, 28–29]

As he and the Queen await Hamlet in her closet, he presumably indicates the same place when he tells her,

> I'll silence me even here.
> 　　　　[III, iv, 4]

In the Quarto of 1603, Corambis (Polonius) is more explicit.

> Madame, I heare yong Hamlet comming,
> I'le shrowde my selfe behinde the Arras.
> 　　　　exit Cor.
> 　　　　　　[Sig. G2ʳ]

Earlier in the play, in preparation for a different observation, Polonius arranged with the King to observe Hamlet as

> 　　　　he walks four hours together
> Here in the lobby. . . .
> At such a time I'll loose my daughter to him,
> Be you and I behind an arras then.
> 　　　　　　[II, ii, 160–163]

As the moment for the observation approaches, the King explains the plan to the Queen.

> Her father and myself (lawful espials)
> Will so bestow ourselves that, seeing unseen,
> We may of their encounter frankly judge.
>> [III, i, 32–34]

Upon hearing Hamlet approach, Polonius calls to the King,

> I hear him coming. Let's withdraw, my lord.
>> [III, i, 55]

This is the same phrase the Queen uses to Polonius in her closet.

> Withdraw; I hear him coming.
>> [III, iv, 7]

The stage direction specifies "Exeunt" for the King and Polonius. In both scenes the observers or observer are to be behind an arras, in both scenes they withdraw at the sound of the unsuspecting Hamlet. The location of the arras behind which the King and Polonius hide is indicated in the First Quarto. Instead of the lines already quoted, which appear in the Folio and the Second Quarto:

> At such a time I'll loose my daughter to him,
> Be you and I behind an arras then.

the First Quarto reads:

> There let Ofelia walke untill hee comes:
> Your selfe and I will stand close in the study.
>> [Sig. D4^v, 14–15]

The word "study" in the Globe plays regularly refers to the enclosure. Therefore, although all texts specify the same place, the Folio and Second Quarto refer to the hanging in front of the study and the First Quarto refers to the study behind the hanging.

A similar observation scene occurs in *Measure for Measure.* While the disguised Duke is consoling Claudio in prison, Isabella, his sister, visits him. Yielding the prisoner to her, the Duke draws the Provost aside and says:

> Bring me to hear them speak,
> where I may be conceal'd.
> [III, i, 52–53]

Kittredge marks an exit at this point and an entrance before line 152. He may be correct, for an "exit" follows the King's and Polonius' withdrawal behind the arras and an "entrance" precedes their emergence. In the First Quarto Corambis' withdrawal behind the arras is also marked "exit." I suggest, of course, that the Duke, like the King and Polonius, withdraws behind the arras to overhear Isabella and Claudio and emerges at the conclusion of their conversation.[15]

There are other scenes where silent observers remain on stage. In these scenes the observers sometimes interrupt the scene that they observe. When this happens, it is not always clear whether or not they hide behind some object or otherwise endeavor to secrete themselves until they make their presence known. Sometimes the observer definitely hides. A scene of this sort occurs in *The Devil's Charter* (III, v). Frescobaldi is waiting for Caesar to enter with the man whom he is to murder. The clock strikes the hour.

> This mine hower appoynted, this the place,
> Here will I stand close till tha' llarum call,
> he stands behind the post.
> [Sig. F3ᵛ]

Immediately thereafter Caesar and the Duke of Candie enter. Frescobaldi observes them from behind the post. The same post, or stage pillar, was probably used in the Shakespearean scenes in the same way although in all but one of the scenes there is no reference to the actor's hiding himself. In *As You Like It* there are two observation scenes (II, iv; III, v) in which no evident action is taken by the observers to hide themselves. The opening scene of *Antony and Cleopatra* is of the same sort. In these instances the need for secrecy is much less pressing than in the other situations. Perhaps it was the practice of the characters to hide only when the situation demanded it.

Those scenes during which the observer speaks involve more complex problems of staging. Of these the "handkerchief" scene in *Othello* (IV, i) is the most intricate. At first, Othello, observing Iago and Cassio, can hear them laugh but cannot hear them speak. Next, he can hear them satisfactorily. Finally, he can see the handkerchief clearly when Bianca flings it at Cassio. The first phase is set by Iago's suggestion to Othello to "encave" himself. Upon Cassio's arrival, Iago asks Othello: "Will you withdraw?" During the scene with Cassio, Iago apparently motions to Othello to come closer, for Othello says:

> Iago beckons me. Now he begins the story.
> [IV, i, 135]

It is hazardous to take the description of the hiding place literally. In the course of the various observation scenes, the stage posts are apparently called "this hedge corner" (*All's Well*, IV, i, 2) and "the turn" (*Timon*, V, i, 50). It is possible, of course, that Othello does not move, the change from his inability to hear the conversation to his ability to hear it being conveyed by his line: "Now he begins the story." But I think it more likely that he does "encave" himself, that is, he partly hides himself behind the arras. When Iago beckons to him, he moves to one of the posts.

There is only one instance for which a property may have been used as a hiding place. In order to see the effect of the forged letter upon Malvolio, Toby, Fabian, and Andrew follow Maria's instructions to get all three "into the box tree" (II, v, 17). If the property were used, it was probably thrust out or carried out from the enclosure and placed in the center of the stage. All the same, the box tree is not really required. No further mention is made of it. To the business and lines of the three observers, it contributes neither humor nor protection. Thus, the completeness and kind of concealment really depended upon the narrative point which had to be emphasized.

Not the credibility of the observation but the clarity of its rendition governed the manner of its staging.

All the devices thus far inspected reveal the same characteristic of being no more conventional than the story requires. This is particularly true of the observation scene. Where the observer is not needed on stage until the scene that he is watching is ended, he is sent off-stage. Where the observer is needed to interrupt at one point, he is hidden simply and conveniently. Where the observer must comment on the scene before him, he is prominently placed. The yardstick is always relevance to the story. The situation is always as credible as it can be, but the creation of credibility is never an end in itself. These conditions hold true for the staging of disguise scenes too.

Several scholars have studied the disguise scene in terms of either its dramatic form or its psychological import.[16] Paul Kreider, for example, emphasizes the careful preparation which precedes the assumption of disguise in Shakespeare's plays. Although he does not consider the methods for staging the disguise, he makes it clear that Shakespeare always informs the audience who is disguised. Here I shall only consider how the character is disguised.

The basic method of disguise is through a change of costume. Almost invariably this change furnishes the foundation for the disguise. In the Shakespearean Globe plays there are seventeen instances of disguise, of which five rely wholly and six mainly on a change of costume (see Appendix C, chart i). In the non-Shakespearean Globe plays, of fifteen cases, four rely wholly and six mainly on a change of costume. Even when a different costume is not the sole method of disguise, it is almost always introduced as an important supplement. Fourteen of the seventeen disguised characters in Shakespeare change their dress; thirteen of the fifteen in the non-Shakespearean plays do so too.

Next in frequency and importance in effecting a disguise is a change of manner. In addition to changing his clothing, the character adjusts or alters his bearing or attitude. The Duke

becomes paternal in *Measure for Measure;* Harbart becomes as
blunt as his alias, Blunt, in *Fair Maid of Bristow;* Vindice in
The Revenger's Tragedy becomes familiar in his first disguise,
then melancholy; Edgar becomes a Bedlamite. The degree of
change in manner depends upon the situation in the play. The
most complete changes, such as Edgar's, have dramatic purposes other than disguise. Of the disguises in Shakespeare's
Globe plays, eight show change in manner. In the non-Shakespearean plays eight definitely and one possibly show change in
manner. A change in voice is occasionally introduced although
the evidence may be deceptive. Kent speaks of "razing likeness"
and "changing accents" but, as *The Revenger's Tragedy* shows,
the latter phrase can refer to manner as well as speech. Vindice,
who has appeared before Lussurioso in one disguise, is about to
assume another one for a new interview. Hippolito cautions
him.

> How will you appear in fashion different,
> As well as in apparel, to make all things possible?
>
> .   .   .   .   .
>
> *You must change tongue:* familiar was your first.
> Vin.   Why, I'll bear me in some strain of melancholy,
>   And string myself with heavy-sounding wire,
>   Like such an instrument, that speaks merry
>   things sadly.
>
> > [IV, ii, 22–29. My italics]

The change of tongue to which Hippolito refers is not a vocal
or dialect change, but as the context clearly shows, a change
of temperament or manner.

Occasionally, but rarely, a dialect aids a disguise. Generally,
Shakespeare seems to call upon the actor to change his voice
somewhat more than his fellow dramatists seem to have done.
There are four examples of change excluding the instance of
Kent examined above. In the non-Shakespearean plays only one
instance occurs. However, it is equally necessary to note that
in the disguises of Rosalind and Viola, particularly that of the
latter, Shakespeare is careful to show that the voices do not
change.

A change in face is rarely employed in disguise. Only one case certainly occurs in Shakespeare, that of Feste in *Twelfth Night*, though two others probably occur. In the non-Shakespearean plays there is only one case of facial disguise. Where facial disguise is introduced, it is always in highly simplified form. Of the four certain and possible examples, two require beards, one depends upon a smirched face, and one introduces a false scar.

In all disguises simplicity is the keynote. Several discoveries of the disguised character's identity require speed in changing costume. The friars remove their hoods to identify themselves. Others may remove a hat or some other part of clothing. Often recognition of the true person comes only when the character names himself. Generally the surprise and wonderment of the other characters at the revelation of the disguise is out of proportion to the device of revelation or the means of disguise. That disproportion emphasizes the conventional element in disguise.

Disguise staging is simple, nominal, and somewhat standardized. At the same time the authors take some pains to make the disguise credible to the other characters. Several scenes occur where the disguised figure is not known in his true person to the other character or characters. In those situations mere assertion of the disguise is sometimes sufficient. In the disguise of Old Flowerdale in *The London Prodigal* a false scar, removed at the end, is a symbol of disguise. Yet in the same play Luce assumes a maidservant's dress and a Dutch accent in order to parade as a Dutch "vrow." Here again the conventional scene is tempered by efforts to account plausibly for the disguise. By and large, symbolic methods play little part in effecting disguise. That is why I have introduced the adjective "nominal." Through uncomplicated means, such as a change of dress, disguise is signified to the audience. But the completeness of the disguise is insufficient to convince an audience that the character would pass undetected. In that sense it is nominal, a token of disguise, without becoming a sign of a deeper disguise, that is, without becoming symbolic. Shakespeare is slightly more realistic in his treatment of disguise than are his colleagues. But the differences are too minute to count. The most complete disguises in Shakespeare, involving all four means examined above, are those of Feste and Edgar. In each case the completeness, as Maria says of Feste,[17] is not to ensure disguise but to elicit for Feste richer comedy and for Edgar deeper pathos and sharper contrast with the mad Lear. Disguise scenes are usually staged according to recurrent principles which are varied no more than the narrative or dramatic purpose demands.

To draw a detailed picture of staging at the Globe, it would be desirable to consider all the recurrent scenes minutely. But this is not feasible in a study of this length. Instead, I must depend upon the dissection of several types of scenes which can best reflect Globe conditions. The remaining scenes which I shall describe, because of the nature of the material or the preciseness of the evidence, complement the scenes already examined. These include the appearances of ghosts, the delivery of greetings and farewells, and the reports of messengers.

There are eight ghost sequences in the Globe plays, six in Shakespeare's plays,[18] two in *The Devil's Charter*. The prologue of *A Warning for Fair Women*, a pre-Globe play, contains evidence that the ghosts were physically represented by being shrouded in a sheet or leather pilch (Sig. A2ʳ). However, Hamlet's father is specifically described as "Arm'd at all points" (I, ii, 200). In the First Quarto a stage direction specifies that the Ghost wears "a night gown" in Act III, scene iv (Sig. G2ʳ), although Hamlet describes him as being in his habit as he lived (III, iv, 135). These contradictions would indicate that there was no regular practice for costuming a ghost.

In the staging of the ghost scenes, however, there seems to have been conformity. The one non-Shakespearean play which portrays ghosts, *The Devil's Charter*, describes the staging exactly.

> [A devil] goeth to one doore of the stage, from whence he bringeth the Ghost of Candie gastly haunted by Caesar persuing and stabing it, these vanish in at another doore.

Later in the same scene,

> He bringeth from the same doore Gismond Viselli,
> · his wounds gaping and after him Lucrece undrest,
> holding a dagger fix't in his bleeding bosome:
> they vanish.
>
> > [Sig. G2ʳ]

Later in the play,

> The Divell bringeth forth from the doore Lucreciaes
> Ghost, and after her the ghost of Candie stabbed.
>
> > [Sig. M2ʳ]

Stage directions early in the scenes place these actions forward on the stage so that there is no doubt that the stage doors are the ones described as the entries for the ghosts.

W. J. Lawrence, some years ago, attempted to prove that the Ghost in the first scene of *Hamlet* rose through the front trap. His conclusion was based on the argument that since Horatio, Marcellus, and Bernardo are seated on stools and are looking ahead, the only way "by which the Ghost could suddenly make itself visible to the three [is] by emerging in front of them through a trap." [19]

The dialogue of the characters contradicts this theory, however. On the entrance of the Ghost, Marcellus cries:

> Peace! break thee off! Look where it comes
> again!
> BERN. · In the same figure, like the King that's dead. . . .
> BERN. See, it stalks away.
>
> > [I, i, 40–41, 50]

After the Ghost leaves the first time, Marcellus describes the visitations of the previous nights.

> Thus twice before, and jump at this dead hour,
> With martial stalke, hath he gone by our watch.
> > [I, i, 65–66]

The First Quarto is more graphic.

> With Marshall stalke he passed through our watch.
> [Sig. B2ʳ]

In the next scene, when Horatio describes the initial events to Hamlet, he states that at first the Ghost appeared before Marcellus and Bernardo,

> and with solemn march
> Goes slow and stately by them. Thrice he walked
> By their oppressed and fear-surprised eyes,
> Within his truncheon's length.
> [I, ii, 201–204.]

All these descriptions suggest that the Ghost entered through one of the doors, crossed the stage, and departed at another door.

When Hamlet awaits the Ghost, Horatio is the first to see it.

> Look my lord, it comes.
> [I, iv, 38]

Hamlet addresses the Ghost, urging it to answer. During this time there is opportunity for the Ghost to cross to the opposite door, then beckon to Hamlet to follow. Hamlet follows the Ghost through the door and five lines later Horatio and Marcellus follow them. Immediately the Ghost, trailed by Hamlet, enters through the door that he first used.

The final exit of the Ghost, according to Lawrence, is through the trap. The fact that the Ghost cries from the "cellarage" makes this suggestion convincing. It must be observed, though, that the Ghost does not speak until fifty-seven lines after he exits, or nearly three minutes later. Furthermore, John C. Adams has shown that the use of the main trap is usually accompanied by thunder to cover the sound of the trap mechanism. If this were the practice, the exit through the trap is unlikely.

The last of the ghost scenes in *Hamlet*, that in the Queen's closet, is reminiscent of the other scenes. The Ghost enters, presumably through the stage door, chides his "tardy son" and departs. Endeavoring to convince Gertrude of his sanity, Hamlet describes the departure.

> Why, look you there! Look how it steals away!
> My father, in his habit as he liv'd!
> Look where he goes even now out at the portal!
> [III, iv, 134–136]

"Portal," in the Oxford English Dictionary, is defined as "a door, gate, doorway, or gateway, of stately or elaborate construction." Only the outer stage doors can satisfy this definition. Thus, Hamlet's description of the departure can pertain only to one of the outer stage doors. I offer a conjectural reconstruction of this scene. After Hamlet slays Polonius, who has been hiding behind the arras at the rear of the stage, he draws his mother forward, seating her upon one of the stools distributed about the stage. The pictures of the royal brothers, probably hanging on a wall of the façade, if the evidence of *A Warning for Fair Women* is applicable,[20] are unveiled by Hamlet, who then comes downstage toward Gertrude. Thus, when the Ghost enters, he comes on stage behind mother and son and in front of his own picture. At the sight of the Ghost, Hamlet falls to his knees. After admonishing his son, the Ghost completes his crossing and "steals away . . . even now out at the portal."

For the staging of the last two ghost scenes, the evidence is scanty. Banquo's ghost enters and sits at the banquet table twice. Since the table is forward on the stage, Banquo presumably follows the same course as the other ghosts, entering at one stage door, sitting, and leaving at the other door. Despite a modern predilection for more elaborate stage trickery, there is no evidence that the stage machinery was employed in the staging of ghost scenes at the Globe. The last of the ghost scenes confirms the evidence of the other plays. Brutus is seated in his tent, reading a book. The Ghost of Caesar appears. The lines of Brutus imply that the Ghost walks toward him. At first Brutus says:

> Who comes here? . . . It comes upon me.
> [IV, iii, 275–278]

Finally, as the Ghost departs, he cries:

> Now I have taken heart thou vanishest.
> [287]

The last verb may be deceptive. In *The Devil's Charter* the stage direction "they vanish" describes the departure of the ghosts through an outer door. In *Jeronimo* a ghost is said to have vanished though he still delivers another five lines before he exits through the stage door. Altogether the evidence indicates that the ghost scenes were staged with a minimum use of stage properties or machinery, with great simplicity and with standard methods.

In Shakespeare's Globe plays there are forty-one farewell or greeting scenes of different degrees of elaboration. These amenities do not seem to have been perfunctory affairs, casually staged, but were ceremonious in manner, much more so than modern productions reveal. Embracing, particularly in farewells, handshaking, and kneeling all played a part in the ritual of greeting and bidding farewell. Whenever one person meets or leaves a group, he does so formally, witness *Troilus and Cressida*, Act IV, scene v, which contains greetings to both Cressida and Hector. Perhaps the hails of the witches to Macbeth were in imitation of courtly greetings. The manner of greeting can be glimpsed through the jaundiced eyes of Apemantus as he watches Timon welcome Alcibiades, obviously with bows and genuflections.

> So, so there!
> Aches contract and starve your supple joints!
> [I, i, 256–257]

To a superior figure, whether King (*All's Well*, I, ii), Protector (*Pericles*, I, iv), or mother (*Coriolanus*, II, i), kneeling was the accepted manner of greeting or being greeted. Although doffing the hat was the accepted sign of greeting a superior, among equals bowing or shaking hands was usual.

Embracing of men appears quite clearly in farewell scenes. Antony and Caesar embrace at parting (III, ii, 61–64), as do Flavius, Timon's steward, and his fellows in *Timon of Athens*, (IV, ii, 29 f.). The farewell without ceremony, which Helen receives from Bertram (*All's Well*, II, v, 59–97) is particularly offensive. In the same way as in greeting, the departing character, when he leaves a group, formalizes his farewells by making the rounds (*Coriolanus*, IV, i). Tears usually flow at such a farewell. Every group farewell scene in Shakespeare where a woman is present is bathed in tears (Virgilia in *Coriolanus*, IV, i; Octavia in *Antony and Cleopatra*, III, ii; Lychorida in *Pericles*, III, iii; Cordelia in *Lear*, I, i, 271). Natural patterns of decorum as well as inclinations toward uniformity characterize these scenes as a whole. Although standard external means of greeting and bidding farewell exist throughout the plays, they are observed with ceremony and rendered with deliberation.

Most of the scenes or devices considered heretofore are relatively uniform in manner and frequency throughout the Globe plays, Shakespearean and non-Shakespearean alike. The messenger, however, is a unique figure peculiar to Shakespeare. On the average, about five messengers appear in each of Shakespeare's Globe plays, compared to an average of about one in each of the non-Shakespearean plays. Shakespeare's messengers may be divided into two classes. Fairly often a character in a play will assume the function of the messenger in order to deliver a report. Essentially, this is what Gertrude does when she describes the death of Ophelia (*Hamlet*, IV, vii). Characters as messengers generally do not assume a special manner but continue to maintain their own identities.

The other type of messenger is the formal messenger. There are forty-three of these as compared to thirty-one character messengers in Shakespeare's Globe plays. The generic messenger usually has no identity. His manner is often theatrical rather than natural. This is particularly evident when he does not inform but directs the superior characters (*Julius Caesar*, V, i,

12–15; *Coriolanus,* II, i, 276–284). Occasionally the situation demands some veil of characterization (*Antony and Cleopatra,* II, v; *Julius Caesar,* III, i). In those instances the messenger takes on the qualities of a servant.

The dramatic function of the messenger was to change the course of the scene, to bring some outside force to bear upon the characters on stage, and, by doing so, to provoke some alteration in the passions or actions of the characters. The salutation accorded the messenger is usually brief, yet attention is clearly focused upon him. The usual respect of servant to master does not seem to be present, but instead it is replaced by an imperious manner. A curious feature of the staging is that no exit is marked for the formal messenger after he delivers his message. Sometimes he is dismissed by the one who receives the message, sometimes he is held back to answer questions, but it is not clear where he goes or how he joins the rest of the actors. I am inclined to believe that he usually exits immediately after delivering his message. There are several scenes in which a series of messengers enter to report a changing situation (*Coriolanus,* IV, vi, 37–79; *Troilus and Cressida,* V, v). The effect of mounting pressure depends upon the repeated entrance and exit of the messengers. The intensification such scenes require could be effectively produced by the entrance of the messenger at one door, and after his report, by his exit at another. If this were regular practice at the Globe, the playwright did not need to mark an exit for him.

The formal messenger is an example of a purely conventional figure who is not symbolic. Whether he had a prototype in Elizabethan life or he was a creation of dramatic technique, he still emerged as a conventional figure, changing little from Caesar's Rome to Macbeth's Scotland. Attention was concentrated on his function—not his character. Therefore, he was granted a forthrightness of expression not found in other stage servants.

Excluded from the study of staging have been many scenes which depend primarily upon acting. In these scenes, which make up large segments of the plays, the qualities of clear speech and passionate action play the major part. A discussion

of their staging would be fruitless because the method of staging them has little influence upon the final effect. Most numerous among these scenes are those devoted to plotting,
singing, word-play, commentary upon character or situation,
railing against another, and pleading. Scenes of mocking and
loving follow closely behind these.

Among these scenes are some of the greatest expressions of
Shakespeare's dramatic powers. For example, there are twenty
pleading episodes in Shakespeare's Globe plays. This score in-
cludes Portia's plea to Brutus for confidence (*Julius Caesar*, II,
i), Isabella's plea to Angelo for Claudio's life (*Measure for
Measure*, II, ii), and perhaps the finest example of all, Volumnia's plea to Coriolanus for Rome's salvation (V, iii). But few
of these derive their powers from elements of staging. Where
they are located on-stage does not matter much, for they create
an environment of their own. Yet scenes such as these need
dimension. If the actors kneel and plead, they need scope to do
so. That is why it is hazardous to depart from the conditions
of the open platform in reconstructing the staging.

The handling of entrance and exit and the representation
of the conventional devices and scenes provide the framework
of the staging. Interwoven and interpolated are those scenes
which rely not on formal presentation but on spontaneous
action. These are the scenes which, through the intensity of
their poetic conception, the penetration of their observation,
or the keenness of their wit, illuminate the stage. But no sharp
distinction exists between the conventional device and the
spontaneous action. They both spring from the need to sustain
and perfect an extended narrative.

V. THE STAGING OF THE FINALES

The art of staging in the Elizabethan theater reaches its cul-
mination in the ritualistic finale which usually brings the narrative to a close. The dramatic nature of the finale has been
fully discussed in Chapter Two. Its theatrical execution may
fittingly conclude this chapter.

Most of the finales depict a sequence of action foreknown

to the audience but not to the figure or figures central to the action. This fact contributes greatly to the ritualistic impression of the finale. Thematically, the finale completes the process of rendering judgment and rewarding faithfulness or love. This process is elaborately and meticulously worked out so that all possible complications of the narrative are unraveled.

Theatrically, it is accomplished in one of two ways. The final "mystery" is solved with the ranking person usually directing the process (*All's Well, Twelfth Night, Measure for Measure*), or a final conflict takes place between a figure rendering judgment, a champion, as in *Lear,* and a figure receiving judgment. Thus, pictorially, there can be one of three centers of focus: the judge, the combat, the revealed mystery. In some cases the rendering of judgment is effected by the central character upon himself, as in *Julius Caesar, Antony and Cleopatra,* and *Othello.* Othello, who has been touched by Christian morality, is conscious of rendering self-judgment. Brutus and Cleopatra, instead, commit suicide in the high Roman fashion.

About two-thirds of the finales begin with only one or two characters on stage who set the conditions for the finale (*Antony and Cleopatra, Twelfth Night, The Merry Wives of Windsor, Othello,* and so on). Once the basic premises are assured, the essential action takes place. In *Twelfth Night* it centers about the contradictory accusations against Viola. In *Julius Caesar* and *Antony and Cleopatra,* Brutus and Cleopatra probe the necessity for death and direct the preparations for suicide, the latter more elaborately than the former, of course. The finales of *Measure for Measure* and *All's Well* follow a similar pattern: a ruler seeks the answer to a mystery by holding a hearing.

All concluding dramatic situations have a courtly or martial formality, except for the finales of *Merry Wives, Othello,* and *Troilus and Cressida.* The finales of *Hamlet, All's Well, Measure for Measure, As You Like It, Twelfth Night,* and *Antony and Cleopatra* reveal a courtly formality of one sort or another. In these scenes the subordinate figures are grouped in relation to the sovereign. This fact alone favors symmetrical balance in the design. For example, the King in *All's Well*, after first welcoming Bertram, is prompted by seeing Helen's ring on his finger to question the manner of her death. 'All action is related to the King. Probably standing at center, he receives and dismisses Bertram from one door and receives Diana from the other. In *Hamlet*, the duel is the focal action of the scene. The placement of the King and Queen, however, dictates the grouping of the court. The stage directions specify that a table with flagons of wine upon it is brought in (*Hamlet*, V, ii, 235f.). The stage direction in the Quarto of 1604 calls for "cushions" which may have been placed on the stools (Sig. N3ᵛ). But apparently no state is introduced. Therefore, the King and Queen probably stand or possibly sit in the center, well enough downstage to be easily seen, the duelists fight before them, and the court is grouped behind them. Until the entrance of Fortinbras, the only speakers are the King, Queen, Hamlet, Laertes, Osric, and, briefly, Horatio, who speaks once when Hamlet is wounded and once when Hamlet is dying. Even this résumé does not convey any idea of the actual sequence of the speeches. No more than two or three people speak in any one part of the scene. The members of the court, placed at the sides and the rear of the stage, are called upon only once to cry "Treason, treason." Otherwise they are virtually ignored. Earlier in this chapter I outlined the finale of *As You Like It* in the same way, to show the division of the scene into episodes of twos and threes. To formalize the grouping, Shakespeare introduced Duke Senior into all the episodes, thus using him as a point of reference.

Where martial conditions prevail at the conclusion, the grouping is governed by the presence of the triumphant general or prince. Malcolm, hailed as King of Scotland, is ringed about by his thanes. At first Alcibiades is engaged in a parley with the Athenian Senators, but when they leave the walls, he is left completely alone. In *Julius Caesar* the opposite happens, for the defeated leader is the center of interest. One by one, Brutus approaches the remnants of his supporters, who are ranged about him, to persuade one of them to slay him. Finally, the last man gratifies his wish. Even when the conquering generals enter, his body remains the center of attention, thanks to Antony's eulogy.

Merry Wives and *Othello*, having neither courtly nor martial finales, rely on a different kind of focal point. In the former play, the place where Falstaff, the object of ridicule, hides from the "Fairies," determines the design of the scene. In *Othello*, the location of Desdemona's bed initially dictates the arrangement of the scene. But when the final truth is known and Iago is arrested, Lodovico supersedes the bed as the keystone of the grouping although Othello naturally remains the figure of greatest interest. This shift of focus from one center to another during the scene and the succeeding diffusion of focus near the end, make staging the finale of *Othello* upon the Globe stage extremely difficult. Constant reference to the bed early in the scene requires the actors to turn toward the rear of the stage, even if the bed is thrust out. The text demands that Othello, Emilia, and Gratiano, at the very least, relate themselves to the deathbed for considerable periods of time. This kind of finale is peculiar to *Othello*, lacking as it does a constant focal point and formal grouping. The explanation may be that the extant texts, Folio and Quarto, embody the version played upon a shallow stage at Blackfriars. Mounted upon such a stage rather than upon the deep stage of the Globe, the finale could be more effectively presented.

The grouping, as I have shown, usually depends upon the placement of the sovereign or triumphant figure. The progress of the finale, however, is controlled in large measure by the degree and kind of activity in which the ranking figure (or figures) engages. In *As You Like It* Duke Senior, being passive, is more a point to which the action relates than a figure who directs the action. Orsino and Olivia in *Twelfth Night* jointly direct the uncovering of the mystery by calling upon others to act rather than by acting themselves. The focus thus lies between them. In contrast, the Duke in *Measure for Measure* not only serves as the center of attention but also acts as the central force in bringing the "mystery" of the action to light. *Lear* reveals an interesting finale which shifts the centers of interest from the single combat of Edmund and Edgar, first to the display of the bodies of Goneril and Regan, and then to the entrance and death of Lear. But throughout these orderly shifts of attention the ranking figure, the Duke of Albany, functions effectively but unobtrusively. It is he who questions Edgar, orders the disposal of the bodies of the evil sisters, directs the burial of Lear, and speaks the final words.[21] Although himself never of central interest, his presence at the center of the action is necessary to the unity of the finale.

The last factor that influences the staging of the finale is the introduction of a resolving figure, found in many of the plays. He may be either of critical or of supplementary importance to the completion of the action. It is his presence which unravels the mystery. Sebastian is the resolving figure in *Twelfth Night*. His entrance unties all the knots at once. However, because *Twelfth Night* contains a double plot, Fabian is needed to explain the trick played upon Malvolio, thus serving as a supplementary resolving figure. Similarly, Edgar and Lear are resolving figures for their respective plots. Further illustrations include the Duke in *Measure for Measure* and Helen in *All's Well*. For a spectacular effect, Shakespeare introduces Hymen as a resolving figure in *As You Like It*. His words to the assembled lovers could very well speak for all the resolving figures.

> Peace ho! I bar confusion.
> 'Tis I must make conclusion
> Of these most strange events.
> [V, iv, 131–133]

It is interesting to see that instead of relying upon the enclosure curtain to effect a sudden discovery, Shakespeare introduced an allegorical figure to make the revelation of Rosalind theatrical. The revelation, therefore, had to be processional, with Hymen acting as marshal. Virtually the same pattern occurs in the finale of *All's Well* where the widow leads in Helen. Under special circumstances, a discovery can be made without using the stage curtain. Enveloped in his friar's hood, the Duke in *Measure for Measure*, as his own resolving figure, can enter undetected. Lucio, by plucking off the friar's hood, accomplishes a sudden discovery.

Ranking figures may also serve as minor resolving figures. Such characters as Fortinbras in *Hamlet*, Caesar in *Antony and Cleopatra,* and Antony in *Julius Caesar* bring events to a close by delivering a eulogy over the fallen hero. Their entrances are processional; their departures are dead marches, in which the body or bodies of the slain are carried off. Another group of minor resolving figures are those entering with information necessary to the disentanglement of the complete narrative. Fabian, as I have shown, is one of these. So also is Fenton in *Merry Wives* and the soldier in *Timon of Athens.*

The entryway through which the major resolving figures come is crucial to the staging. For this the plays provide no satisfactory clues. Diana's lines which precede the revelation that Helen lives could easily imply a discovery.

> He [Bertram] knows himself my bed he hath
>   defil'd,
> And at that time he got his wife with child.
> Dead though she be, she feels her young one kick.
> So there's my riddle: one that's dead is quick—
> And now behold the meaning.
>   Enter Helen and Widow.
> KING.   Is there no exorcist
>   Beguiles the truer office of mine eyes?
>   [V, iii, 301–306]

Similar situations occur in *As You Like It* and *Twelfth Night.* In *As You Like It* the revelation is heralded by music which suggests a processional entrance. In *Twelfth Night* Sebastian follows Toby on stage in order to justify his treatment of Toby. These scenes by analogy indicate the unlikelihood that Helen was discovered by the drawing of the curtain of the enclosure. Yet in all these scenes the resolving figures must enter prominently, for upon their entrance they occupy the center of attention. I suggest, therefore, that to achieve maximum effect and to preserve symmetry, these entrances were made through the curtain at the rear of the stage.

Throughout this chapter I have stressed dramatic factors usually ignored, and minimized factors usually stressed. The theory of staging which emerges, therefore, departs in some ways from the views generally accepted. I have emphasized that, in re-creating Globe stage practices, we must be cautious:

(1) Not to reconstruct staging only in terms of settings;

(2) Not to disregard or underestimate the vital role that the entrances and exits played in the artistic organization of the productions;

(3) Not to neglect the inclination of the Globe company towards uniformity in staging;

(4) Not to overvalue the necessity or even the desirability of novelty in staging;

(5) Not to underestimate the ability of the Elizabethan narrative to shape its own principles of staging;

(6) Not to assume that staging at the Globe occupied as crucial a role in rehearsing and performing a play as it does, aesthetically and organizationally, in the theater today.

Chapter Six

THE STYLE

THE CONCLUSIONS which I have drawn in this essay apply only to production at the Globe playhouse from 1599 to 1609. From them it is clear that the staging of the plays was influenced less by the structure of the stage than we have hitherto thought. When William Poel undertook to demonstrate how a knowledge of the use of an Elizabethan stage is conducive to a proper appreciation of Elizabethan plays, he embarked upon a necessary and salutary crusade. Almost every recent Shakespearean production attests to its success. However, the effect of his campaign has led to an overemphasis upon the importance of Elizabethan stage structure to production. Such studies as those of V. E. Albright, J. C. Adams, G. F. Reynolds, and Ronald Watkins are based on the assumption that the stage structure and its machinery played the decisive role in the presentation of an Elizabethan drama. This premise is not supported by the evidence. Certainly the basic form of the stage affected both the structure of the plays and the manner in which they were produced. The large platform and formal façade determined the fundamental conditions of production. But the actual production of a drama relied upon specific parts of this stage much less than we have thought. Style in staging was inherent in the dramatic form, not the stage structure.

The style of acting at the Globe played as much a part in the shaping of production as the stage structure itself. But Elizabethan acting lacked both the histrionic traditions and the fertile conditions for the development of a self-perpetuating style. Instead, the actor, endowed with a keen tongue, an agile body, and most of all, a passionate heart, fitted his skills and talents to the needs of the plays. Unlike the *commedia* actors or the naturalistic actors of the Stanislavsky school, the Elizabethan actor did not impose a mode of presentation upon the individual scripts. This fact in no way reduces his importance to the production; it merely means that his style of playing was derived from the drama. Although the actors employed the playwrights, they did not dictate the kind of roles which were to be provided.

All factors of production, of course, were modified by the exigencies of the repertory system. Simplicity and recurrence in staging were direct results of such a system. It demanded flexibility from the actors and from the stage. Because of the practice of doubling in most plays, and the daily change of bill, the system prevented the development of special "lines." Altogether the strenuous demands it made upon the actors encouraged individual brilliance and bold strokes but discouraged intricately designed spectacle, ensemble playing, or extensive rehearsal.

Subject to the conditions of the repertory system, the script played the dominant part in shaping the style of production. Naturally the form of the script harmonized with the structure of the stage and the manner of acting. The platform stage encouraged the growth of a panoramic narrative form of drama. The actor's rhetorical and poetical skill, and his freedom of emotional release enabled the author to provide him with speeches of swelling passion. But it was the script which united these elements into a harmonious theatrical style.

This style, within certain limits, was realistic, not because of the subject matter of the narrative but because of the many opportunities that it offered for the description and portrayal of passion and thought. True, the framework of the passion and thought was conventional, but the conventionality had its source, for the most part, in the ceremony of Elizabethan life, which was artificial only in the Elizabethan sense of having art. Within this conventional framework, which facilitated narration as well as imparted form to the acting and staging, there operated a spontaneous, lyrical, and intensely emotionalized reality. A conventional framework, however, must not be equated with a symbolic method.

Recent scholarship has looked with increasing favor upon George Reynolds' contention that Elizabethan staging was fundamentally symbolic. Kernodle has shown how symbolism functioned in medieval art and continental staging but has been less successful in showing its presence upon the English stage. Both scholars have pointed out individual instances of symbolic staging during the Globe period, but neither of them has demonstrated the consistent use of symbolism throughout a number of plays or an entire production. Nor is there evidence that a pattern of symbolism pervaded the action of the Globe plays. It is significant that few of the properties which we know were used at that playhouse reveal a symbolic purpose. For the most part they are utilitarian. Those properties which are most readily suited to symbolism, such as trees, have no certain representatives at the Globe playhouse. Although I have pointed out several instances where symbolic staging was or may have been introduced at the Globe, its occasional appearance did not establish the over-all style.

This style is chiefly characterized by its reconciliation of the contradictory demands of convention and reality. The two forces were maintained in delicate balance through the poetic vision of the playwrights, most completely by Shakespeare, to a lesser extent by his contemporaries. To call this style realism leads us to confuse it with the realism of modern drama. To call this style symbolism, even though it avails itself of symbols to a limited extent, leads us astray. Perhaps it is necessary to reflect the dual nature of the style in a compound term. For the conventional framework, the adjective "ceremonial" is appropriate. For the passion which lies within the conventional framework and which even permeates its interstices, the adjective "romantic" is appropriate. For the scope of the theme and the elevation of the tone, the adjective "epic" is appropriate. Thus, the style of production at the Globe playhouse may be defined as at once, ceremonial, romantic, and epic.

APPENDIX A

i. Comparison of Plays Known Only Through Henslowe with Plays Otherwise Known

Total number of plays listed in the performance lists of Henslowe's *Diary*	113	
Plays known only through Henslowe's *Diary* ...	62	54.9%
Plays known only through the *Diary* and Henslowe's *Papers*	5	4.4
Plays known otherwise than through Henslowe's *Diary* or *Papers*	24	21.2%
Plays which scholars have identified with works otherwise known	[22]	
Identification is probable for	10	8.9
Identification is improbable for	12	10.6
Plays definitely and probably unknown but for Henslowe	69.9%	
Plays definitely and probably otherwise known		30.1%

Of those known otherwise than through Henslowe .. 34 plays gave
403 performances

Of those unknown but through Henslowe .... 79 plays gave
496 performances

ii. Length of Runs of Plays Listed in Henslowe's *Diary*, ed. W. W. Greg, I, 13–22, 24–25, 27–28, 30, 42, 49–54

1. Number of Performances

No. of Perfs.	No. of Plays between 1592–1597 *	No. of Plays between 1594–1597 †	No. of Perfs.	No. of Plays between 1592–1597 *	No. of Plays between 1594–1597 †
1	19	5	13	3	2
2	15	5	14	4	3
3	8	1	15	2	2
4	7	4	16	2	2
5	4	0	17	2	1
6	3	2	21	1	1
7	7	4	22	2	2
8	5	4	25	2	2
9	4	3	29	1	0
10	6	2	32	1	1
11	6	4	36	1	0
12	8	7			

* Full performance list, 1592–1597: 113 plays. Average number of performances: 7.9; mean number of performances: 7.

† Partial performance list, June, 1594–February, 1597, limits of the most stable period. Average number of performances: 10; mean number of performances: 10.

2. Length of Time

Years	Mos.	1592–1597 * (No. Plays and Percentage)		1594–1597 † (No. Plays and Percentage)		Years	Mos.	1592–1597 * (No. Plays and Percentage)		1594–1597 † (No. Plays and Percentage)	
	1	30	26.5	9	15.8	1	0	2 ⎫		2 ⎫	
	2	16 ⎫		5 ⎫		1	1	2		2	
	3	6		2		1	3	2		2	
	4	7 ⎬ 31.0		3 ⎬ 22.8		1	4	1 ⎬ 8.0		1 ⎬ 15.8	
	5	5		3		1	7	1		1	
	6	1 ⎭		0 ⎭		1	8	1 ⎭		1 ⎭	
	7	7 ⎫		5 ⎫		2	0	1 ⎫		1 ⎫	
	8	7		6		2	2	3 ⎬ 3.5		2 ⎬ 5.3	
	9	3 ⎬ 24.8		2 ⎬ 33.3		3	2	1	.9	1	1.8
	10	5		4							
	11	6 ⎭		2 ⎭		Revived ‡		6	5.3	3	5.2

* 1592–1597, 113 plays.

† June, 1594–February, 1597, 57 plays.

‡ Length of run is counted continuously when a play is performed regularly, there being no more than four months between performances. Otherwise the play is considered to be a revival.

iii. Summary of Court Performances, 1590–1642

Total number of plays that were or may have been presented at Court, 1590–1642	144	
1. Plays definitely produced publicly before appearance at Court	67	46.5%
2. Plays where initial performance is uncertain .... (Notice of Court performance is *only* or *first* reference to play.)	39	27.1%
3. Plays for which there is evidence public playing preceded Court performance	8	5.5%
4. Uncertain. Title pages indicate performances in public and at Court	6	4.2%
5. Plays the title pages of which refer only to public performance	4	2.8%
6. Plays which received licenses shortly before Court performances	8	5.5%
7. Old plays revived, possibly with additions for Court ...	4	2.8%
8. Plays definitely presented at Court first	7	4.9%
9. Plays probably presented at Court first	1	.1%

The total number of plays presented at Court is calculated from the lists appearing in E. K. Chambers, *The Elizabethan Stage* and Mary Steele, *Plays and Masques at Court*. The investigation of the circumstances under which the plays received their first presentations employed a wide variety of primary and secondary sources. It is beyond the scope of this book to give the evidence for each conclusion.

APPENDIX B

i. Localization in Shakespeare's Globe Plays

Play	Type of Locale						Total Scenes
	Particular		General		Neutral		
	P	D	P	D	P	D	
Julius Caesar	6		2	9	1		18[1]
As You Like It	1		3	18			22
Twelfth Night	2		4	9		3	18
Hamlet	1	3	10	6			20
Merry Wives of Windsor	3	13	1	5		1	23
Troilus and Cressida	4	6	2	11	1		24
All's Well	1		1	17	1	3	23
Measure for Measure	6		4	2	4	1	17[2]
Othello	1	3	5	2	4		15
Lear	2	1	2	14	1	3	23[3]
Macbeth	1	2	8	9		7	27
Antony and Cleopatra	4		8	15	8	7	42
Coriolanus	3	4	9	8	3	2	29
Timon of Athens	4	1	4	5	1	2	17[4]
Pericles	2	5	4	12		4	27[5]
Total	41	38	67	142	24	33	345

[1] IV, ii and iii treated separately.
[2] Number of scenes for *Measure for Measure* is based on Folio numbering.
[3] II, ii–iv are treated as one scene following Quarto and Folio.
[4] IV, iii–iv are treated as one scene.
[5] Choruses involving dumb shows are treated as scenes.

P. probably
D. definitely

ii. Properties Required in the Globe Plays

THE SHAKESPEAREAN PLAYS:

Property	Plays	Scenes	Method of Introduction
Tables	Othello	I, iii	probably discovered
	Pericles	II, iii	no indication
	Antony and Cleopatra	II, vii	brought on
	Antony and Cleopatra	I, ii	brought on
	Timon	I, ii	brought on
	Timon	III, vi	brought on
	Macbeth	III, iv	probably brought on
	As You Like It	II, v	probably brought on
	Hamlet	V, ii	brought on
	Macbeth	V, i	use uncertain
	Julius Caesar	IV, iii	use uncertain
Seats	Antony and Cleopatra	II, vii	brought on (stool)
	Coriolanus	II, ii	brought on (stool)
	Othello	V, ii	brought on
	King Lear	IV, vii	brought on
	Julius Caesar	III, i	probably brought on
	Hamlet	I, i	probably brought on
	Measure for Measure	V, i	probably brought on
	All's Well	II, i	probably brought on
	Pericles	V, i	probably brought on
	Pericles	V, i	probably discovered
	Antony and Cleopatra	III, x	probably brought on
	Coriolanus	I, iii	probably brought on
	Hamlet	III, iv	no indication
	King Lear	III, vi	no indication
	Julius Caesar	IV, iii	no indication
	Pericles	I, ii	no indication
	All's Well	II, iii	no indication
	Coriolanus	V, iii	no indication
	Antony and Cleopatra	II, ii	no indication
	Macbeth	III, iv	probably discovered
	Hamlet	III, ii	no indication
	King Lear	III, vii	no indication
Beds	Antony and Cleopatra	V, ii	taken off
	Pericles	III, i	probably discovered
	Othello	V, ii	probably discovered
	Julius Caesar	IV, iii	no indication (cushions)
	King Lear	III, vii	probably discovered (cushions)
	Pericles	V, i	discovered

Property	Plays	Scenes	Method of Introduction
Scaffold	Antony and Cleopatra	IV, xvi	probably brought on
	Julius Caesar	III, ii	brought on
	Troilus and Cressida	I, ii	probably brought on
Tombs	Timon	V, iii	no indication
	Pericles	IV, iv	no indication
Tents	Julius Caesar	IV, ii	use uncertain
	All's Well	III, vi	use uncertain
	Troilus and Cressida	I, iii	use uncertain
Trees, Rocks, etc.	As You Like It	III, ii	use uncertain
	All's Well	IV, i	use uncertain
	As You Like It	II, v	use uncertain
	King Lear	V, ii	use uncertain
	Antony and Cleopatra	IV, xiii	use uncertain
	Timon	IV, iii	use uncertain
	Twelfth Night	II, v	no indication
	Hamlet	III, ii	no indication
Straw	King Lear	III, iv	discovered
	Julius Caesar	V, v	no indication
	Julius Caesar	V, iii	use uncertain
	Merry Wives of Windsor	V, vi	use uncertain
Statue	Julius Caesar	III, i	use uncertain
Desk	Merry Wives of Windsor	I, iv	use uncertain
Stocks	King Lear	II, ii	brought on
Cauldron	Macbeth	IV, i	taken off
Chest	Pericles	III, ii	brought on
Corpses	Pericles	I, i	probably discovered

Total number of properties 65
Less properties whose use is uncertain 15
Total number of properties used 50

Properties brought on .... 12 · 24% ⎫
Properties probably brought on .... 11 22% ⎬ 50%
Properties taken off .... 2 4% ⎭

Properties discovered .... 2 4% ⎫ 18%
Properties probably discovered .... 7 14% ⎭

Properties for whom method of introduction is
· not indicated 16   32%

THE NON-SHAKESPEAREAN PLAYS: [1]

Property	Plays	Scenes	Method of Introduction
Tables	Every Man Out of His Humour	II, ii	use uncertain
	Every Man Out of His Humour	V, iv	no indication
	Cromwell	vii	brought on
	Devil's Charter	IV, iv	use uncertain
	Devil's Charter	Prologue	probably brought on
	Devil's Charter	IV, iii	brought on
	Devil's Charter	V, vi	brought on
	Devil's Charter	V, iv	brought on
	Fair Maid of Bristow	i	use uncertain
	Miseries of Enforced Marriage	xii	brought on
	Revenger's Tragedy	V, iii	brought on
Seats	Merry Devil of Edmonton	Prologue	discovered
	London Prodigal	ii	probably brought on
	Yorkshire Tragedy	viii	brought on
	Miseries of Enforced Marriage	xii	brought on
	Devil's Charter	IV, v	probably brought on
	Devil's Charter	V, vi	discovered
	Devil's Charter	V, vi	brought on
	Devil's Charter	I, v	brought on
	Devil's Charter	Prologue	brought on
	Devil's Charter	II, i	no indication
	Devil's Charter	I, iv	discovered
	Cromwell	vi	discovered
	Every Man Out of His Humour	II, ii	probably brought on
	Every Man Out of His Humour	Chorus	brought on
	Sejanus	II, ii	no indication
	Sejanus	III, i	probably brought on
	Volpone	V, xii	probably brought on
	Volpone	IV, v	probably brought on
	Volpone	V, iii	brought on
	Revenger's Tragedy	I, ii	no indication
	Revenger's Tragedy	V, i	probably discovered

[1] This list of properties does not include properties from *Satiromastix* or *The Malcontent*.

Property	Plays	Scenes	Method of Introduction
Beds	Merry Devil of Edmonton	Prologue	discovered
	Devil's Charter	IV, v	taken off
	Volpone	I, ii	no indication
	Revenger's Tragedy	I, iv	discovered
	Revenger's Tragedy	II, iv	no indication
Tents	Devil's Charter	Prologue	probably brought on
	Devil's Charter	IV, iv	no indication
Scaffold	Volpone	II, ii	brought on
	Fair Maid of Bristow	xiii	taken off
Raised Struc-ture	Every Man Out of His Humour	III, ii	no indication
Writing Desk	Miseries of Enforced Marriage	iii	use uncertain
	Miseries of Enforced Marriage	iv	use uncertain
	Cromwell	iii	discovered
	Volpone	V, ii	no indication
Trees, Rocks, etc.	Merry Devil of Edmonton	x	use uncertain
	Merry Devil of Edmonton	x	use uncertain
	Merry Devil of Edmonton	i	use uncertain
	Miseries of Enforced Marriage	ix	no indication
	Miseries of Enforced Marriage	ix	use uncertain
	Every Man Out of His Humour	III, iii	use uncertain
Gibbets	A Larum for London	viii	use uncertain
	A Larum for London	xi	use uncertain
Post	A Larum for London	xiv	use uncertain
	Cromwell	v	use uncertain
	Every Man Out of His Humour	III, i	use uncertain
Tortoise	Volpone	IV, iv	no indication
Chest	Volpone	I, i	no indication
Altar	Sejanus	V, iv	no indication
Magic Glass	Devil's Charter	IV, i	discovered
Statue	Devil's Charter	I, ii	use uncertain

Property	Plays		Method of Introduction
Earthen			
Vessel	Devil's Charter	IV, i	brought on
Prop			
Lion or			
Dragon	Devil's Charter	IV, i	brought on
Cupboard	Devil's Charter	V, iv	brought on
Hearse	A Larum for London	ii	brought on
Cannon	A Larum for London	II, ii	use uncertain
Corpse	Revenger's Tragedy	V, i	no indication

Total number of properties 68
Less properties whose use is uncertain 17
Total number of properties used 51

Properties brought on	18	35.3%
Properties probably brought on	8	15.7% } 54.9%
Properties taken off	2	3.9%
Properties discovered	8	15.7% } 17.6%
Properties probably discovered	1	1.9%
Properties for which method of introduction is not indicated	14	27.5%

APPENDIX C

i. Disguise

Play[1]	Character	Dress	Manner	Voice	Face
As You Like It	Rosalind	II, iv, 4–8	I, iii, 122–124; III, ii, 313–315		
Twelfth Night	Viola	I, iv, s.d.	I, v, 177–236	I, iv, 29–34	
Twelfth Night	Feste	IV, ii, 1	IV, ii, 22–23	IV, ii, 71–72	IV, ii, 2
Measure for Measure	Duke	I, iii, 45–48	I, iii, 45–48; II, iii, 1–42		
Coriolanus	Coriolanus	IV, iv, s.d.; IV, v, 59 ff.			
Pericles	Pericles	II, ii, 48–52			
Pericles	Thaisa[3]	V, iii, 13–15			
Julius Caesar	Lucilius[3]				
Merry Wives of Windsor	Ford[4]	II, ii (?)			
Merry Wives of Windsor	Falstaff	IV, ii, 190 ff.			
Merry Wives of Windsor	Children, Evans	V, iv, 49–52; V, v			

Play[1]	Character	Dress	Manner	Voice	Face
Othello	Roderigo				I, iii, 346(?)
King Lear	Kent	I, iv, 1–4	II, ii, 1–180	I, iv, 1 f.	
King Lear	Edgar (Poor Tom)	II, iii, 10; III, iv, 66	II, iii, 9–20; III, iv	II, iii, 14–20	II, iii, 9(?)
King Lear	Edgar (Peasant)	IV, i, 40–44	IV, vi	IV, vi, 7 f., 45 ff.	
King Lear	Edgar (Cornishman)			IV, vi, 235–251	
King Lear	Edgar (Champion)	V, iii, 117, 142			
Devil's Charter	Candie, Caesar	F3v			
Merry Devil of Edmonton	Raymond as Friar	D2r			
London Prodigal	Old Flowerdale	A2r	A2r		G4v 18–20
London Prodigal	Luce	F1v	F1v	F1v	
Cromwell	Hodge, Bedford	C4v 26–D1v 27	C4v 26–D1v 27		
Miseries of Enforced Marriage	John, Thomas				
Fair Maid of Bristow	Harbart	B1v 28–2v 16	B1v 28–2v 16		

[1] *The Malcontent* is not included in this list although its plot is based completely upon a disguise. In this play the basic disguise is manner (see I, i). Malevole and Celso converse about the former's loss of his dukedom (213–255). On the entrance of Bilioso, however, "Malevole shifteth his speech," that is, he adopts his satiric manner. This treatment of disguise is similar to that in *The Revenger's Tragedy.*

[2] Time here helps to disguise Thaisa.

[3] Lucilius claims to be Brutus, but he is immediately recognized.

[4] Ford may have a change of clothing, particularly considering that Falstaff sees him at his house in IV, ii, and Ford visits him again in V, i.

Play[1]	Character	Dress	Manner	Voice	Face
Fair Maid of Bristow	Challener	B1ᵛ			
Fair Maid of Bristow	Sentloe	E3ʳ 20	E3ʳ⁻ᵛ		
Fair Maid of Bristow	Anabell	E4ᵛ	(?)		
Volpone	Volpone (Scoto)	II, iv	II, iv, 30–36		
Volpone	Volpone (sick)		I, iii–v; III, iii–v, vii, ix; IV, vi		
Volpone	Volpone (Commandant)	V, iii			
Volpone	Peregrine	V, iv, 1			
Revenger's Tragedy	Vindice	I, i	I, i		

ii. Formal Scenes in Shakespeare's Globe Plays requiring more than five characters

Single Combat Scenes
As You Like It, I, ii; *Merry Wives of Windsor*, III, i; *Troilus and Cressida*, IV, v; *Coriolanus*, III, i.

Banquet Scenes
As You Like It, II, vii; *Macbeth*, III, iv; *Antony and Cleopatra*, II, vii; *Timon*, I, ii.

Hearing or Trial Scenes
Merry Wives of Windsor, I, i (?); *Measure for Measure*, II, i; *Othello*, I, iii; *Lear*, II, ii; *Coriolanus*, III, iii.

Council or Senate Scenes
Hamlet, I, ii; *Lear*, I, i; *Othello*, I, iii; *Coriolanus*, II, ii; *Julius Caesar*, III, i.

Play-Within-Play Scenes
Hamlet, II, ii; III, ii.

Procession Scenes
Hamlet, V, i; *All's Well*, III, v; *Troilus and Cressida*, I, ii; III, iii; *Macbeth*, IV, i; *Coriolanus*, II, i; *Pericles*, II, ii; *Julius Caesar*, III, i.

Welcoming Scenes
Troilus and Cressida, IV, v; *Othello*, II, i; *Macbeth*, I, vi; *Timon*, I, i.

Alarum Scene
Macbeth, II, iii.

Parley Scenes
Antony and Cleopatra, II, ii; II, vi; *Julius Caesar*, V, i.

Finales
As You Like It, V, iv; *Twelfth Night*, V, iv; *Merry Wives of Windsor*, V, v; *Hamlet*, V, ii; *All's Well*, V, iii; *Measure for Measure*, V, i; *Othello*, V, ii; *Lear*, V, iii; *Macbeth*, V, viii; *Coriolanus*, V, vi; *Antony and Cleopatra*, V, ii; *Pericles*, V, iii.

The only plays whose finales do not fall into this category of group scenes are *Julius Caesar, Timon of Athens,* and *Troilus and Cressida.* Their finales fall into the first category of group scenes, less than five characters with mute supernumeraries. Each of three scenes (*Troilus and Cressida,* IV, v; *Othello,* I, iii; and *Julius Caesar,* III, i) contains two types of formal actions within the single scene.

iii. The Use of the Above: Two Special Instances

Julius Caesar, V, iii

The stage direction "Pindarus above" together with the stage direction, "Enter Pindarus," makes it almost certain that the above and not a platform was used. None of the scaffold scenes has a stage direction "above" or an "enter." In this instance, then, we must suppose that either Cassius spoke very slowly or Pindarus moved very quickly, for only two and a half lines cover his ascent and two lines his descent.

Antony and Cleopatra, IV, xv

The physical factors that have to be satisfied in staging the monument scene are (1) Cleopatra is aloft with her women; (2) Diomedes reports Antony's suicide and then tells her to look out the other side of the monument to see Antony; (3) Antony is heaved aloft as Cleopatra calls for aid, but not specifically from Diomedes. Diomedes, it is necessary to note, is Cleopatra's, not Antony's, servant; (4) Antony's body is carried out at the end of the scene.

Warren Smith suggests that a scaffold was utilized for the monument ("Evidence of Scaffolding on Shakespeare's Stage," *R.E.S.*, N.S. II (1951), 29). This is unlikely in view of the specific direction placing the action "aloft." Wherever scaffolds are otherwise used (*Troilus and Cressida*, I, ii; *Julius Caesar*, III, ii; *Volpone*, II, ii; *Fair Maid of Bristow*, Sig. E4ʳ–F2ᵛ), the term "aloft" or "above" is never introduced. Smith also fails to satisfy the final direction, "Exit bearing Anthony." The monument must be connected to the tiring house. At the same time there is no indication of a curtain. Consequently, I suppose the monument to be located above. What of factor (2)? It is generally supposed that the stage direction, "Enter Diomed," refers to an entrance on the platform. Kittredge adds "below" after this stage direction. But this is not the necessary interpretation. If Diomedes entered above, and reported in messenger fashion to his mistress, Cleopatra, his injunction to "Look out o' th' other side your monument" could easily mean "Look out front." In messenger fashion he leaves after making his report. The last problem concerns raising Antony. The agency for doing so was the combined energy of more than four boys (Cleopatra, Charmian, Iras, and her maids who appear for the first time) and of at least four men. How high the body had to be raised is uncertain. J. C. Adams calculates the above was 12' above the floor and had a 2'6" railing. Hodges' estimate is less, about 10'. Neither 10' nor 12' are prohibitive heights although a railing would be difficult to work over. Perhaps it was, possible to remove a portion of the railing. Despite the obstacles, however, Antony was raised in a manner which, we must suppose, was not ludicrous.

NOTES

INTRODUCTION

1. C. W. Wallace, *The First London Theatre* (Lincoln, Neb., 1913), p. 24.

2. Gerald E. Bentley, "Shakespeare and the Blackfriars Theatre," *Shakespeare Survey*, I (1948), p. 47.

3. Peter Streete agreed, in this contract dated January 8, 1600, to complete his construction by July 25, 1600 (E. K. Chambers, *The Elizabethan Stage* (Oxford, 1923), II, p. 438), a period of about twenty-eight weeks. However, it was covenanted that "the saide Peeter Streete shall not be chardged with anie manner of pay[ntin]ge in or aboute the saide fframe howse or Stadge or anie parte thereof, nor rendringe the walls within" (Chambers, II, p. 437). Consequently, we must add to the twenty-eight weeks an indeterminate period during which the playhouse was painted, thus bringing the estimated completion of the Fortune to some time in August at least. It is probable that in computing the schedule for the Fortune, Streete utilized his experience at the Globe, particularly since the new stage was to be so much like the Globe's. Streete would find such computation easy after allowing for differences in building conditions. On the one hand the fact that the timber from the Theatre was to be used for the Globe suggests that the frame for the Globe took less time to erect. On the other hand, the fact that the Globe had to be built on piles might reasonably suggest that laying its foundations required more time. If Henslowe's notation of payment "to the laberers at the eand of the fowndations the 8 of maye 1600" (Philip Henslowe, *Papers*, ed. W. W. Greg, p. 10), correctly reflects the time consumed in erecting these of the Fortune, a matter of about sixteen weeks, then we must assume that the base of the Globe was not ready to take a frame until the middle of June. As Henslowe's *Diary* and *Papers* indicate, Streete probably consummated his portion of the contract somewhat later than he had estimated, that is, about the first week in August (Henslowe, p. 11). But even if there were some delay, as Greg believes, Streete had erred merely by a matter of two weeks. I believe that his initial estimate, fundamentally reliable, reflected his experience at the Globe.

4. Among others Heminges testified that he shared in profits from the presentation of plays at Blackfriars for four years previous to 1612 (Kirkham vs. Painton, as reprinted in F. G. Fleay, *A Chronicle History of the London Stage* (London, 1890), pp. 225, 235, 238, 244, 249). The only time when the plague bills declined sufficiently to permit the possibility of performances was in March, 1609. The weekly count of plague deaths was thirty-two as of March 2, forty-three as of March 9, and thirty-three as of March 16. Thereafter, the plague increased in severity and the weekly number of deaths fell below forty only once again before December, 1609. (Statistics from John Bell, *London's Remembrancer* (London, 1665) as reprinted in J. T. Murray, *English Dramatic Companies* (London, 1910), II, pp. 186–187.)

5. E. K. Chambers, *William Shakespeare* (Oxford, 1930), I; Alfred Harbage, *Annals of the English Drama* (London, 1940); William Shakespeare, *The Complete Works of*, ed. G. L. Kittredge (New York, 1936); James McManaway, "Recent Studies in Shakespeare's Chronology," *Shakespeare Survey,* III (1950), 22–33. In composing the list of plays performed by the Globe company, I have relied on Chambers, compared with Harbage and Kittredge, and checked against McManaway's survey of studies in the chronological order of Shakespeare's plays. Later theories on particular plays have been examined when relevant.

6. *Twelfth Night,* ed. J. D. Wilson (Cambridge, 1930); Leslie Hotson, *The First Night of* Twelfth Night (New York, 1954).

7. Percy Allen, "The Date of *Hamlet*," *T.L.S.*, January 2, 1937, 12; Chambers, *William Shakespeare*, I, p. 423; also "The Date of *Hamlet*," *Shakespearean Gleanings* (London, 1944), pp. 68–75; *Hamlet*, ed. J. D. Wilson (Cambridge, 1936), 2nd ed.; H. D. Gray, "The Date of *Hamlet*," *J.E.G.P.*, XXX (1932), 51–61; L. Kirschbaum, "The Date of *Hamlet*," *S.P.*, XXXIV (1937), 168–175.

8. Leslie Hotson, "Love's Labour's Won," *Shakespeare's Sonnets Dated* (New York, 1949), 37–56.

9. A. Hart, "The Date of *Othello*," *T.L.S.*, October 10, 1935, 631; A. Cairncross, "A Reply to Hart," *T.L.S.*, October 24, 1935, 671; Richmond Noble, "A Reply to Hart," *T.L.S.*, December 14, 1935, 859; W. W. Greg, "The Date of *King Lear* and Shakespeare's Use of Earlier Versions of the Story," *Library*, XX (1940), 377–400.

10. Chambers, *William Shakespeare*, I, p. 522.

11. *Macbeth*, ed. J. D. Wilson (Cambridge, 1947), pp. xl–xlii. Wilson offers a fanciful argument to support his theory that the play was first performed before James in Edinburgh in 1601–1602. Kenneth Muir (Arden edition, 1951), p. xxvi, reviewing this argument, concludes, "It is reasonable to assume that the play was first performed in 1606, first at the Globe, and afterwards at Court—perhaps with a few minor alterations."

12. Leslie Hotson, *Shakespeare vs. Shallow* (Boston, 1931), pp. 111–122; P. Alexander, *Shakespeare's Life and Art* (London, 1939), p. 125; William Green, *Shakespeare's Garter Play* (unpublished dissertation, Columbia University, 1959), believes that Lord Hunsdon commissioned Shakespeare to write the play for performance on April 23, 1597. However, his explanation for the omission of the play's title from Meres' list is essentially hypothetical (pp. 249–251).

13. Eight early plays of Shakespeare's were actually revived during the Globe period, or supposedly revived according to the title pages of early editions. These plays were *The Comedy of Errors, Love's Labour's Lost, The Merchant of Venice, A Midsummer Night's Dream, Richard II, Richard III, Romeo and Juliet,* and *Titus Andronicus.* Seven of the eight, all but the first, were printed in quartos. However, the texts of later editions were set up from the early editions without appreciable alterations. The Folio text of *Dream* does include some additions to the stage directions which may be illuminating but which do not change the theatrical elements. The Fourth Quarto (1608) of *Richard II* is the first edition to contain the abdication scene, and the Folio text of *Titus Andronicus* contains additional stage directions and a new scene. But these omissions in the early copies do not seem to be a result of staging conditions. There are two possible inferences. Either the later texts had no connection with the playhouse and therefore merely copied the earlier texts, or the productions did not change suffi-

ciently over the years to cause variations in the texts. As a result I have decided to use these plays for occasional reference only.

14. The dating of these and the succeeding plays is based upon Chambers, *Elizabethan Stage*, III, pp. 214, 293, 431, 513; IV, pp. 1, 8, 12, 27, 30, 42, 54.

15. Baldwin Maxwell, *Studies in the Shakespeare Apocrypha* (New York, 1956), pp. 99–106, dates the play between 1599 and 1600.

16. *A Yorkshire Tragedy* has been identified with *Miseries of Enforced Marriage* by F. G. Fleay and others. Mark Friedlaender, "Some Problems of *A Yorkshire Tragedy*," *S.P.*, XXXV (1938), 238–253, in his reconsideration of the evidence rejects this theory. He suggests that both plays were made from a single original play. In a more recent study Baldwin Maxwell (pp. 153 ff.) considers the plays to be independent works. Whatever the theory, it is certain that both plays were staged and must be enumerated separately.

17. Thomas Kyd, *The Works*, ed. Frederick S. Boas (Oxford, 1955), p. xlii. Chambers, *Elizabethan Stage*, IV, p. 23, suggests that the present text was the one presented at the Globe about 1604. However, the suggestion is hedged with so many qualifications that I thought it better to exclude this piece.

CHAPTER ONE. THE REPERTORY

1. The material for the succeeding pages comes from an analysis of Philip Henslowe's *Diary*, ed. W. W. Greg (London, 1904–1908), the dates being based on Greg's correction of Henslowe. Mention must be made of the new edition of Henslowe's *Diary*, prepared by R. A. Foakes and R. T. Rickert (Cambridge, 1961), which appeared while the present work was in press. The editors offer slight correction of the primary evidence and some fresh interpretations of its significance.

2. Chambers, *Elizabethan Stage*, IV, pp. 322–325.

3. Henslowe, I. The list of plays from November 10, 1595–January 17, 1596 may be found on page 27. Fuller descriptions of the plays mentioned by name may be found in Volume II, pp. 167–168, 175–177.

4. Performances: Nov. 24–25, *Hercules*, I and II; Nov. 26, *Longshank;* Nov. 27, *New World's Tragedy;* Nov. 28, *Henry V* (new); Nov. 29, *The Welshman;* Dec. 1, *A Toy to Please;* Dec. 2, *Henry V;* Dec. 3, *Barnardo and Fiametta;* Dec. 4, *Wonder of a Woman;* Dec. 6, *Crack Me This Nutte.*

5. *Belin Dun* was performed regularly from June 10 to November 15, 1594, and regularly from March 31 to June 25, 1597, yet there was an isolated performance on July 11, 1596. See Henslowe, II, p. 164.

6. Chambers, *Elizabethan Stage*, II, pp. 143 ff.; Henslowe, II, pp. 118–119, 124–127.

7. Chambers, *Elizabethan Stage*, II, pp. 165–172, 177–180. From 1597 to 1603 nine men, Chettle, Day, Dekker, Drayton, Hathway, Haughton, Munday, Smith, and Wilson, furnished sixty-four of the eighty-eight plays which were finished and produced.

8. These are: *Phaethon, Earl of Godwin and His Three Sons* I and II, *King Arthur* I, *Black Bateman of the North, Madman's Morris, Pierce of Winchester, Civil Wars of France* I and II, *Fount of New Fashions, Brute, The Spencers, The Page of Plymouth, Troy's Revenge or Polyphemus, Cox of Collumpton, For-*

tunatus, Patient Grissel, Seven Wise Masters, Strange News out of Poland, Cupid and Psyche, Six Yeomen of the West, Cardinal Wolsey, Thome Strowd III, The Conquest of the West Indies, Judas, Malcolm King of Scots, Love Parts Friendship, Jephthah.

9. Henslowe, II, p. 112.

10. F. G. Fleay, *A Chronicle History of the London Stage*, p. 117.

11. Sir Henry Herbert, *The Dramatic Records of Sir Henry Herbert*, ed. J. Q. Adams (New Haven, 1917), pp. 66–67.

12. *The Virgin Martyr* involved the addition of a scene, *The Tragedy of Nero* was allowed for printing, *Come See a Wonder* is listed for "a company of strangers," and "the company at the Curtain" is in dispute.

13. 1604–1605: 10 plays presented, 7 by Shakespeare; 1611–1612: 23 plays, 2 by Shakespeare, 5 by others, 16 unidentified; 1612–1613: 20 plays, 8 by Shakespeare, 12 by others; 1618: 3 plays, 2 by Shakespeare, 1 by another poet; 1633: 22 plays, 4 by Shakespeare, 18 by others; 1636: 19 plays, 3 by Shakespeare, 16 by others; 1638: 7 plays, 1 by Shakespeare, 6 by others; 1638–1639: 17 plays, 2 by Shakespeare, 15 by others. See Chambers, *Elizabethan Stage*, IV, pp. 171–183; Mary S. Steele, *Plays and Masques at Court* (New Haven, 1926).

14. Chambers, *Elizabethan Stage*, IV, pp. 350–351. Periods during which plague forced the closing of the theaters between 1599 and 1608 were: March–December, 1603, c. October 5–December 15, 1605, July–December, 1606, July–November 19, 1607, August–December, 1608.

15. Days without performances because of Lenten observance are not counted.

16. Chambers, *William Shakespeare*, II, p. 332.

17. Henslowe, II, pp. 83, 124–125, 149.

18. The eight plays are Suckling's *Aglaura* (1638), Cartwright's *The Royal Slave* (1636), and Habington's *Cleodora* (1640), which were presented for Their Majesties by courtiers seeking favor (see Steele, pp. 265, 268; Herbert, p. 58); Carlell's *The Deserving Favourite* (1629) and Mayne's *City Match* (1639) (see Steele, pp. 263, 274, 277); *Two Merry Milkmaids* (1620), which may or may not have been presented publicly (Steele, p. 206); Middleton and Rowley, *A World Tost at Tennis* (1620), which was conceived as a masque, but apparently presented publicly (Steele, p. 227); and *As Merry as May Be* (1602–1603).

19. Herbert, p. 32. Also see pp. 19, 19 n., 36.

20. *Ibid.*, pp. 22, 35, 54; also Bentley, II, p. 675.

21. J. C. Adams, *The Globe Playhouse* (Cambridge, 1942), pp. 59–89; T.W. Baldwin, *The Organization and Personnel of the Shakespearean Company* (Princeton, 1927), pp. 332–338; Alfred Harbage *Shakespeare's Audience* (New York, 1941), p. 33.

22. Chambers, *Elizabethan Stage*, IV, pp. 166–175. From Elizabeth the Lord Chamberlain's men received £30 (3.6 per cent) in 1599–1600, £30 (3.6 per cent) in 1600–1601, £40 (4.8 per cent) in 1601–1602, and £20 (2.4 per cent) in 1602–1603. The percentages indicate that portion of their income derived by the players from the Court. (Based upon Baldwin's low estimate of £840 annual income.)

23. Frances Keen, "The First Night of *Twelfth Night*," *T.L.S.*, December 19, 1958, 737.

CHAPTER TWO. THE DRAMATURGY

1. The recognition of this deficiency forced Thomas W. Baldwin to develop his theory of Shakespeare's five-act structure in reference to the Renaissance critics of France, Italy, and Germany (*Shakespeare's Five-Act Structure*, Urbana, 1947). Henry Popkin, *Dramatic Theory of the Elizabethan and Jacobean Play-wrights* (unpublished dissertation, Harvard, 1950) endeavors to show that the Elizabethan and Jacobean playwrights were aware of prevailing theories of drama, but he does not go on to show that they introduced what they knew into what they wrote.

2. Baldwin, *Shakespeare's Five-Act Structure*, pp. 305, 315, 321, 326.

3. Muriel C. Bradbrook, *Themes and Conventions of Elizabethan Tragedy* (Cambridge, 1935), p. 5.

4. Madeleine Doran, *Endeavors of Art* (University of Wisconsin, 1954), p. 5.

5. Heinrich Wölfflin, *Principles of Art History* (New York, 1932), pp. 14–16, 159; Doran, p. 6.

6. George Puttenham, *The Arte of English Poesie* (1589), as reprinted in Gregory Smith, *Elizabethan Critical Essays* (Oxford, 1904), II, pp. 19–20.

7. Francis Fergusson, *The Idea of a Theater* (Princeton, 1949), pp. 229–230.

8. Hardin Craig, "Shakespeare's Development as a Dramatist in the Light of His Experience," *S.P.*, XXXIX (1942), 226; also S. L. Bethell, *Shakespeare and the Dramatic Tradition* (London, 1944), p. 70.

9. Doran, pp. 103, 263.

10. *Ibid.*, p. 296.

11. *Ibid.*, p. 264.

12. Bradbrook, pp. 30, 75.

13. Doran, p. 295.

14. See especially *Twelfth Night*, I, i–iii; *Hamlet*, I, i–iii; *Lear*, I, i; *Measure for Measure*, I, i; *The Devil's Charter*, dumb show.

15. The other ranking figures are Antonio in *The Revenger's Tragedy*, Malevole, revealed as Duke Altofronto in *The Malcontent*, young Flowerdale in *The London Prodigal*, and the husband in *A Yorkshire Tragedy*. The prodigal son plays, *Miseries of Enforced Marriage*, *The London Prodigal*, and *A Yorkshire Tragedy*, have a double figure, the husband who judges himself and the wife who grants forgiveness.

16. Discovery: *As You Like It*, *Twelfth Night*, *Merry Wives of Windsor*, *All's Well*, *Pericles*; discovery-single combat: *Hamlet*, *Lear*; discovery-suicide: *Othello*; discovery-trial: *Measure for Measure*; single combat: *Macbeth*; suicide: *Julius Caesar*, *Antony and Cleopatra*; trial: *Coriolanus*; siege: *Timon of Athens*.

17. Curtis B. Watson, "Shakespeare's Dukes," *S.A.B.*, XVI (1941), 33. Watson insists that the Duke employed in this fashion is unique to Shakespeare's plays. However, as the non-Shakespearean plays reveal, the same functions are carried out by father, king, or lord.

18. G. Wilson Knight, *Principles of Shakespearean Production* (Harmondsworth Middlesex, 1949), p. 21.

19. *Ibid.*, p. 21; W. J. Lawrence, "Some Reflections on Shakespeare's Dramaturgy," *Speeding Up Shakespeare* (London, 1937), p. 43; Richard G. Moulton, *Shakespeare as a Dramatic Artist* (Oxford, 1893), p. 217.

20. Moulton, p. 217. He persists in finding a "point" for the climax although he more clearly than any one of the other writers perceives the extended nature of the climax. On page 209 he treats the scenes of Lear's madness as a "Centerpiece," apparently realizing their climactic interconnection. Yet he fails to take the next step by abandoning the conception of a climactic moment.

21. Harley Granville-Barker, *Prefaces to Shakespeare* (Princeton, 1947), I, p. 274.

22. The appearance of the "climactic plateau" late in *Troilus and Cressida* is further support for the theory of a two-part play suggested by T. W. Baldwin in *A New Variorum Edition of Troilus and Cressida*, ed. Harold N. Hillebrand, supplemental ed. T. W. Baldwin (Philadelphia, 1953), p. 452.

23. The climax is also associated with the subsequent disappearance of the central figure, a characteristic pointed out by W. J. Lawrence. Both comedy, for example, *Twelfth Night* and *Measure for Measure* (Angelo is absent for the third and almost all of the fourth act) and tragedy display the same pattern.

24. Levin L. Schücking, *Character Problems in Shakespeare's Plays* (New York, 1922), p. 114.

25. Elmer E. Stoll, *Shakespeare Studies* (New York, 1942), p. 37, corrected edition; G. Wilson Knight, *Wheel of Fire* (New York, 1949), pp. 13–14.

26. G. Wilson Knight, *Wheel of Fire* and *Principles*, pp. 140–155, for his proposed *Macbeth* production.

CHAPTER THREE. THE STAGE

1. G. F. Reynolds, "What We Know of the Elizabethan Stage," *M.P.*, IX (1911), 68.

2. V. E. Albright, *The Shakesperian Stage* (New York, 1909), p. 45.

3. The figures are suggestive rather than definitive. See Appendix B, chart i, for breakdown according to plays.

4. H. Granville-Barker, "A Note on Chapters XX and XXI of *The Elizabethan Stage*," *R.E.S.*, I (1925), 68.

5. Ashley Thorndike, *Shakespeare's Theater* (New York, 1916), pp. 102 ff.

6. *Twelfth Night*, II, ii; *Measure for Measure*, V, i; *Lear*, II, i; II, ii; III, i; *Othello*, V, ii; *Antony and Cleopatra*, II, vi; III, ii; *Troilus and Cressida*, IV, i; *Coriolanus*, I, viii; I, ix; *Timon of Athens*, I, i; III, iv–vi; IV, ii; *Pericles*, Chorus, II; II, v; Chorus, III; *The Devil's Charter*, prologue; I, i; IV, i; *Fair Maid of Bristow*, scene xiv.

7. W. J. Lawrence, *The Physical Conditions of the Elizabethan Public Playhouse* (Cambridge, Mass., 1927), pp. 22 ff.

8. W. J. Lawrence, *The Elizabethan Playhouse and Other Studies*, Series One (Stratford-on-Avon, 1912), p. 23.

9. Lawrence, *Physical Conditions*, pp. 22 ff.; J. C. Adams, p. 146.

10. G. F. Reynolds, "*Troilus and Cressida* on the Elizabethan Stage," *Joseph*

Quincy Adams Memorial Studies, ed. James G. McManaway *et al.* (Washington, 1948), pp. 229–238.

11. *Julius Caesar*

BRUTUS. How many times shall Caesar bleed in sport,
That now on Pompey's basis lies along
No worthier than the dust!

(III, i, 114–116)

ANTONY.   Then burst his mighty heart;
And in his mantle muffling up his face,
Even at the base of Pompey's statuë,
(Which all the while ran blood) great Caesar fell.

(III, ii, 191–194)

Plutarch, *Julius Caesar.* in *Shakespeare's Plutarch,* I, p. 102. "But when [Caesar] saw Brutus with his sword drawn in his hand, then he pulled his gown over his head, and made no more resistance and was driven either casually or purposedly by the counsel of the conspirators against the base whereupon Pompey's image stood, which ran all of a gore-blood till he was slain."

12. See Appendix B, chart ii, for the list of properties in Shakespeare.

13. Henslowe, *Papers,* pp. 116–118.

14. *Antony and Cleopatra,* I, ii; II, vii; *Timon of Athens,* I, ii; III, vi; *Cromwell,* scene vii; *The Devil's Charter,* V, iv; *The Revenger's Tragedy,* V, iii.

15. Probably *Macbeth,* III, iv; *As You Like It,* II, v; undetermined *Pericles,* II, iii.

16. Brought out: *Hamlet,* V, ii; *The Devil's Charter,* IV, iii; V, vi; probably brought out: *The Devil's Charter,* prologue; uncertain: *Every Man Out of His Humour,* V, iv; discovered: *Othello,* I, iii.

17. A parallel instance is found in *Volpone.* In the last scene in which the bed is employed, Mosca says to Volpone, then lying in the bed:

Patron, go in, and pray for our successe. (III, ix, 62)

The line suggests that the bed was removed rather than hidden by a curtain.

18. Warren Smith, "Evidence of Scaffolding on Shakespeare's Stage," *R.E.S.,* n.s. II (1951), 22–29.

19. Richard Hosley, "The Discovery-Space in Shakespeare's Globe," *Shakespeare Survey,* XII (1959), 35–46. Many of my own conclusions parallel those of Mr. Hosley. See my dissertation, *The Production of Shakespeare's Plays at the Globe Playhouse, 1599–1609* (Columbia University, 1956).

20. *Ibid.,* 46. Both *Cromwell,* sc. vi, and *Merry Wives of Windsor,* III, iii, require similar facilities.

21. Richard Southern, "On Reconstructing a Practicable Elizabethan Public Playhouse," *Shakespeare Survey,* XII (1959), p. 33.

22. Hosley, 44–45.

23. Alone: *Devil's Charter,* IV, i; I, iv; *Cromwell,* sc. iii, vi; attended: *Devil's Charter,* V, vi; *Cromwell,* sc. xii.

24. *A Yorkshire Tragedy,* sc. v; *The Revenger's Tragedy,* II, iv; *The Merry Devil of Edmonton,* prologue.

25. *The Revenger's Tragedy,* I, iv; V, i.

26. Fastidious Briske takes down a "base viol" from a wall. Such action may depend upon the discovery of an interior. (III, ix, 81)

27. Concealment: *As You Like It*, III, ii (?); *Twelfth Night*, IV, ii; *Hamlet*, III, i, III, iv; *Merry Wives of Windsor*, III, iii; *Measure for Measure*, III, i; *Lear*, III, vi; *Coriolanus*, II, i; discovery: *Othello*, I, iii, V, ii; *Timon*, V, iii; *Pericles*, I, i, III, i, V, i; tents: *Julius Caesar*, IV, ii–iii; *Troilus and Cressida, passim.*

28. See *Two Elizabethan Stage Abridgements: The Battle of Alcazar and Orlando Furioso*, ed. W. W. Greg (The Malone Society, 1922), pp. 34–35.

29. *Merry Wives of Windsor*, II, ii, III, v; *Every Man Out of His Humour*, V, iv; *Merry Devil of Edmonton*, sc. i; *Miseries of Enforced Marriage*, sc. v; *A Yorkshire Tragedy*, sc. iii–v.

30. Adams, p. 289.

31. *Devil's Charter*, II, i, IV, iv; *Timon*, V, iv; *Coriolanus*, I, iv; *A Larum for London*, sc. ii. There is no stage direction specifying Sancto Davila's appearance on the walls. However, he is "walking about Castle" and he answers to the question, "Whose that above?" (sig. B2ᵛ).

32. *Othello*, I, i; *Volpone*, II, ii; *Every Man Out of His Humour*, I, ii; *Devil's Charter*, III, ii.

33. Richard Hosley, "The Gallery over the Stage in the Public Playhouse of Shakespeare's Time," *S.Q.*, VIII (1957), 31.

34. J. C. Adams, pp. 209–215. Also G. F. Reynolds, *The Staging of Elizabethan Plays at the Red Bull* (New York, 1940), p. 188.

35. *Macbeth*, IV, i; *Hamlet*, V, i; *A Larum for London*, scene xii; *The Devil's Charter*, prologue; III, v, IV, i, V, vi. For *Hamlet*, I, iv and v, see Chapter Five.

36. Leslie Hotson, *Shakespeare's Wooden O* (London, 1959), p. 13.

37. Hotson, *The First Night of Twelfth Night*, p. 67, also p. 119; Nagler, p. 11.

38. Thomas Dekker, *The Gull's Hornbook*, in Alois Nagler, *Sources of Theatrical History* (New York, 1952), p. 135.

39. Hosley, "The Gallery," 28.

40. Alois Nagler, *Shakespeare's Stage* (New Haven, 1958), pp. 10–11.

41. George R. Kernodle, *From Art to Theatre* (Chicago, 1944), pp. 87–89, 120–121, 124, 129.

42. C. Walter Hodges, "The Lantern of Taste," *Shakespeare Survey*, XII (1959), 8.

43. J. C. Adams, pp. 135, 233, 259.

44. John Summerson, *Architecture in Britain 1530–1830* (London, 1953), p. 59.

45. C. Walter Hodges, *The Globe Restored* (New York, 1953), Appendix A, pp. 170–177.

46. Kernodle. Quotations were selected from pp. 7, 70, 110, 134 respectively.

47. J. A. Gotch, *Architecture of the Renaissance in England* (London, 1894), I, p. xix.

48. Ellis Waterhouse, *Painting in Britain 1530–1790* (Baltimore, Md., 1953), p. 1.

49. *A Calendar of Dramatic Records in the Books of the Livery Companies of London 1485–1640*, The Malone Society. Collections, Volume III (1954), p. xxvi.

50. *Ibid.*, pp. 9 (1521), 21 (1534), 26 (1535), 27–29 (1536), 33 (1541), 38 (1546), 39 (1556), 41 (1561), 47 (1568), 53 (1581), 58 (1601), 59 (1602).

51. *Ibid.*, pp. 18 (1529), 37 (1540), 46 (1566), 47 (1568).

52. Charles M. Clode, *The Early History of the Guild of Merchant Taylors* (London, 1888), II, p. 267. For Harper, see II, p. 267; For the Merchant Tailors Company, I, p. 187.

53. *The Dramatic Records of the City of London*, The Malone Society, Collections, Volume II, Part III (1931). See p. 311 for example.

54. Clode, I, p. 187.

55. Robert Withington, *English Pageantry* (Cambridge, Mass., 1918–1920), II, p. 23.

56. Gotch, p. xxii; Summerson, pp. 22 ff.

CHAPTER FOUR. THE ACTING

1. Alfred Harbage, "Elizabethan Acting," *P.M.L.A.*, LIV (1939), 687. Although Professor Harbage modified his views later ("B. L. Joseph, *Elizabethan Acting*," *S.Q.*, II (1951), 360–361. A Review.) and arrived at the position that I describe on pp. 157 ff., his original thesis has served as the basis for most discussion of the subject and may well be used as a point of departure. In *Theatre for Shakespeare* (Toronto, 1955), he reprints his original article as a "personal indulgence."

2. W. F. McNeir, "E. Gayton on Elizabethan Acting," *P.M.L.A.*, LVI (1941), 579–583; Robert H. Bowers, "Gesticulation in Elizabethan Acting," *So. Folklore Quarterly*, XII (1948), 267–277; A. G. H. Bachrach, "The Great Chain of Acting," *Neophilologus*, XXXIII (1949), 160–172; Bertram L. Joseph, *Elizabethan Acting* (London, 1951). In a later book, *The Tragic Actor* (London, 1959), Joseph disclaims any intention of associating formality with oratory. Both acting and oratory "had the same object, the imitation of human emotions as they are to be recognized in human beings in life" (pp. 19–21). In effect, he adopts the position of the naturalists (p. 27).

3. Joseph, *Elizabethan Acting*, p. 1.

4. Harbage, "Elizabethan Acting," 698. Quoted from the ms. of *The Cyprian Conqueror*.

5. Joseph, *Elizabethan Acting*, p. 60.

6. John Russel Brown, "On the Acting of Shakespeare's Plays," *Quarterly Journal of Speech*, XXXIX (1953), 477–484; Marvin Rosenberg, "Elizabethan Actors: Men or Marionettes?" *P.M.L.A.*, LXIX (1954), 915–927; R. A. Foakes, "The Player's Passion: Some Notes on Elizabethan Psychology and Acting," *Essays and Studies*, VII (1954), pp. 62–77.

7. Foakes, 76.

8. Leonard Cox, *The Arte or Crafte of Rhethoryke* (1527–1530), ed. Frederic I. Carpenter (Chicago, 1899); Richard Sherry, *A Treatise of the figures of grammar and rhethorike* (1555); Richard Rainolde, *A Book called the foundation of*

Rhetorike (1562); Roger Ascham, *The Schoolmaster* (1570); Gabriel Harvey, *Rhetor* (1577); Dudley Fenner, *Artes of Logicke and Rhetoric* (1584); Henry Peacham, *The Garden of Eloquence* (1593), ed. William G. Crane (Gainesville, Fla., 1954); John Hoskins, *Directions for Speech and Style* (c. 1590), ed. Hoyt H. Hudson (Princeton, 1935); Edmund Coote, *The Englishe Schoole-Maister* (1596); Alexander van den Busche, *The Orator*, tr. L. P. (Anthony Munday?) (1596); Sir Francis Bacon, *Works*, ed. James Spedding (London, 1858), vols. iv–vi.

9. Abraham Fraunce, *The Arcadian Rhetorike* (1588), ed. Ethel Seaton (Oxford, 1950), p. 107. Succeeding material has been taken from pp. 112–128.

10. Baldassare Castiglione, *The Courtier*, tr. T. Hoby (1561), reprinted in Everyman's Library Edition (London, 1944), p. 56.

11. Fraunce, p. 106.

12. Hoskins, p. 2.

13. Peacham, Sig. U1v–U2r.

14. Sir Thomas Elyot, *The Boke named the Governour* (1531), folios 48–49.

15. William G. Crane, Introduction to Peacham, p. 23.

16. Sir Francis Bacon, *The Advancement of Learning*, in *Works*, IV, pp. 456–457.

17. Alan S. Downer, "The Tudor Actor: A Taste of his Quality," *Theatre Notebook*, V (1951), 77; Leslie Hotson, *Shakespeare's Motley* (New York, 1952).

18. Albert L. Walker, "Conventions in Shakespeare's Description of Emotion," *P.Q.*, XVII (1938), 26–56.

19. Examination of Augustine Phillips. Chambers, *William Shakespeare*, II, p. 325.

20. *Two Elizabethan Stage Abridgements: The Battle of Alcazar and Orlando Furioso*, ed. W. W. Greg. The parallel texts of the 1594 Quarto and Alleyn's part occupy pages 142–201.

21. Compare part line 221 with play line 1171; part lines 223–224 with play line 1175; part line 165 with play line 1012.

22. Thomas W. Baldwin, *The Organization and Personnel of the Shakespearean Company* (Princeton, 1927). See charts opposite p. 229.

23. *Ibid.*, pp. 197, 232, 248.

24. Hardin Craig, *The Enchanted Glass* (New York, 1950), pp. 225–226.

25. Louise Forest, "Caveat for Critics against invoking Elizabethan Psychology," *P.M.L.A.*, LXI (1946), 657.

26. Foakes, 65.

27. Theodore Spencer, *Shakespeare and the Nature of Man* (New York, 1943); Lily B. Campbell, *Shakespeare's Tragic Heroes. Slaves of Passion* (New York, 1952); E. M. W. Tillyard, *The Elizabethan World Picture* (London, 1948); John W. Draper, *The Humors and Shakespeare's Characters* (Durham, N. C., 1945).

28. Timothy Bright, *A Treatise of Melancholie* (1586), pp. 51–52.

29. Bacon, IV, 432.

30. Elyot, pp. 146 ff.

31. Bacon, IV, 457.

32. F. N. Coeffeteau, *A Table of Humane Passions*, tr. Edward Grimeston (1621); Ruth Anderson, *Elizabethan Psychology and Shakespeare's Plays* in *University of Iowa Studies*, III (March 15, 1927), 72 ff.; Campbell, p. 69.

33. Thomas Wright, *The Passions of the Minde* (1601), p. 88, as quoted by Lawrence Babb, *The Elizabethan Malady* (East Lansing, Mich., 1950), pp. 17 ff.

34. Babb, p. 13.

35. Craig, p. 124.

36. The display of wit as an individualizing element is usually limited to the following types: ladies, pages or boys, satirists such as Jaques and Thersites, clowns, gulls, braggarts, and occasional generic figures such as gentlemen and citizens. The only characters outside of these types who engage in wit play in Shakespeare's Globe plays are Paris (*Troilus and Cressida*, III, i), Lafew, Abhorson, Shallow, and Evans (*Merry Wives of Windsor*, I, i), also in the same play, Pistol and Nym (I, iii) and the Host (II, iii; III, i). Also Iago (who may be considered a satirist) and Polonius (II, ii).

37. Draper, for example, considers Cassio a choleric type, yet his description of the sanguine personality would fit as well (p. 15). The sanguine type, as Draper describes it, displays a predominance of blood, a handsome physique, ruddy color, a full body, susceptibility to love, honesty, trueness, and gaiety (pp. 18–23). This description fits Cassio.

CHAPTER FIVE. THE STAGING

1. Ronald Watkins, *On Producing Shakespeare* (New York, 1950), p. 104.

2. Summerson, pp. 30–51. See especially the plans of Wollaton Hall, p. 34; Hardwick Hall, p. 36; and Charlton House, p. 48.

3. The determination upon the figure of more than five characters composing a group scene is not arbitrary. Five actors can function on such a stage as the Globe without encountering problems of covering each other or vying for attention. Furthermore, Shakespearean scenes jump from those with five characters to those with appreciably more. Exceptions are noted in the text of the chapter, especially in the discussion of category two of the group scenes.

4. A. H. Thorndike, *Shakespeare's Theater* (New York, 1916), p. 83. Chambers expresses a similar but less sweeping version of this view in *Elizabethan Stage*, III, p. 86.

5. Alfred Harbage, *Theatre for Shakespeare* (Toronto, 1955) pp. 31 ff., estimates that in the 1,463 scenes of the 86 plays produced in the popular theater between 1576 and 1608, only 90, or slightly more than 6 per cent of the scenes require "the use of a curtained recess or equivalent stage enclosure."

6. Sir Mark Hunter, "Act- and Scene-Division in the Plays of Shakespeare," *R.E.S.*, II (1926), 296 ff. J. Dover Wilson, writing shortly afterward, concurred in this definition. "Act- and Scene-Division in the Plays of Shakespeare: A Rejoinder to Sir Mark Hunter," *R.E.S.*, III (1927), 385.

7. C. M. Haines, "The 'Law of Re-entry,'" *R.E.S.*, I (1925), 449–451.

8. W. W. Greg, *Two Elizabethan Stage Abridgements*, pp. 32–33.

9. The difference between the figure of 339 entrances and 644 entrances and exits results from a difference in dividing scenes in the plays. For the purpose of considering split entrances and exits, I thought it best to eliminate any instances where it was even probable that a scene continued, as in *Hamlet*, from III, iv, to IV, i.

10. A. C. Sprague, *Shakespeare and the Audience* (Cambridge, Mass., 1935), p. 66.

11. Examples occur in *True Tragedy of Richard III*, 475–477, 581 ff.; *Love and Fortune*, 1370 f., *Sir Clyomon and Sir Clamydes*, 828, 852 f., and *Cambises*, 127 ff., 602 ff.

12. Sprague, pp. 67–68.

13. Warren Smith, "The Third Type of Aside in Shakespeare," *M.L.N.*, LXIV (1949), 510.

14. There are five speeches which may or may not be asides. These are not included. *Macbeth*, I, iii, 116–117; V, iii, 20–28; *Lear*, I, iv, 244–245, 251, 255–256; IV, ii, 83–87; *Hamlet*, III, ii, 191. Four additional speeches are written to that the character either speaks loudly enough for the sound but not the sense to be overheard or fears being overheard. *Caesar*, II, iv, 39–43; *Twelfth Night*, III, iv, 1–4; *Othello*, IV, i, 238–249; *Antony and Cleopatra*, III, vii, 6–10.

15. *Coriolanus*, II, i, shows the same characteristics. Brutus and Sicinius who have been talking to Menenius step aside, according to the stage direction (106), when the Roman ladies enter. Shortly after they do so, the triumphal procession for Coriolanus enters, then moves on to the Capitol. Upon this exit Brutus and Sicinius, according to the Folio, "enter" (220 ff.) conversing about what they have seen. Apparently they had gone off and yet they are aware of what has taken place. The circumstances fit the conditions of the observation scene that I have been describing.

16. Paul V. Kreider, *Repetition in Shakespeare's Plays* (Princeton, 1941), Chapter One, "The Mechanics of Disguise"; M. C. Bradbrook, "Shakespeare and the Use of Disguise in Elizabethan Drama," *Essays in Criticism*, II (1952), pp. 159–168; Victor O. Freeburg, *Disguise Plots in Elizabethan Drama* (New York, 1915).

17. *Twelfth Night*, IV, ii, 69–70. Maria. "Thou mightst have done this without thy beard and gown. He sees thee not."

18. *Julius Caesar*, IV, iii, 267–308; *Macbeth*, III, iv, 38–73, 93–107; *Hamlet*, I, i, 18–69, 126–175; I, iv, 38–91; I, v, 1–113; III, iv, 102–136. From this list I exclude the show of kings in *Macbeth*, IV, i. The apparitions do not pass over the stage immediately, but assemble upon it until Banquo's ghost "points at them for his." The lines that follow being of doubtful authenticity, they offer no assistance in determining how the apparitions depart, though nothing in the text conflicts with the conventional manner of staging ghost scenes.

19. W. J. Lawrence, *Pre-Restoration Stage Studies* (Cambridge, 1927), p. 106.

20. *A Warning for Fair Women*, Sig. E3ᵛ. In the midst of a dumb show which takes place on the platform, the following direction occurs: "Chastitie, with her haire disheveled, and taking mistres Sanders by the hand, brings her to her husbands picture hanging on the wall, and pointing to the tree [above the center trap] seemes to tell her, that that is the tree so rashly cut downe."

21. In the Folio Edgar speaks the final lines, but in this respect the Quarto follows general usage. Of the other fourteen Shakespearean Globe plays, the ranking figure definitely speaks the final lines in eleven of them (*All's Well,* King; *Measure for Measure,* Duke; *As You Like It,* Duke; *Twelfth Night,* Duke; *Coriolanus,* Aufidius; *Timon,* Alcibiades; *Macbeth,* Malcolm; *Hamlet,* Fortinbras; *Othello,* Lodovico; *Antony and Cleopatra,* Caesar; *Pericles,* Pericles). The other three plays present special instances. *The Merry Wives of Windsor* has no ranking figure, but it is appropriate for Ford to conclude the action. *Julius Caesar* apparently has two ranking figures, Antony and Octavius. But the fact that Octavius speaks last points to his triumph in *Antony and Cleopatra.* Pandarus concludes *Troilus and Cressida.* This play, as I have shown, has a unique structure.

INDEX TO THE GLOBE PLAYS

GENERAL INDEX

DATE DUE

CPSIA information can be obtained
at www.ICGtesting.com
Printed in the USA
BVHW052308140223
658549BV00002B/65